A Five Finger Feast

A Five Finger Feast

Two Years in Kazakhstan,
Lessons from the Peace Corps

Tim Suchsland

PEACE CORPS WRITERS

A Five Finger Feast:
Two Years in Kazakhstan, Lessons from the Peace Corps

A Peace Corps Writers Book—
an imprint of Peace Corps Worldwide

Copyright © 2022 by Tim Suchsland

For more information, contact
peacecorpsworldwide@gmail.com.
Peace Corps Writers and the Peace Corps Writers colophon
are trademarks of PeaceCorpsWorldwide.org.

Illustrations and cover design by Tim Suchsland.
Book cover art: *A Five Finger Feast (Beshbarmak)*, 2015.
www.TimSuchslandArt.com

ISBN 13: 978-1-950444-38-0
Library of Congress Control Number: 2022906705

First Peace Corps Writers Edition, May 2022

A PEACE CORPS WRITERS BOOK

For William...
Never stop exploring!

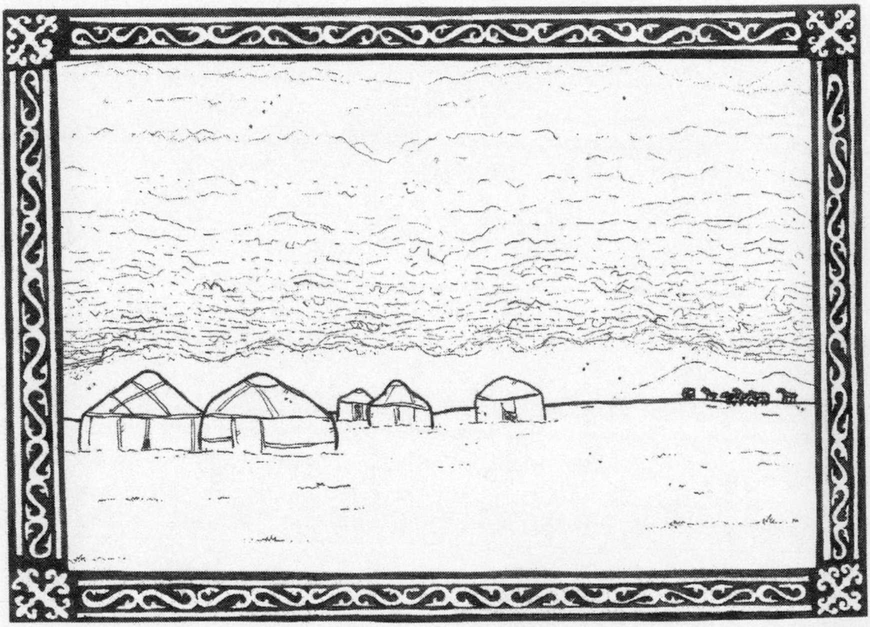

«Бала жүруді жығылудан үйренеді.»
"The child learns to walk by falling down."
A Kazakh Proverb

A Five Finger Feast

List of Illustrations

Preface

Although the material rewards of the Peace Corps are minimal—a certificate "signed" by Barack Obama and $5,000, after taxes—I wouldn't trade my two years of service for anything in the world. When I returned from Kazakhstan, I recounted this life changing experience to friends and family, but it never quite translated well. Kazakhstan became a blurred spot on the map of my mind, and I have been trying to figure out this nebulous space ever since.

A Five Finger Feast is my exploration of Kazakhstan, its people and its culture. My story is about two years of ambition, triumph and exhilaration, but it is also about loneliness, loss and failure. My "lessons" reflect the emotions and labors of being a young American living in a faraway place that is vastly different from home. *A Five Finger Feast* explores the universality of friendship and family. It is also a travelogue of sorts—a journey through time (2007-2009) and space (mostly Kazakhstan).

I changed most of the names to honor the privacy of those I

served and the friends I made there. While the stories are true, I took some artistic license with dialogue and some of the storytelling so the book would read better for the audience. Memory is a funny thing. It is never one hundred percent linear. It tends to jump around in our jumbled, spinning heads. Doesn't it?

In the decade plus it took me to write *A Five Finger Feast*, a lot has changed in the world. Don't get me wrong, much is still the same, but things change as this is the nature of time. The Peace Corps no longer operates in Kazakhstan. The Ukraine, where part of my story embarks, is the unfortunate target of Putin and his war machine. Even the omnipresent president of Kazakhstan, Nursultan A. Nazarbaev, "retired." His newly built capital, Astana, was even renamed after him. The COVID Pandemic happened, and that put a pause on the Peace Corps' operations around the world. Even typically "unnewsworthy" Kazakhstan made its debut on the American news cycle. Unrest took place there in early 2022. Many of the people I befriended have moved on with their lives, with many of them leaving my Peace Corps site, Yavlenka.

In a way, the world feels less "open," less accessible than it did in the 2000s. Maybe it is the world that put up its guard or maybe it is me, probably a little of both. Today, for me to join the Peace Corps would be too much of a commitment to take. As people get older and gain more responsibilities (jobs, families, mortgages, etc.), it is harder to leave those lives behind. I feel nostalgic for those two years in the late 2000s. I have not been back to Kazakhstan since I left in 2009, and I may never be able to go back. Time will tell. It is okay though, because the memories are there, and they will remain with me.

Tim Suchsland
Spring 2022
Seattle, Washington

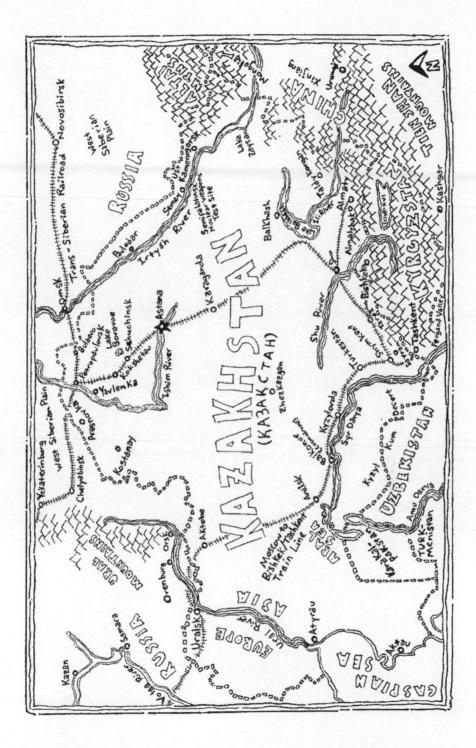

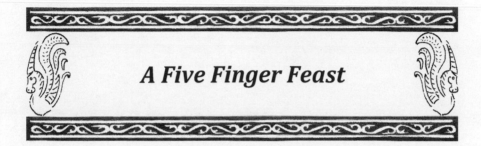

A Five Finger Feast

Part I
A Prelude,
Three Months of Training

Lesson 1
Culture Shock

"Peace Corps is one of the great US people-to-people achievements of the twentieth century, now continuing into the twenty-first century. As the advertisement says, 'It's the most difficult job you'll ever love!' And it's one of the most important things we as a nation do..."

Richard Hoagland
US Ambassador to
Kazakhstan, 2009-11

Brochure for the Peace Corps

I refused to wake. I just couldn't do it. I woke up and fell asleep. I woke up and fell asleep again. I laid there with my eyes closed for what seemed like hours, vacillating between sleep and consciousness. I was exhausted. I felt hungover, drunk, wasted on time and travel. Sunlight began to creep into the room. It seeped through the cracks in the blinds, creeping towards my face. I finally opened my eyes. They were crusted shut with gunk and grit. I stared at my watch. I had slept for over ten hours, and during that time I had been transported to a new world, another parallel universe.

I poked my head out from my bed covers to see my new surroundings. I cautiously glanced around my new bedroom.

The room was small, but it was filled with things—foreign things, weird things, stuck in a time passed on by the rest of the world. A desk leaned against one of the walls. A stack of aging books sat on top. Indecipherable Cyrillic patterns whirled on their leathery spines. An old wardrobe loomed in one corner of the room. It looked worn. At some point in time long ago, a child had placed animal stickers at the base of the wardrobe. Shapes of rabbits and bunnies stuck to the varnish. They were faded now, mostly outlines and blobs of gloss. The walls of the room were faded too, plastered with aging floral wallpaper. Its corners and edges were discolored and peeling back from the wall. A black-and-white photograph hung above the bed. A grimacing Kazakh man in an old-fashioned military uniform looked down at me, judging me for idling so long in bed.

Where am I? I asked myself. *What am I doing here?*

Even after so many hours in bed, I still couldn't get myself up. It pained me to think, to conceive even vaguely, what waking up and rising from bed meant. It all just felt so foreign.

Move one leg at a time from under my sheets. I told myself. *Place my feet on the ground and rise...*

Nothing happened. My brain had forgotten how to communicate with the rest of my body. My legs felt tired and dulled. My whole body felt fatigued and exhausted. I looked down to the ground where my feet would have landed. A large rug swirled with oriental patterns. I felt dizzy and nauseated.

Get up, whispered a voice inside my head. *Take on the day!* This time the voice shouted. *This is, after all, a new place and a new day. Adventures await outside.*

Yet, I didn't want to leave my bed. I felt too tired to rouse myself and take on the unknowns that waited for me today.

Why did I sign up for this, the Peace Corps? I cursed my existence faintly under my breath. *This feeling... this feeling of dread, it's awful!*

These feelings of fatigue and uncertainty had been conveniently glossed over in all of the Peace Corps' brochures that I read before departing. These were the pamphlets that sold me on this "adventure" across the planet. They were filled with pictures of smiling Americans working with happier-looking people from places like Africa and Latin America and the tropical paradises of the Pacific. They were filled with slogans and statistics promoting international friendship and a "spirit" of volunteerism.

Spirit of volunteerism? I laughed to myself. *Here I am in Kazakhstan, finally enlisted in the Peace Corps, and I can't even volunteer to get myself out of bed to face my new reality.*

Culture shock and jet lag hit me hard. The world outside was new and strange, and most of all, it was scary—too much for me to face in this fragile state. My bed, on the other hand, was warm and comfortable, and I had made it mine. For ten hours, it was all mine.

Outside, beyond my sheets and blankets, beyond my bedroom door, that wasn't mine. It was an alien, inhospitable world outside. It was a parallel universe, eight thousand miles from anything remotely resembling home, anything looking like the norm. Outside my door came weird smells, seeping through the cracks. Strange clanging noises sometimes banged their way through the walls unexpectedly and with force. From outside came untranslatable jibber jabber and nonsense—amorphous and antipodal, nebulous and bipolar.

My joints and back were beginning to ache from lying in bed

for too long. The sagging relic of a mattress didn't make my bones feel any better, nor did the anxiety and fear that oozed deep down to the marrow. My bladder burned. I needed to pee. My stomach growled. I needed to eat. It was time to face this new world outside.

Traffic Jam

I had already been in Kazakhstan for three days. I had spent three days with seventy-five other Peace Corps trainees at Tabagan, a ski resort in the mountains near Almaty.[1] Our group's codename was Kaz 19, the nineteenth group of Peace Corps volunteers in Kazakhstan. At the resort, the Peace Corps staff kept us comfortable and well-fed. They sheltered us as if we were children, and most of us were at twenty-one or twenty-two. A few of us were *almost* adults at a wise twenty-five. At Tabagan, we created an American bubble in the antipodes.

On the third day, the bubble burst. It was time to leave the comforts of the resort. Peace Corps staff loaded the trainees onto two big charter busses. We were heading for five training villages in the vast plains below the Tien Shan.[2]

The bus ride was noisy. We were strangers when we had left the States a few days prior, but in the twenty-four hours of flights and layovers to Kazakhstan and with three days in our American bubble at Tabagan, many began to mingle and make friends. On the bus we paired off when we took our seats. Some leaned over the backs of seats or across the aisle to talk to groups of newfound friends. The trainees, most young with big egos, shouted over each other to get the attention of their partners seated next to them. Some told college drinking stories. Others bragged about their times backpacking Europe. Most seemed to have little concern for the scenery passing us by out-

---

[1] Almaty ("Full of Apples") is the largest city in Kazakhstan (pop. 1,500,000).
[2] The Tien Shan or "Heavenly Mountains" is a range in Kazakhstan, China, Kyrgyzstan and Uzbekistan. The highest peak is Jengish Chokusu (24,406 ft).

side the bus as we descended the mountains.

For me, though, I still felt like an outsider amongst this crowd of American strangers. I was beginning to feel the pangs of homesickness, and maybe this was stopping me from feeling at ease. Even with all the comforts provided at the mountain resort, jetlag, sleepless nights and an underlying anxiety of things to come didn't provide me the energy to be an extrovert among my present company. While the other trainees talked and laughed, I sat silently staring out the window at my new reality racing down the mountain.

The drive down the mountain was bumpy and tortuous, swerving down a ravine lined with pines and wild apple trees. Rain-bearing thunderclouds rolled over the massive mountains. Like our bus, the clouds barreled down toward the hot plains below. The energy of the storm was fueled by the afternoon's August sun. Our view began to open up to the vast steppe as we went farther down the mountainside. The steppe seemed to stretch ahead of us into a field of golden infinity. The winding, bumpy roads began to flatten and straighten out. From here, orderly trees lined the thoroughfares. The leaves of the trees were weighed down with heavy grey grit. Fields of wheat began to give way to brick and concrete. A cityscape quickly emerged. We continued to speed towards Almaty's city limits.

As we entered Almaty, once called Alma Ata or the "Grandfather of Apples," we drove past rickety stands along the roadside. Women were selling everything from watermelons to motor oil, and even beer—a quick refreshment for drivers passing by. Small groups of men squatted along the sides of the dusty road. Most were playing cards and smoking cigarettes. They seemed to have little concern for the darkening clouds looming overhead.

At first glance, the city seemed to exist in a void between developing boom and apocalyptic bust. It was a purgatory of rubble and construction. A mixture of bricks and plastic bags strewed the sides of the road. Piles of trash dotted the dirt sidewalks. Some smoldered with smoke and flame, others lay charred and dormant. Shiny buildings of steel and glass were being erected right next to old decaying Soviet-era apartments overgrown with weeds.

The closer we got to the city center the more the bus slowed, and the mercury steadily rose. It was hot inside the bus, and outside the traffic was maddening. Vehicles swerved in and out of each other in a yo-yo of bursts of speed and a caterpillar's crawl. Busses cut off cars, cars cut off trucks, trucks cut off busses. It was a vicious cycle.

I glanced at our bus driver a few seats up from mine. His balding, wrinkled scalp was oozing beads of sweat. He noticed me staring at him when he looked up into his rearview mirror. He stared back at me with bloodshot eyes. I quickly averted my gaze towards the world outside. At that moment, I saw a bus stalled on the road. Five or six men had jumped out of the bus, and they were pushing it to jumpstart the large beast.

Culture Shock

I turned to look around the bus. The other trainees continued conversing amongst themselves. They didn't seem to notice the chaos outside. They went about talking with each other nonchalantly, seeming apathetic to this chaotic world outside.

After a long while, our bus escaped the madhouse of Almaty when we popped out the opposite side of the city. The highway began to open up again, and it was an open road for ten or more miles. City turned into suburbs, and suburbs became farms and fields once again.

We eventually turned off the main highway onto a long tree-lined road. The road was asphalt, but potholes were strewn across its surface like craters on the moon. Cars on the road swerved around the potholes and dips. Our bus simply rolled through the crevasses with a loud *THUMP!* The farther we drove, the more the road disintegrated into gravel and dirt.

We entered Almalybak.[3] Its old name was КИЗ (*KIZ*), the Russian acronym for the Kazakhstan Institute of Agriculture, which was located here during Soviet days. The Peace Corps staff pointed out the ivy-covered and graffitied remains of the institute as we drove by.

By now, the sky outside the bus had turned from a sweltering hazy blue to dark and grey. It began to rain. The bus continued to bounce along the wet streets of *KIZ*.

A Peace Corps staff member named Stasia stood up in front of the bus. She was a slender Russian woman in her late fifties or early sixties.

"Hello!" shouted Stasia with enthusiasm.

The trainees continued to talk over her.

"I want your attention," announced Stasia again.

The trainees continued to talk.

"*Vnimanie!*" screamed Stasia. *Attention!*

---

[3] Almalybak ("Apple Garden") and neighboring Zhalpaksai are villages on the outskirts of Almaty (pop. 8,000). They are commonly referred to as *KIZ*.

The bus became silent.

"Okay, much better," smiled Stasia with glee. "Eleven of you on this bus are to be taken to the local school here in *KIZ*. This is your training site. From here, you will be sent off with your new families. This is your new home."

These host families were locals who would take care of us through our three-month-long training. During training, we would learn Russian and Kazakh, the inner workings of Kazakhstani culture and our Peace Corps job roles.

"Get excited," stated Stasia in her barely noticeable accent. "Do not look so scared." She stared at me and continued. "It will not hurt, not one bit. Well, a little, but not much, and remember you will be reporting back to this very spot for the start of your language classes in two days' time, eight-in-the-morning."

The bus drove through the gates of the school yard. I saw the families waiting, middle-aged women and children mostly. They looked nervous.

I bet they have never seen an American before. At least, a real-life one. I wondered, peaking from the safety of my window. *Perhaps they're thinking what an American looks like, or what Americans might eat. How does an American even talk? Will they be able to even communicate with us?*

The rain was coming down harder now. The smell of ozone filled the bus as its doors opened. On Stasia's command, eleven of us rose to our feet. Eleven of us said our farewells to our new colleagues. Eleven of us headed towards the exit of the bus. This was the moment of no return.

Culture Shock

Could the Peace Corps recruiters—the ones who scouted Kaz 19 as new recruits back home on our college campuses, the recruiters with their pages of promotional literature and glossy pamphlets, the recruiters with their informational sessions and Q and As—could they have really prepared us for this moment? Could the Peace Corps have fully prepared us in three months of training and two years of service for the life-changing events that would come? Lifelong friendships, marriages to locals and to each other, travel to unknown places, career paths opened, and other doors closed—the list of unique experiences goes on and on. Through all the pains and triumphs that we would experience in this far off place, light years from home, Kazakhstan would be the sole and common glue in the experiences of Kaz 19. Kazakhstan would help define us and our lives, no matter how long we spent there. The initial shock and awe of Kazakhstan would burn an everlasting impression on me as I stepped off that bus.

Mars

I stepped off the bus onto the Martian surface. I gagged for a breath of air. The shock set in instantly. My hands became sweaty. My heart began to race. I should have been brimming with joy. Instead, I felt apprehension and angst.

The host families huddled under the awning of the school, avoiding the sudden downpour of rain. They approached my ten American companions warily and introduced themselves, but no one came to me. My heart sunk deeper as each trainee was led off with a family to his or her new home.

Stasia approached me.

"Tim, well, how do I say this? Äje, your host mum," stuttered Stasia, "she called a few minutes ago and she will be late. We wait for her before we take the bus onto the next stop."

I waited with Stasia. Rain pattered loudly on the awning above. The echoing noise grew louder by every minute that I waited. The bus, still filled with most of the remaining trainees waiting to go to other training villages, idled in the school yard. It felt as if everyone on the bus was staring at me as I waited. I felt anxious over my uncertain future.

You could hear the car coming from blocks away, even with the rain drowning out most noise. A white Soviet-made sedan came bouncing down the street. The engine clanged and rattled loudly. An elderly Kazakh man smoking a cigarette and topped with a cabby hat drove the car. Äje, I assumed, sat in the passenger seat. They quickly drove up to the school and jumped out of the car.

Like old friends, Stasia and Äje jested and chatted in Russian when they greeted each other. The old man stood by the car, aloof, smoking his cigarette, not seeming to care that it was raining. Äje finally approached me. The Kazakh woman was older than I expected, with short dyed-brown hair. She wore glasses, making her dark eyes look smaller than they really were.

"Aww, you are Teem," greeted Äje with a smirk.

She speaks English! I was stunned.

"My name is Äje. Let us go now. We must scurry home."

She grinned with delight as she led me to the car.

Despite the rain, my back-pack was latched to the top of the car. My tall six-foot-one frame was stuffed into the back seat. The car reeked of cigarettes and gasoline. I was rocketed away, leaving the busload of Americans. My driver launched down the road with his new American package. He swerved along the muddy road, avoiding some potholes and bouncing through others.

Gold-Toothed Smiles

My body bounced uncomfortably from bed after my long slumber. I needed to pee. I put on shorts and a t-shirt. I walked to the bedroom door, and I slowly opened it. The door creaked. The whole house creaked as I stepped into the hall.

I emerged into my new world. Things looked old and worn. There were dusty tables with old vases and books on them. Faded pictures hung on the walls, framed by slightly stained, floral wallpaper. I went down the dark corridor toward the light. The door to the outside was wide open, letting in a mid-morning breeze. Flies buzzed in. I followed them into the kitchen.

I found a young Kazakh woman in the kitchen helping Äje. It appeared that Äje was grinding meat with a metal crank. Flies buzzed about the pile of freshly minced flesh on the kitchen table. The woman was much younger than my new host mom, and she was dressed in a sort of bathroom robe with floral patterns. She wore a silk head scarf wrapped around her hair. The young woman gave me a big smile, flashing a mouthful of shiny gold teeth. Äje quickly told the woman something in Kazakh. The strange guttural sounds seemed just that, rough and alien. The words of their conversation sounded as if they were being coughed up with visceral force. Without even catching the woman's name or relation to Äje, she was out the front door and through a gate in the yard.

"Aww, Teem, you have awoken," grinned Äje—no gold teeth. "I am making our dinner, *manti*."

I had no idea what *manti* meant, but she continued talking without an explanation.

"I will have Qizi take you around town today. Aww, she and you will like that. Yes, you will like it."

Qizi was Äje's eleven-year-old daughter. She was her only

daughter. Äje and her husband, Atasi, must have had her while they were in their late forties since they looked more like grandparents to her rather than parents.

"Qizi!" screamed Äje. "Qizi!"

Qizi came bolting in from the yard outside through the front door. Qizi was skinny as a twig. She wore stained clothes that were becoming too small for her as she grew in spurts and spasms. She was full of energy, and she bounced frequently from point A to point Z.

Äje rattled off a word in Kazakh. Qizi nodded in compliance.

"Meester Teem, come, pleez," commanded Qizi with a silver-toothed smile and rough, basic English.

As Qizi led me to take a seat at a table on their front porch, the anxiety I had felt earlier in the morning was gone, at least, for the time being. A slight discomfort remained since I still needed to pee, and I was hungry. She began to set the table. Her hands were visibly dirty.

"*Tarelka*," said Qizi, and a small plate was placed in front of me. "*Vilka!*"

She set down a fork in front of me. *Chai* came next, and she hastily poured me a cup of tea.

"*Yaytsa i khleb*," spurted Qizi.

She placed a greasy fried egg on my dish and some crumbly white bread slices on the table. There was an exotic smell to my otherwise mundane meal, but I couldn't quite put my finger on it at first. I sniffed. Then I got a bigger whiff. It was the distinguishable smell of dill. Large amounts of dill covered my *yaytsa*, my greasy fried egg.

"*Pochti zabyla!*" shrieked Qizi. "*Maslo!*"

She ran and grabbed butter from a small refrigerator sitting outside on the porch. I could see the refrigerator wasn't plugged in, and flies buzzed out of it when she opened the door.

My morning hunger vanished as I ate my dill-encrusted egg

and drank tea. I avoided the butter. One basic need was satisfied, but another had still gone unsatiated since the evening prior.

Turkish Toilet

The Peace Corps had conveniently left this part out of their advertisements. The toilet wasn't really a toilet, at least by Western sensibilities. Some call them "Turkish toilets," but this wasn't even that. It was a hole carved in the wood floorboards of an outhouse. Deep down beneath this hole was a cesspool and quagmire of nastiness. Flies and a foul odor drifted up from the dark cavern below.

I avoided the outhouse the night before. My primordial fears of what lay below in the dark frightened me, but I could avoid it no longer. The pain in my groin and abdomen was unbearable.

SMACK! The door slammed behind me, and I was engulfed by darkness in the small wood shack. I squatted uncomfortably, with my feet planted firmly on each side of the small hole, trying not to fall in. I waited, but nothing came, so I squatted there a bit longer, waiting. It was difficult to balance with feet planted flat on the wood floor and my buttocks hanging over the abyss. I hummed a simple tune in my head, still waiting. I continued to balance there, hovering above the foul sewage that lurked in the darkness below.

I noticed the toilet paper. It wasn't the soft, quilted quality of American sensitivity. No, it was a pile of newspapers and old torn-up books. A wicker trashcan was next to this pile. It was filled with torn-out pages of Tolstoy and Dostoevsky, smeared brown and denigrated.[4]

My upper arm itched.

Damn shots. I thought.

A couple of days before, I had been poked a dozen times by the Peace Corps medical staff. It was the Peace Corps' attempt to make me immune to every bug and germ endemic to Central Asia: hepatitis A, rabies, some tick diseases, and a half-dozen other maladies.

After sitting for a long time, I gave up. I felt constipated.

As I left the outhouse, I saw my host dad, Atasi. He was standing nearby in his garden, smoking a cigarette, inspecting his vegetables.

"*Salem.*" I spouted out the only Kazakh word I knew.

"*Salem,*" smiled Atasi.

He didn't have gold teeth. Instead, he opted for no teeth. Yet, his smile was welcoming and playful, slightly devious. He was short, dark-skinned with a white balding head of hair. His loosely worn sweatpants and ragged t-shirt made his potbelly pop out.

We both stood face to face awkwardly in his garden, neither of us knowing what to say to each other. Awkwardness was becoming a theme for the day.

"*Ogurtsy,*" spat Atasi as he held out two cucumbers in his right hand. "*Das ist ein ogurtsy.*"

He thought German was a good substitute for the English he didn't know.

"*Pomidory. Das ist ein pomidory.*"

He handed me a vine of tomatoes, and we began to walk together through the yard. As we walked, Atasi grabbed a large

---

[4] Leo Tolstoy (1828-1910) wrote *War and Peace* and *Anna Karenina*. Fyodor Dostoevsky (1821-81) wrote *Crime and Punishment*. He was exiled by the Russian tsar to Kazakhstan (1854-59).

red apple off the ground. It had fallen from a tall tree in the center of the yard. Apple trees grew everywhere in *KIZ*. He handed me the cucumbers in his hand while he whipped out a knife from his pocket. He cut away an area of the apple where bugs had burrowed through the fruit. He cut a piece of apple and handed it to me.

"*Dyesert*," grinned Atasi.

I put the piece in my mouth. It was tart, but subtly sweet and quite refreshing.

"*Timka*, come, pleez," commanded Atasi.

He took me over to a pair of grubby-looking dogs, both mutts, lounging in the dirt. They were chained to the fence. One was black with pointy ears. It growled and showed its teeth—no gold teeth. The other was scruffy with shaggy hair and floppy ears. He wagged his tail playfully.

"*Eta Bashki*," said Atasi, and he pointed to the mean one with pointy ears. "*Eta Bashki, kak Presidyent* Booosh. *Khorosho nyet.* Ahh, *eta* Rex," continued Atasi, and he pointed to the scruffy dog. "*Alles klar?*"

"*Ja, alles klar.*" I nodded in agreement, even though most things weren't very clear.

The Stadium

"Meester Teem!" screamed Qizi. Qizi woke me from an afternoon nap. I had slept for two more hours since my late-morning breakfast.

"Come, pleez!" ordered Qizi.

She led me to the yard. It was hot under the August sun, but Qizi wanted to introduce me to the world outside, this alien planet called *KIZ*. We walked towards the metal gate to the street. A high iron-rod fence shielded the yard and the house from the dusty street outside.

As she opened the rickety gate, anxiety crept back into my thoughts. It pulsed through my veins and oozed from my pores.

The irrational fears that my brain had conjured earlier rushed back all at once. The panic seemed to last forever.

No time to worry. Qizi was already on the other side of the gate. The late-afternoon light hit my eyes with a glare as I followed her through the looking glass.

I stepped onto the street outside. It was a dirt road, dusty and uneven. Gates and tall metal fences framed the road. A few apartment blocks rose above houses and dusty trees in the distance. Whiffs of burning diesel and melting plastic percolated through the air, reaching my nostrils in noxious doses. Qizi led me along, kicking up dust as she ran and bounced ahead.

"*Na stadion*," shouted Qizi.

"Nahhh stadium?" I replied, perplexed and confused.

"*Nu*, *da*, *idti*," shouted Qizi.

I had no clue what she was saying to me.

We walked a few blocks, passing by hunched-over *babushka* along the road. They were dressed in coats and shawls, though it was quite hot outside. They had warm gold-tooth smiles on their faces.

Na stadion! It wasn't much of a stadium, or even a playing field for that matter. Qizi and I arrived at a large field lined with trees and trash piles. The grass was worn down and patchy. Dirt paths crisscrossed the field where passersby frequented. A group of young men were playing soccer on the opposite side of the field. A group of girls sat and watched. Vodka bottles and glass shards littered the field. The glass pieces dangerously poked up like blades of grass, neither affecting Qizi nor bothering the men playing soccer. We crossed the crabgrass-freckled *stadion* towards the group of girls.

"*Amerikanets*, Meester Teem, *Amerikanets*," yelled Qizi, and she pointed to an American playing soccer in the dust.

I was surprised and relieved to see Will, one of the eleven who had been left behind by the Peace Corps in *KIZ*. I desperately wanted to go up to this American and talk—make plans for our escape, at least for a brief moment, to somewhere away from the madness of *KIZ* and Kazakhstan. I tried to get his attention. A glance. A wave. A shout. Nothing seemed to work. Instead of acknowledging me, Will continued to play soccer so coolly with the local men. He didn't even give me a simple nod to recognize my existence.

Did he not see me? I asked myself. *A tall redheaded American with glasses is hard to miss around these parts.*

I felt slighted and miffed. I had the notion that those in the Peace Corps shared a common bond with each other—*Semper Fi*, and what-not. But here he was not following through with this unspoken agreement. Instead, Will continued to play. He played so coolly and spoke to the other men as if he knew them like old friends. He spoke with them as if he had some special password to the local lingo. He looked as if he had already figured out this whole Kazakhstan thing in less than a day.

"*Druzya*," exclaimed Qizi. "My friend!"

Qizi walked up to a group of five girls. The oldest two were in their early teens, but most looked the same age as Qizi's eleven years. Qizi rattled off Kazakh to the oldest girl, a lanky girl. This girl gave me a smile and giggled—only one gold tooth. The rest of the girls followed suit and giggled.

There I was in the *stadion*, standing awkwardly with a group of giggling tweens. After being led around like a dog on a leash by an eleven-year-old, I felt emasculated. I was surrounded by people, yet I felt utterly and completely alone.

This is my "adventure." I begrudgingly thought. *So this is the "adventure" I had signed up for with the Peace Corps...*

"The most difficult job..."

My mood had slipped from anxiety into depression. Stress and sadness had taken the best of me in that moment.

How would I last two years here, I began thinking as Qizi and I started back towards the house from the stadium, *if I can barely get through one day?*

Qizi and I continued back to the house in silence. During this walk my senses were raised and guarded. I didn't want to face the crushing tasks and itching sensations of Kazakhstan.

Then I noticed two Kazakh boys ahead on the side of the street arguing. A third boy stood nearby watching, egging them on. We continued down the road, getting closer to the boys. They looked as if they were twelve or thirteen. They shouted at each other louder and louder as we got closer. By the tone of the encounter, they seemed to be using nasty, crude words.

"*K chortu!*" yelled one boy.

"*Khui! Suka!*" responded the other.

Qizi and I walked closer. The boys were in our direct path

home. There was no avoiding them.

The shoving came next. Both boys grabbed each other by their shirts, pushing and shoving. Dust was scuffled into the air by their feet. The third boy watched, laughing and yelling at the two. He was yelling unrecognizable Kazakh words.

I looked at Qizi. She looked nervous and worried, not knowing what to do. We were coming within ten feet of the fight.

What to do? What to do? What to do? I thought in a panic as adrenaline started flowing through my brain and body. *What to do? What to do? What to do?*

Throughout the day, I had been pushed to my limits in every way. Everything that day had confused and baffled me. This day had taken me for a ride of uncertainty, toying with my senses and logic. My brain began to race. The prefrontal cortex furiously scanned and skimmed for an answer. Nothing in any of the Peace Corps' handbooks or training sessions at Tabagan had mentioned what to do for this sort of situation.

I suppose, though, some things are too complex for words and text to sum up. Yet, on the other hand, they are simple and universal. Some things, most things in life, don't have a handbook or brochure written on how to answer them. There are too many shades of grey, too many tones and textures, colors and luminosities, to include them in a tiny pamphlet or even a thousand-page book. There are too many sights and smells, ideas and thoughts. Have an open mind to get through the shocks and the bumps and the madness of the world. Live so your actions and intentions are good. That is the simplest, yet most complicated thing to do.

I'm in the Peace Corps, damn it! I reminded myself. *Doing nothing while these boys beat each other up, well, that defeats the purpose of whatever I am doing in Kazakhstan!*

In that moment, I acted.

"Stop! Stop! Stop!" I yelled at the boys in English.

I ran over to the group of boys before they could take their first punches at each other. In one swift move, I got in between the two boys. The third boy watched in bewilderment. He stopped laughing. I held my hands out—one to the boy on my right, the other to the boy on my left.

"No!" I said in a stern and curt voice.

They looked at me puzzled. I motioned and mimed for them to shake hands and be done with the argument. They didn't shake. Instead, the boys quickly walked away in opposite directions. The third boy continued to watch in a stupor.

Over a decade and a half has passed since that first roller-coaster of a day in *KIZ*, and I still think back and wonder what those kids must have thought when this gangly foreigner accidentally landed in the middle of their brawl. This was the shock and awe of grassroots diplomacy.

As Qizi and I scurried back to the house after stopping the fight, I could tell that something was fundamentally different for me—for both of us. My mindset had changed. During the quick blitz of my intervention between the boys, the fear, sadness, anger, anxiety, loneliness and all the other emotions that clouded my experience in Kazakhstan up to that point in time had been washed away in one swift action. I was filled with relief, and simple curiosity and wonder. Yes, that's what it was—curiosity and wonder.

Qizi and I continued along our way back to the house. Smiles were on both of our faces—gold-toothed smiles. Maybe the Peace Corps' ads and brochures had been right all along.

Lesson 2
Корпуса Мира (A Corps for Peace)

A Brief Introduction

At one million square miles, Kazakhstan is the ninth largest country on earth. Yet, it only contains nineteen million inhabitants. It is the population of the New York City metro area—spread from Phoenix to Chicago, Dallas to Bismarck. Aside from the Altai and Tien Shan Mountains in the east of the country and some pine and birch-tree forests on the fridges of its Siberian north, much of the country is empty, flat, arid steppe land. There are places that I have seen there that are so far removed from civilization that it feels like nothing else exists except for the infinite horizon of the steppe and the blue sky. This land of vast nothingness is, strangely, one of the most exotic and beautiful places I have ever encountered in my life.

Shrouded by a cloud of secrecy, closed off from the outside world by the Soviet Union, most Americans know little-to-nothing about this country. When *Borat* hit theaters in 2006, many Americans thought the country was made up by comedian

Sacha Baron Cohen.[5] However, as I learned when I landed in Almaty in August of 2007, it is very real.

Qaz

Golden Warrior, Almaty

Tucked away between Russia to the north, China to the east, Europe in the west and the numerous Stans (e.g. Uzbekistan, Afghanistan) to the south, Kazakhstan is at the center of Eurasia. At the crossroads of East and West, it's not European nor is it quite Asian. It is Central Asian in culture, but it is also Russian. It was believed to be the edge of the world by Alexander the Great.[6] It was a land conquered by Genghis Khan.[7] Yet, so immense in size, much of Kazakhstan has never been "conquered" by anyone. It remains wild, untamed.

The Kazakhs emerged as a distinct ethnic group sometime during the late-medieval period (circa 1500). They descended from Turkic, Mongolic and ancient Scythian tribes of the vast and expansive Eurasian steppe. They lived aptly by the name, *Qazaq*, which scholars believe is derived from the Turkic word *qaz* ("to wander").

For generations, the people of the steppe lived a nomadic life from the Volga River in the west to the Altai and Tien Shan thou-

---

[5] *Borat! Cultural Learnings of America for Make Benefit Glorious Nation of Kazakhstan* (2006) is a comedy film starring Sacha Baron Cohen.
[6] Alexander the Great (356-323 B.C.E.) was a Greek king who conquered the Persian Empire. His conquest took him to the Fergana Valley, a region in Uzbekistan, around 329 B.C.E.
[7] Genghis Khan (c. 1155-1227) was the founder of the Mongol Empire, which spanned Mongolia to Europe. His army arrived in Kazakhstan in the 1220s.

sands of miles to the east.[8] They herded their livestock from one pasture to the next, living in large circular tents called yurts. From the Arabs and Persians, they adopted a shamanistic form of Islam, convenient to a wandering lifestyle. Life repeated itself in this nomadic way for hundreds of years.

The Russians entered the picture by the eighteenth century. By the end of the medieval period, the Russians had overthrown the "Tatar Yoke." The Golden Horde had ruled Russia since the Mongols overwhelmed much of humanity in the 1200s. First came fur traders and remote outposts manned by Cossacks (Slavic frontiersmen). Petropavlovsk, the city near my Peace Corps village, was one such frontier fort. In the 1800s, the British and Russian empires competed in a colonial land grab for Turkestan (Central Asia). This "Great Game" or "Tournament of Shadows" cemented Russia's claim on Kazakhstan. In the late nineteenth century, Russians began colonizing deeper into the steppe. This disrupted the Kazakhs' nomadic way of life.

The twentieth century was ever-changing for Kazakhstan. The tsar (Царь or emperor of Russia) was overthrown in the Revolution of 1917. For five years, civil war raged across the old empire. Vladimir Lenin founded the Soviet Union (USSR) in 1922, imposing communism on Kazakhstan.

It was the Soviet Union that codified a "Kazakh" ethnic nationhood. At the same time, the Soviets forced the Kazakhs to abandon their nomadic life, settle down and learn Russian. Kazakhs became just one of many ethnicities in Kazakhstan. "Troublesome" groups—like Volga Germans, Germans who settled in the Volga region in the 1700s, and *Koryo-saram*, Koreans who lived in the far eastern region of Russia—were forced to resettle there from other parts of the Soviet Union. General Secretary Stalin was not trusting of his multi-ethnic union.[9] Con-

---

[8] The Volga River is the longest river in Europe. It flows into the Caspian Sea.
[9] Joseph Stalin (1878-1953) was the ruler of the Soviet Union from 1927-53.

centration camps called *gulag* became the some of the largest population centers in Kazakhstan.

The Nazi invasion of the Soviet Union sparked the Great Patriotic War (WWII) in 1941. The War saw ten percent, around 600,000, of Kazakhstan's population perish and more forced relocations of ethnic groups. The War brought large scale industrialization to Kazakhstan.

After Stalin's death in 1953, Nikita Khrushchev became the leader of the Soviet Union. He initiated the Virgin Lands Campaign to stimulate grain production in the arid steppe. This program was largely a failure. However, this enormous undertaking promoted more immigration to Kazakhstan. With an influx of Russian and Ukrainian settlers, Kazakhs became the minority in Kazakhstan.

During the Cold War, the Semipalatinsk Polygon in northeast Kazakhstan became the testing grounds for the Soviet Union's military-industrial complex. Like my home state of Nevada, nuclear weapons were extensively tested in Kazakhstan. Nuclear testing left a legacy of contamination that will last for tens of thousands of years on the "infinite" landscape of the steppe.

The Aral Sea would be the next to fall victim to the Soviet's folly in Central Asia. It was once the fourth largest lake in the world. The Sea was an oasis in the deserts of Central Asia. Starting in the 1960s, the Aral Sea was drained to irrigate cotton fields in Uzbekistan and southern Kazakhstan.[10] Like the Virgin Lands Campaign, "progress" turned into failure. The region surrounding the Sea dried, becoming contaminated with pesticides, sandstorms and drought.

During the Great Game, Afghanistan had been the staging ground for Russian and British exploits. First, the British sent a military expedition to Kabul in the 1840s, believing Afghan

---

[10] Uzbekistan is a former Soviet Republic south of Kazakhstan.

tribesmen were colluding with imperial Russia. The occupiers were driven out by the tribes in 1842. The Soviets would repeat history from 1979-89, attempting to prop up a communist regime in Kabul. The war against the Mujahideen—Islamic jihadist fighters who used US-funded weapons, with one such fighter being Osama bin Laden—would take 15,000 Soviet lives. Many of those who were drafted to fight for the communists were Muslim recruits from the Soviet's Central-Asian republics. My host father was one of the young Kazakhs drafted to fight. The defeat was a disaster and humiliation for the Soviet Union.

Although the Soviet Union had flaws, it was a stabilizing force. It has been thirty years since the Soviet Union's collapse, yet many in Kazakhstan nostalgically reminisce about the "good ole' days." The Soviets promised a utopian future, uniting and modernizing people from the Baltic Sea to the Bering Strait. The Soviet Union helped bring millions out of serfdom. The Soviets educated millions. Today, the countries of the former Soviet Union have some of the highest literacy rates in the world. Though modernization came at a price, there were great strides in the sciences. Baikonur Cosmodrome—where Yuri Gagarin was launched in 1961, becoming the first person to space—is the best example in Kazakhstan.

Nevertheless, the writing was on the walls for the collapse of the Soviet state. In the 1980s, the last Soviet leader, Mikhail Gorbachev, enacted two reform programs: *Glasnost* (political and social openness) and *Perestroika* (economic restructuring). These programs quickened the demise of the USSR. In Kazakhstan, the anti-nuclear movements like Nevada Semipalatinsk created open dissent against the state. Food and consumer goods became scarcer. Black markets operated on the streets in a sort of proto-capitalism. At the same time, the military machine was bankrupting the country. The war in Afghanistan and the nuclear meltdown at the Chernobyl power plant (1986) not only humiliated the Soviets, but it also highlighted to its citizens the incompetence of their state. The system was unraveling.

In 1989, a politician named Nursultan A. Nazarbaev took power over the Kazakh SSR. Two years later in December of 1991, Kazakhstan declared independence from the collapsing Soviet Union. Nazarbaev would be the only name on the ballot for president. He ruled Kazakhstan until 2019. In his thirty years of rule, he saw the ups and downs of a nation in transition.

As Kazakhstan's economy was integrated into the global economy, a few technocrats profited immensely from selling off the Soviet's state-run industries, particularly oil and gas in Kazakhstan. At the same time, Nazarbaev saw Kazakhstan's living standards plummet in the 1990s. Men's life expectancy dropped to a low of fifty-eight in 1996. Millions of people fled Kazakhstan in the 1990s. Most of the Volga Germans, who numbered around a million in 1989, left Kazakhstan, taking advantage of Germany's "right to return" laws.

By the 2000s, Nazarbaev's nation was connected to the rest of the world through the internet. At the same time, Kazakhstan is still one of the least politically free nations in the world. Free speech is far from free.

In early 2022, protests and unrest broke out over gas prices. In a rare instance, Kazakhstan was catapulted into the news cycle. Underlying frustrations with government corruption and a lack of economic opportunities and liberties boiled over. The government cracked down, the internet was shut down, Russian troops arrived to restore order and thousands of citizens were arrested. Long before the unrest, many journalists in the country had learned the consequences of speaking out against those in charge.

Despite Nazarbaev's shortcomings (corruption, familial nepotism, megalomania) he saw living standards rise again in the 2000s. He walked a fine line of diplomacy with the USA, Europe,

Корпуса Мира (A Corps for Peace)

China and Putin's Russia, bringing a burgeoning, yet tenuous prosperity to the Kazakhstani people.[11]

Mr. Nazarbaev's desire to bring Kazakhstan onto the world's stage ushered

The Capital, Astana (now Nur-Sultan)

the US Peace Corps to Kazakhstan. From 1993 to 2011, over a thousand volunteers served in English education and community development programs in Kazakhstan. Kaz 1 would be the first group of volunteers to arrive in Kazakhstan in 1993.

At twenty-two and a recent graduate of the University of Nevada, I followed in August 2007 in Kaz 19.

Senator Kennedy

At midnight on October 14, 1960, then presidential candidate John F. Kennedy spoke to an energized crowd at the University of Michigan. In his speech he asked these students: "How many of you who are going to be doctors, are willing to spend your days in Ghana? Technicians or engineers, how many of you are willing to work in the Foreign Service and spend your lives traveling around the world?" In his short speech, Kennedy sparked a promise to create a Peace Corps, to send Americans abroad to countries in need, helping in the development and cooperation between nations. This promise was made at the height of the Cold War. The Cuban Missile Crisis would bring the Soviet Union and the US to the brink of nuclear destruction just two years after the University of Michigan speech.

The Peace Corps was inaugurated by Executive Order 10924 on March 1, 1961. It was formalized by Congress with the "Peace Corps Act." The first group of Peace Corps volunteers arrived in

---

[11] Vladimir Putin (b. 1952) is the leader of the Russian Federation.

Ghana by that August.

Since its founding, the Peace Corps has served in more than 140 countries. It follows three simple goals:

1) Help interested countries in meeting their needs for trained men and women;
2) Promote a better understanding of Americans for host countries and the people being served there;
3) Create an understanding for Americans of host countries and their people. (This book is part of that third goal.)

Over 200,000 volunteers have served. These Americans—many of whom were young recent-college graduates, like me—have worked in the fields of education and youth engagement, healthcare, technology, environmental work, agricultural improvement, community development, and business and economic development. We sacrificed twenty-seven months of our lives to work abroad in communities far away from home. The places are not always the easiest of places to live. Comforts of home are often non-existent. Family and friends are left behind for two years. Yet, the experiences are life changing for those who serve. As the Peace Corps' advertisements went, it's the "toughest job you'll ever love."

In terms of impact, it is difficult to quantify. The Peace Corps attempts to do this through audits and reports to warrant the couple hundred million allocated to it by Congress every year. Financially, it is a small part of the federal government's budget, especially when put side-by-side to the military. Nevertheless, the impact of the Peace Corp has been one of the greatest forces for goodwill in the American story. Millions of lives around the world have been improved and forever changed because of a relationship they had with a Peace Corps volunteer. The work of the Peace Corps is grassroots diplomacy at its finest.

Корпуса Мира (A Corps for Peace)

I am proud to have been a part of this effort. In the spirit of the Peace Corps' third goal, this book is my attempt to bring the Peace Corps and Kazakhstan home.

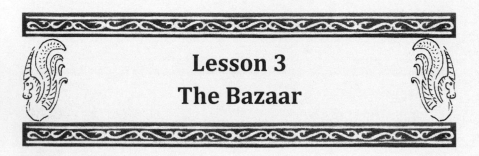

Lesson 3
The Bazaar

"Boys, these are our own tracks, and we've actually been circussing round and round in a circle for more than two hours, out here in this blind desert!"

From Roughing It
by Mark Twain

Harbinger of Winter

It was the beginning of October. The leaves were changing colors. Vibrant oranges, yellows and reds dotted *KIZ*. The rains were coming more frequently now, quenching the arid foothills of the Tien Shan. With northerly winds off the steppe cooling the hot air, the summer passed away.

"*Segodnya my poydem na rynok,*" shouted Lyudmila Aleksandrovna as we gathered in front of the village school.

None of us ten trainees listened to our teacher.

"Listen!" She shouted again in her thick, accented English.

The Bazaar

"Please, quiet," whispered our other teacher, Muğalïma. "Please, listen to Lyudmila Aleksandrovna."

"Listen up!" shouted Muğalïma and Lyudmila Aleksandrovna in tandem.

We all shut up.

"Okay, much better," continued Lyudmila Aleksandrovna. "Today, vee are going on a vield trip to the bazaar. You must buy vinter *dublenka* today. *Dublenka* is a big jacket."

We called Lyudmila by her formal patronymic Aleksandrovna, daughter of Aleksandr, as a sign of respect that students give to teachers.[12] She was a Russian woman in her late forties. She hailed from a town several hours from nowhere in the middle of the steppe. It was a tough, cold place, and from first impressions, Lyudmila Aleksandrovna looked like a tough, cold woman. That was mostly a façade. In reality, she was a sweet person who cared about her young Peace Corps trainees. She had been teaching Russian to trainees for years.

As a complete antithesis to Lyudmila Aleksandrovna, there was Muğalïma. She was a new teacher to the Peace Corps. Although she was our other teacher, we didn't call her by her patronymic. For one, none of us could spit out the right pattern of letters and syllables to say her Kazakh father's patronymic. *Zhiz... Zhoo... Zhizhoo... something like that...* She also seemed more like a peer to us than a teacher. She was only twenty-two. She was from the northern city of Petropavlovsk, Petro for short.[13] After training ended, I would be heading to a village called Yavlenka near Petro. Petro was, for several centuries, a Russian outpost in the land of nomadic Kazakhs. Because of Petro's Russian history, Muğalïma was russified to her core. She

---

[12] The patronymic is derived from a father's first name. It acts as a middle name in the Russian language.

[13] Petropavl (fmr. Petropavlovsk) is the northernmost city in Kazakhstan (pop. 200,000).

dressed the part of a Russian. She talked the part of a Russian. She was like so many other Kazakhs, Russian in every which way except in face and name.

"Vee are going to take the bus to the bazaar," continued Lyudmila Aleksandrovna with her announcement. "It is called the Baraholka Bazaar. It is on the outskirts of Almaty."

The announcement to go to the bazaar was a welcome one for the group of trainees. For several weeks, we had been begging Lyudmila Aleksandrovna and Muğalïma to take us to the bazaar. Today the bazaar would be one of our few reprieves in training, an excuse to play hooky and skip the endless hours of language classes and workshops.

Six days a week we spent toiling away at learning the complexities and tongue twisters of the Russian language, with a few interjections of Kazakh here and there. In the hours not learning the local languages, we labored in teacher practicums, English tutoring sessions with the local children, community projects and cultural lessons by Peace Corps staff. The Peace Corps made sure we had no idle time, no time to get us into trouble and even less time to get homesick.

"I vant you to mind your belongings," continued Lyudmila Aleksandrovna. Her voice was deep and raspy as if she had once been a smoker. "Be careful on the bus ride and inside the bazaar. To my mind, there are many, many *vory* there. They vill take your belongings iv you do not vatch out!"

"*Vory* are thieves," clarified Muğalïma.

Our group began for the bazaar, walking from the school to the bus stop.

It was mid-October. Only a month was left in *KIZ*. Soon we would be leaving for our permanent sites, even smaller villages in the middle of nowhere. Some of us would be heading to sites up north, where winter, or so we had heard through hearsay, had already arrived in the northern reaches of the country. The auguries and omens pointed to a harsh, long and unforgiving winter—at least, that's what I was told by my host mom, Äje.

Äje's laughter from the previous evening rang in my head…

"Aww, Teem," laughed Äje shrilly as I showed her my ski jacket from America. *"You cannot have thought this jacket would work in the north."*

My host mom, a southerner all her life, had only been to the north of Kazakhstan once.

"But this jacket is great!" I told her. *"It's the best jacket."*

I was exaggerating. Nevertheless, it was a decent jacket. Plus, I had paid a lot of money for it back in the States.

"Oh, no, indeed it cannot work," continued Äje. *"Aww, you will freeze to death. That is certain."*

"But it's high quality."

"No, it will not work," reinforced Äje. *"You are going to, what's the village of yours? Yes, Yavlenka. It is in Siberia. You know of Siberia, yes?"*

"Yes, I know of Siberia." I said in a tone of irritation.

"Aww, it snows there now as we speak," said Äje with great conviction. *"You will buy one of our fur dublenka at the bazaar. Yes, a good Kazakh dublenka. That's what you will do."*

"Frak you?!"

Ten of us trainees continued to walk through the village with Lyudmila Aleksandrovna and Muğalïma. We made our way towards the bus stop.

The original eleven trainees who had been dropped off in *KIZ* in August had been reduced to ten now. The eleventh, Leo, had been transferred within the first week to another training village to prepare for his university teaching placement. He was slightly older than the rest of us, and back home, he had some actual real-life teaching experience, so he was promoted. He replaced the spot of a dropout, a girl who left within a week of landing in Kazakhstan.

A Five Finger Feast

The rumors milled from training site to training site. Who-ever retold the gossip had a different story of why this girl had left. Some claimed the girl couldn't hack it; the Peace Corps wasn't for her. Medical Separation was the term others threw around. Some said it was because of adverse effects to the end-less regiment of vaccinations we took at the hands of the Peace Corps medical staff. Others claimed it was a terrible bout of diarrhea. Throughout training, the medical staff warned us of the "poop problems" we would face.

The girl who Leo replaced wasn't the only one to leave Kaz 19. Three additional trainees were also gone by now. The ru-mors milled about them too. Diarrhea. Host family problems. Homesickness. The rumors always seemed to be milling, and they churned not just about the ones who left early (Early Termination or ET). The trainees even knew the gossip and rumors of the 140 volunteers (groups Kaz 17 and Kaz 18) already scattered around Kazakhstan, and we had yet to meet most of them.

It wasn't a surprise to me that so much gossip and drama went around. Mix seventy-five trainees, most in their early twenties, into a pressure cooker with varying temperaments, attitudes and personas, add Peace Corps incest, and *voila!* Nothing could be kept secret.

In addition to all the rumors floating from training village to training village, there was an inexplicable divisiveness to the ten of us in *KIZ*. I sensed the divisions from the very beginning of training. There were cliques in the small group of ten, if you could call two or three people a clique. Trainee 1, 2 and 3 were best friends with Trainee 4, until they unexpectedly dropped Trainee 4 from their group one day. Trainee 5 and 6 were never far apart, and sometimes they brought along Trainee 7 when-ever the whim struck them. Trainee 5 hated Trainee 2, and vice versa. The dynamics of social life in *KIZ* was made more awkward than it needed to be. The dynamics meant that some were friends—sometimes, as the rumors went, more than friends—others not so much. Some were nice about not being friends in careful, not-so-off-putting ways. Others, they were nice enough to give the person they disliked the middle finger behind their back. In Kazakhstan, this was known as the "evil eye" (Көз).

I never totally understood the divisiveness and cliques, and looking back on it today, I still ask myself why some couldn't get along. After all, we were supposed to be the proponents of peace. We shared many of the same values. We were all college graduates from mostly middle-class, mostly liberal-minded America. Then again in any group I suppose it was just natural for personalities to clash and others to pair off, mix and match in their own strange ways as circumstances allowed. The cliques made things in *KIZ* tricky and difficult to navigate since we were forced to work together on projects around the village. Even with this necessity, some still just couldn't get along.

The clique situation left me—I guess that made me Trainee 8—with the loner Alexander (Trainee 9), a socially awkward redhead or *ryzhiy*. I too am a *ryzhiy*. As the Russian children's saying goes: *"Ryzhiy, ryzhiy konopatyy, ubil dedushku lopatoy."* Translated: "Redhead, redhead with freckles, you killed your grandfather with a shovel." The saying confuses me, even to this day. But, like so many things in Kazakhstan, it was easier to just not ask questions.

There was also Jose (Trainee 10). Jose—who is today still a close friend of mine, a brother, in fact—was quiet at first, but we slowly became friends over the months of training. Jose and I seemed to have agreeable temperaments that allowed us to go peacefully between the various cliques and deal with the daily stressors that Kazakhstan threw at us from time to time. Jose was already an old man when he joined the Peace Corps, an elderly twenty-five. He was born and raised in the tropics of

Central America and, later, California. He was a native Spanish speaker who also spoke French, a perfect candidate for Peace Corps Africa or Latin America. Yet, here he was in Central Asia, where winters were long, dark and cold, learning his fourth language, Russian.

Our large group continued along on our walk through *KIZ* with Lyudmila Aleksandrovna and Muğalïma. We walked down the dusty road towards the bus stop.

Aside from the internal politics of our training group, it was always a bit awkward walking through *KIZ* together as a foreign gaggle. Wherever the gaggle went, it was gawked at by the local villagers. It seemed that the Americans had landed into a bit of celebrity. Whenever and wherever we encountered a child or group of children on the street, they shouted our names. They knew all our names. Children approached us and shook our hands. The children of *KIZ* were endearing, friendly and enthusiastic towards their American guests. The kids never sensed the internal tensions among the trainees. They didn't care if the trainees didn't get along. To them, we were all best friends, like the Beatles were—well, before Paul sued John, George and Ringo, and before Yoko split up the band for good.

Along the road to the bus stop, our gaggle passed children and teenagers on their way to school. They were dressed up in their finest outfits. The boys were in shiny satin suits and pointy loafers, and the girls dressed in black-and-white blouses and skirts. Some girls wore dresses akin to a French maid's outfit. All the girls, no matter what age, attempted to wear high-heel shoes as if the muddy and dirty pot-holed roads didn't exist.

As we passed one group of teenage boys, the females in our gaggle continued ahead while the male trainees stopped and greeted the group of boys. A few jests in our elementary Russian and Kazakh welcomed the village boys. We went around shaking hands. By this time, we had been trained to shake hands in the

The Bazaar

Central-Asian fashion—not firm and not long lasting, instead bashful and somewhat limp. With some of the boys, we taught them to give us high fives and fist bumps. Apparently, the high five and fist bump weren't universally known in *KIZ* until our arrival. We made them popular with our American celebrity.

We left the teenagers and continued along to catch up with our group. Meanwhile, some of the timider boys who hadn't approached our group to shake our hands shouted from afar.

"Hellooo!"

"How are you?"

"What *is* your name?!"

"*Frak you?!*"

Labyrinth

I would learn to love and hate the bazaar in my two years in Kazakhstan. The bazaar was complex and stressful, but also exciting and every visit an adventure. The bazaar reflected the labyrinth of Kazakhstani society and the economic complexities existing in the larger scheme of the former Soviet Union.

Before its collapse in 1991, the Soviet Union had been the second largest economy in the world. The state ran everything: heavy industry, department stores, farms, utilities, transportation, etc.

> "*Turning and turning in the widening gyre the falcon cannot hear the falconer; things fall apart; the centre cannot hold; mere anarchy is loosed upon the world, the blood-dimmed tide is loosed, and everywhere the ceremony of innocence is drowned; the best lack all conviction, while the worst are full of passionate intensity.*"[14]

Even before its collapse, people began hawking family heir-

---

[14] From "The Second Coming" by William Butler Yeats (1919).

looms on the streets so they could buy a loaf of bread. People raided abandoned buildings, stripping pipes and wiring from the walls to trade for goods and vodka. Millions emigrated abroad, and those weren't even the worst things that happened to people during the collapse. Meanwhile, a select few technocrats and former Party insiders made billions and billions and BILLIONS off the demise of the Soviet Union. Policies and plans! *Perestroika* and fledgling capitalism! Defaults and collapse! Oil and corruption! Inflation and black markets! It had been a labyrinth of economics indeed. Yet, to most people, the maze simply meant bread and vodka.

To me that day we arrived at the bazaar, the economics simply meant how to get the lowest price for a *dublenka* jacket.

The maze of the Baraholka Bazaar was situated through a mess of traffic and congestion on the outskirts of Almaty. It was the largest bazaar in Almaty, and truck loads of cheap goods and merchandise flowed into the bazaar from China, Russia, Turkey and India. Likewise, busloads of buyers from as far away as Uzbekistan, Siberia and western Kazakhstan would load up boxes and fill rice sacks to haul their newly purchased goods back to wherever they had come from before. It was a new-age Silk Road.[15] Baraholka was a maze of tarps strung together and shipping container crates pushed side by side. It was a mismatch of cavernous paths and stalls jammed with men pushing carts of pirated Britney Spears CDs and fake Adidas t-shirts. Everything ever conceived and created by the gods—Deng Xiaoping and Steve Jobs alike—could be bought and sold at Baraholka.[16] Boots, radios, fur hats, fake-leather jackets, cars, carrots, chickens, carpets, rugs, cutlery, pots, pans. You name it and Baraholka shall provideth.

---

[15] The Silk Road was an ancient trading route between Asia and Europe.
[16] Deng Xioping (1904-97) was the leader of China in the 1980s and 1990s. Steve Jobs (1955-2011) was the founder of Apple.

The Bazaar

Into the Beast

The ride to the bazaar had been stifling and cramped. The bus driver had overloaded the small bus with each new stop heading into the city. The luckier passengers, mostly women and elderly, had taken seats while most had to stand body to body, holding on with their dear life to the straps that hung from the ceiling. Armpits were jammed into faces. The smell of bad breath and sweat mixed into the already stuffy air of the vehicle.

Upon arrival at Baraholka, our group unloaded from the bus like tightly packed sardines in a can. We stumbled and tripped over the other passengers to speedily vacate the large over-crowded vehicle. *Honk! Honk! Beep! Beep!* We had been let off the bus in the middle of traffic on a car-jammed road. Like a game of Frogger, we ran around honking cars and stalled busses to get to safety.

"Peace Corps! Over here," shouted Muğalïma.

Muğalïma beckoned our group to the curbside. She began to organize the group of shell-shocked Americans. Lyudmila Alek-

41

sandrovna arrived and quickly supplanted Muğalïma at the task.

"My little children," said Lyudmila Aleksandrovna. "Vee have arrived at bazaar. Get a partner and do not become lost. To my mind, vee vill meet at this spot again in thoooree hours."

We began to partner up.

"And I remind you all to vatch vor *vory*," inserted the concerned Lyudmila Aleksandrovna.

The trainees grouped up into their cliques and entered the bazaar. I paired up with Jose—and Alexander, the loaner and *ryzhiy*, came along too. The three of us were on the search for *dublenka* jackets since we were all headed to the frigid north.

We made our way toward the busy entrance of the bazaar, a tight opening in between two shipping containers. The three of us stood at the entrance of the beast. The narrow, dark passage was framed by crates, tarps, plywood and plexiglass.

Beggars loitered at the entrance, a few old men, but most were small children. They loitered among the humdrum and commotion of shoppers and cart pushers going in and out of the bazaar. Kazakhstanis called these beggars *Tsygane*. Kazakhs and Russians alike hated the *Tsygane*. To them, *Tsygane* and *vory* were synonymous. The *Tsygane* children wandered barefoot through the crowd of people, and even outside to the road and traffic, offering up dirty hands to beg for a *tenge* (T) or two. The older *Tsygane* just sat and waited patiently near the entrance. They collected what the children gathered.

We ventured deeper into the entrance of the dark cavern towards the vendors inside.

"*Samsa! Samsa!*" shouted a vendor, selling fried pastries.

"*Shashlyk!*" yelled another, standing next to a smoky barbecue and selling kebabs of mystery meat.

The entrance area was jammed full of vendors. A woman stood next to a port-a-potty charging people to use her toilet. A few women sat on blankets on the ground, pawning trinkets of no worth. One woman was selling decapitated sheep heads, a delicacy in Kazakh culture. She used a cardboard box as a table to display her choice meats. Bootleg VHS tapes, CDs and DVDs of blockbuster movies hung from the walls of vendors. The bourgeois laws and Western notions of intellectual property didn't seem to exist here. "Illegal" was such a subjective term in Kazakhstan, after all. I'd learn if you can pay off the police with a small bribe, titles and terms such as "legal" and "illegal" had almost no difference.

Germans?

We descended deeper and deeper into the dark cave of the bazaar. In every which way, small alleys and narrow aisles spread out, playing tricks on the eye, looking as if the bazaar stretched on for miles and miles. *Maybe it did...* Murmurs of commotion and shouting resonated through the air. Delivery people with dollies going about with their huge loads of goods pushed past us. They honked and shouted at us in Russian and Kazakh. As we walked along, merchants began hustling us to buy their goods.

"Buy my beautiful rug for your house," said one merchant.

"Buy my shiny gold jewelry for your lovely, beautiful wife," said another.

"But dear merchants," we laughed, "we don't have houses to lay down these wonderful rugs, nor do we have wives to provide these beautiful gems."

Merchants continued to hound us with disorienting speed

and confusion. *Buy this and buy that!* It was difficult enough getting through the crowded paths and narrow aisles of the bazaar, but it was made even more difficult with the merchants trying to pull us into their stalls to buy their junk. Our foreign guise must have made for easy targets on our backs. As redheaded *ryzhiy*, Alexander and I brought even more attention upon ourselves—more than we had hoped. Kazakhstan doesn't have many people with red hair. Jose, being Hispanic, also didn't fit in amongst Kazakhs or Russians. People gawked at us.

"*Ryzhiy, ryzhiy!*" shouted one emaciated merchant from his dark stall, like a hunter cooing his prey. "*Guten Tag! Dublenka?*"

The Kazakh man held up a large fur jacket. Somehow, he read our minds. The merchant baited us, and we took the bite. The two *ryzhiy* and Jose walked into the merchant's trap.

The stall was cramped and small and it went back less than twenty feet. The odor was overwhelming with a strange, artificial chemical smell. On the walls hung fur jackets and hats of different styles, shapes and textures. Another Kazakh man was inside the stall working. He was larger than his counterpart. He had a grumpy ogre-look to him.

"*Nyemtsy?*" asked the thin man with a toothless grimace and a pockmarked face.

Nyemtsy? He thought we were German tourists. Other merchants in the bazaar had asked this same question to us. It seemed that Germans were the most-common foreign travelers in Central Asia. A place seldom traveled by the rest of the world.

"*Nyemtsy?*" repeated the merchant.

"*Nyet,*" answered our crew in unison.

"*Amerikantsy?*" asked the man, looking at Alexander and me.

"*Da, amerikantsy.*" I answered yes to being American.

The merchant nodded in affirmation while the ogre simply stared at us from across the stall.

"*Pakistanets?*"

The Bazaar

He pointed to Jose with an expression of confusion.

"He thinks you're Pakistani," clarified Alexander to Jose.

"*Vse amerikantsy*," replied Jose, assuring the man that we were all Americans.

The man looked at Jose up and down, doubting his statement. For many Kazakhstanis, we would learn, they had the very biased view that all Americans were either white or black. This left little room for the many shades in American society. Still, for this merchant, Jose meant money.

"*Nu*," started up the man, "ferrrend fraaam *Ameriki i Pakistana*." He was determined that Jose was from Pakistan, as he continued in a hybrid of English, German and Russian, "*dublenki* zhaaakkkets! *Guten* zhaaakkkets!"

The toothless man pointed to the jackets on the walls. He shouted something to the ogre who was working in the back of the stall. The man stopped what he was doing. He approached the group with a grinning face.

"*Amerikantsy*," whispered the thin man to the ogre with eagerness and a smirk, calling us "suckers with money."

The ogre nodded in agreement. He came forward to stand over us, awkwardly watching our every move.

"Maaany *dublenki* zhaaakkkets!" continued the thin toothless merchant. He spat up saliva as he talked, and he began grabbing jackets down from the wall. "*Dublenki* zhaaakkkets from Cheena, Germanee, Indeeya, Rasha..." He trailed off listing the many countries of his products' provenance.

While the merchant continued on about the quality of his products, his ogre counterpart grabbed Alexander with a sweaty hand. He began forcefully putting a coat on him. Alexander, unsuspecting of the ogre's action, looked at us with a tense, uncomfortable smile. Droplets of sweat beaded on his forehead. He overheated from nervousness and the large jacket in the stuffy stall. The large man next grabbed another jacket. It looked as if it was made of fake leather and trimmed with fake fur. He manhandled Jose and suited him with the jacket.

As I watched what was happening to Alexander and Jose, I began to back out of the stall slowly. I didn't want to fall victim to the forceful fashion show. I could see Alexander had already pulled out *tenge* (T30,000, roughly $250) from his wallet. It didn't take long for the toothless merchant and his ogre henchman to convince him to buy the overpriced, cheaply made jacket. Jose wasn't so easily sold. He, at least, bargained the price down for the jacket. The haggling didn't look like it was going well. He pulled out T25,000 (about $200).

While I backed out of the stall, I bumped into someone behind me. It was a merchant from a neighboring stall. The blonde-haired man was young, more of a boy, a kid, than a man. It seemed that he had caught wind of the alien gibberish coming from next door. He forcefully pulled me into his booth next door.

"Wha... What are you doing?" I demanded in English.

His booth was filled with *shapki* or hats—different sizes and shapes, some fur and some cotton, others leather.

"*U menya shapki!*" said the Russian kid forcefully. "Buy hat! Good hat!" demanded the merchant as he clenched a hat in his sweaty hand.

This boy was pushy. He spoke English with rude roughness, unpleasant to the ear. He plopped a big fur hat onto my head.

"*Nyet!* I don't want your hat." I yelled.

I tried pulling myself out from the stall.

"*Amerikanets!* Give me *dengi!* Maaanney! Maaanney!"

The boy gestured with his hands for me to fork over the cash I carried in my wallet. At this point, it didn't seem to matter to him whether we exchanged money for goods rendered or not.

"*Nyet!*" I said angrily.

I threw the hat at him, and I ran out of the booth. Just at this same time, Jose and Alexander were exiting the other stall wearing newly bought *dublenka* jackets.

"What's going on Tim?" asked Jose.

"Uhh, let's get out of here." I replied. "And fast!"

The Russian boy walked out from the stall. He glared at us with the "evil eye" as we walked away quickly.

"*Blyat*! Foog yoo, Ger-man *MAN*!" shouted the young Russian.

We walked away even faster, escaping the boy and the merchants—Alexander and Jose with *dublenki* zhaaakkkets in hand. Their wallets were hundreds of dollars lighter than before encountering the merchants, and Lyudmila Aleksandrovna's final words rang in the air: *"remind, vatch vor vory!"*

Pelmeni

We continued along with speed, pushing our way through the crowd, avoiding eye contact with anyone selling anything—which was pretty much everyone. We twisted and turned and went down small aisles and paths. Jose and Alexander knocked into people with their cumbersome mass of fake fur and leather.

As we turned and twisted, we made it to a section of the bazaar where vendors sold nuts, spices, candies, meats, fruits and vegetables. Long links of dark leathery horsemeat sausages hung from  vendors' stalls. Chunks of beef and mutton lay atop countertops.

Women in white aprons, some stained red with blood and guts, gestured for us to come over to them. They held out a rainbow of colors to us—oranges, reds, greens and whites, all samples of carrot coleslaws, beet salads, pickles and fermented yogurts. The food was slimy and smelled of strong vinegar.

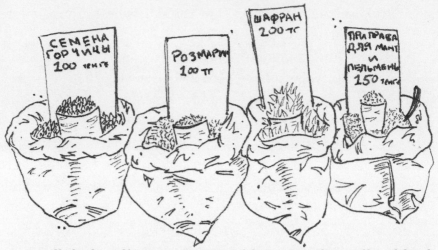

Small dark cafés were scattered between the stalls of food. They were cramped-looking with only a few tables for sitting. Vodka and cognac bottles lined their walls.

We popped into one of these cafés. It was empty except for a waitress. Alexander led the way in and grabbed a table in the back corner of the café. Their jackets took up one of the table's seats. After a few minutes' wait, a large waitress approached us. The Kazakh girl looked like she had never smiled in the twenty-something years of her life.

"*Chto hotite*?" huffed the girl as she came to get our order. *What do you want?*

We looked at each other with uncertainty.

"Menu?" asked Jose since the waitress had yet to give us menus to browse.

"*Cho*?" replied the waitress in an aggravated, disbelieving tone as if we should have known better than to ask a question.

"Menu?" repeated Jose.

"*Nyet* menu," assured the girl.

"No, menu!" I informed Jose and Alexander. "A restaurant without a menu!"

They seemed to understand without my translation.

"*Yeda*?" I asked for food.

"*Yeda?*" replied the girl as if I was the dumbest human alive.

"Food," blurted Alexander while he mimed eating.

She huffed and puffed as she listed their short list of options: "*Vodka, cognac, pivo, borscht, manti, kirieshki...*" She trailed off. "*Tozhe pelmeni.*"

The menu was short and sweet. There were three types of alcohol: vodka, cognac and beer. She also had beet soup called *borscht;* steamed dumplings called *manti; kirieshki* were salty snacks, like flavored croutons sold in packaged bags; and then ravioli-like *pelmeni*.

"*Manti*," ordered Alexander.

"*Skolko?*" demanded the waitress.

"What? *Chto? Skolko*-wha?" replied the *ryzhiy*, perplexed at the waitress' question.

"*Da! Skolko?*" repeated the girl.

Her countenance turned even more grimacing. She began tapping her foot impatiently.

"What does she want?" He asked us, getting flustered.

"She wants to know how many *manti* you want," said Jose.

"Oh, umm, *pyat*," said Alexander as he held up five fingers.

"*A vy?*" She turned to Jose and asked what he wanted.

"*Borscht*," stated Jose.

"*Vodka?*" replied the girl.

It was only noon, but it was already drinking time. She was trying to upsell Jose's order. She wanted to liquor him up with the customary *sto gramm*, a large glass of vodka.

"*Nyet, spasibo.*" He replied with a "no, thank you" politely since it was too early in the day to get drunk.

"*Cognac?*" asked our waitress, seeming intent on Jose ordering an alcoholic drink.

"*Nyet, spasibo*," said Jose again.

"*Pivo?*" asked the girl, but this time for beer.

She was persistent, so Jose ordered a beer. Alexander decided to order one too.

She then looked at me, still annoyed, but without saying a word. She just waited for me to say something to start my order.

"Uhh, *pelmeni*." My words fumbled and jumbled.

The small dish of boiled meat dumplings was a simple one, but it was a difficult word for me, a novice in the Russian language, to say.

"*Cho*?" asked the girl rudely.

"*Pelmeni*." I ordered again.

"*Cho*?" repeated the waitress peevishly.

"*Pelmeni!*" I repeated, annoyed that she didn't understand.

She gave me that look again as if I were the stupidest person she had ever met.

"*Cho? Ne ponimau*." She didn't understand what I wanted.

"*Pell...myen...ee...*" I said slowly and clearly. "*Pell...myen... ee...*" I repeated myself again and again. Then with a slightly different pronunciation. "*Pill-men-yi*." And again. "*Peel-men-ee! Pill-myen-ee! Pyel-myen-yee! Pell-myan-yee!*"

She looked at me stupefied.

"*Pill-myan-ee! Peel-man-yi! Pell-myon-ni!*" I continued.

"*Pelmeni*," interrupted Jose.

"Ahh... *pelmeni!*" said the waitress in an epiphany.

"*U nas nyet*," declared the waitress. "No! No! *Nyet pelmeni*."

After the confusion and tongue twisting, the waitress acknowledged that the café didn't have any more *pelmeni*.

Annoyed, I ordered *borscht*.

The waitress left and we didn't see her for a good thirty minutes. She eventually emerged with a basket of cut *lepeshka*, a type of flatbread, and three glasses of *sto gramm*. She placed the items on our table. Jose tried to call for her attention to correct the mistaken order, but she walked away before acknowledging him. The rest of our food came out next. Three bowls of *borscht* soup. Alexander's order of *manti* never manifested. We gave up and started into the bread.

We were starved. We clanged our glasses of *sto gramm* together and took down the poison in one large gulp. We proceeded to scarf down our soups.

"Following our own tracks…"

We left the café, slightly buzzed and bellies slightly full. It was time to return to our teachers at the entrance of the bazaar. Jose, Alexander and I looked at each other confused about which direction to go. We were lost.

"Don't worry." I said, assuring Jose and Alexander. "I am like a human GPS. I can find our way out of here."

Jose and Alexander looked at me uneasily. They didn't seem to believe in my professed navigational abilities, but they had no other choice but to follow. We walked and walked. The stalls all looked the same.

We stopped at one stall to buy a *dublenka* jacket for me. The deal was simple and hassle-free. A nonchalant merchant let me set my own price. It was Т15,000 ($150) for a Chinese-manu-factured fake-fur and fake-leather jacket. The merchant also gave me a deal on a tight-fitting pair of winter boots for only Т10,000 ($100).

Before we left the merchant's stand, the merchant pointed out *vory* that he claimed were following us. We looked around, but we could only make out shoppers and merchants—a few homeless *Tsygane* children, as well. We left his stall, more vigilant of these phantoms following us.

Three of us now carried cumbersome jackets, bumping into people and knocking over merchandise. We continued through the maze of the bazaar. Merchants bombarded us with questions and demands to buy their goods. We walked and walked, faster and faster, to escape the merchants' fervor.

"I feel like we are going in circles," said Jose.

"We are on track." I assured him. "Trust me!"

"But we just passed by that café we ate at for lunch, again."

He was right. We were walking in circles. We were back at the café. We were lost and following our own tracks. My human compass had been put to shame by a blizzard of stimuli in the labyrinth of the bazaar. By this time, our vodka buzzes had worn off, turning into headaches. Jose and Alexander didn't look pleased, but we pressed on. We continued through the bazaar and continued some more. Through the maze we went, awkwardly bumping into people and merchandise with our large jackets—keeping a watchful eye for the supposed *vory* following behind. The time for meeting the rest of our group for our rendezvous had now passed. Our teachers, Lyudmila Aleksandrovna and Muğalïma, would not be happy waiting for us.

"This place is familiar." I exclaimed with some certainty.

To be honest, the area of the bazaar that I landed us in looked the same as the rest—small stalls and shipping crates, tarps and merchandise everywhere. Nevertheless, I knew we had been to this part of the bazaar before. Then I realized we somehow looped back around to the original merchants who had sold Jose and Alexander their overpriced jackets. We saw the thin man with a toothless grin and his large ogre. Of course, next to them sat the Russian boy who harassed me earlier. He sat in his lair looking like a jackal scoping for prey.

We walked by briskly, not saying a word and not making eye contact with the men and the boy. The Russian boy quickly sniffed out the foreigners in his presence. He stepped out of his stall and glared at us with his angry eyes, the "evil eye," as he cursed us under his breath. As we sped past his stall, I swore he lipped "foog yoo," the closest words to English he could conjure.

We trekked on through the endless desert of the bazaar,

searching for our exit. We attempted to trace our steps backwards. We passed rug merchants and jewelers. They tried to lure us into their stalls with shiny trinkets. We passed the bootlegs. Jarring Russian pop music blasted from stereos, propelling us further through the labyrinth. Then we passed the port-o-potty. The stench was atrocious, repulsing us even further through the maze. Finally, we came to the end of the tunnel. The afternoon light was blinding when we emerged from the bazaar. Our eyes were not used to the daylight after being in the dark bazaar for so long. The air was fresher outside—at least, as fresh as Almaty's pollution allowed.

"My little children have returned," roared Lyudmila Aleksandrovna as we approached her and Muğalïma.

She gave us a big smile when we came closer. We expected her to be angry for being late. We were thirty minutes late for the meeting time, after all.

"You're the first to come back," informed Muğalïma.

"To my mind," interrupted Lyudmila Aleksandrovna, "others vill come back soon. I hope they vill return soon. Iv they do not come, vee have a problem."

"You get extra credit," laughed Muğalïma, "for getting back here on time."

Muğalïma winked at us.

We underwent our first "real-world" test in Kazakhstan. It was a test to tackle language barriers and post-Soviet economics, but it was a test of temperament and flexibility.

The other trainees filtered back to our meeting spot. Some carried winter jackets and boots, others came back with pirated DVDs. We all came back with weird stories to tell about *vory* and the strange merchants we met. When the final trainee was accounted for, we hailed down a bus passing through the traffic. We all loaded up in the crowded vehicle, and we started back to the safety of *KIZ*.

Lesson 4
Power Outages

Ivy League

"You need to tell Drotos," demanded Ben. "Tell him, tell him he needs to send you on the next flight back home!"

When he talked, he stared intensely. His long glaring forehead inched closer and closer to mine with every word he spoke.

I backed away as he inched into my personal space.

"You need to march up to Drotos," he continued, "and tell him how it is going to go down!"

John Drotos, the Peace Corps' country director, was standing nearby in the brisk fall air mingling with Peace Corps staff. The trainees and our new Kazakhstani teacher counterparts were also mingling amongst one another. We were all waiting anxiously for busses to arrive at the juniper-lined courtyard of the Sanatorium Kazakhstan in Almaty.[17]

The Soviet-built resort was the type of luxury spa the mem-

---

[17] A *sanatorium* is a type of resort or health spa.

bers of the communist *politburo* used to frequent. Although the resort was in the posh neighborhood of Medeu, the old building, with its marble façade, was dirty and decaying from the city's pollution. Its old brutalist structure and solid concrete build, planned to forever exude Soviet power, was slowly crumbling.

The resort, where we had just gone through three days of workshops with our new counterparts, was our jumping off point from Almaty. We were all heading for a week-long visit to our future Peace Corps sites, the places where we would eventually live and work for two years of service. In the beginning of November, we would be sworn in as volunteers and finally shipped off for service.

Here at the sanatorium, as we waited to leave, this seemed like the last chance for any trainee to make that final decision to quit and leave Kazakhstan forever. From this point on, this decision would be made more difficult and complicated.

"Tell him," demanded Ben.

"Umm, Ben," I replied, "I don't think that's how it works."

"Agreed," interrupted Jose. "If Tim leaves training, I think it's over for him. Peace Corps has its rules. You can't leave country for the first six months."

Jose and I had been talking about my family's situation back home in Nevada, before Ben overheard and butted in. I felt like I had gotten to know Jose well enough to tell him what was happening. He was the only trainee I told, at least by choice, in nearly two weeks since my family's crisis emerged.

"It's rough enough to already be far from home," I continued, "especially to have this going on."

"I'm sorry to hear about your grandmother," followed Jose.

"Screw that!" butted in Ben. "Dammit! You need to be there with your family, now!"

Although a graduate of the Ivy League—he made his *alma mater* known to all—Ben wasn't the most eloquent with his words. I knew he was trying to help, but he only made me feel worse, and in doing so, he was beginning to hit a nerve.

I already knew what I needed to do for my family, but I was stuck in Kazakhstan, and in Kazakhstan I remained. I wanted to be home. I needed to be home, but I also needed to be here. I knew my family would have liked me to be home with them, but I knew they... I knew she wanted me here.

"Tim, I'm serious, and"—his sweaty forehead inching towards me—"you need to tell Drotos now. Send you home, or... or maybe... I'll do it for you! That's what, exactly, that's what you need to do! I'd be on the first plane home, no doubt."

I knew that he didn't really know what he would do. His act was a front, a tough guy act. How can any of us really know what we will do when one of our loved ones is on the precipice of life and death? To make matters more complicated, what do you do if you are stuck on the far side of the planet, a distant and almost-unreachable place from home?

For the past two weeks since receiving the phone call, I had been thinking it over and over about what I should do or what I wanted to do or what I could do. Each outcome of every situation came down to one thing, my lack of ability to do anything. Perhaps I should have left at the first heartbeat when I received word from home. Instead, I stalled. I stayed.

I should have felt happy and excited because I would be heading to my future site, a village called Yavlenka in the far north of Kazakhstan. Instead, I felt horrible. I felt guilty. I kept on thinking it over and over about what was happening eight thousand miles away in Nevada. My family was going through hell back at home, and I was helpless to do anything. Instead of doing anything to help them, I had to listen to this Ivy League know-it-all tell me what to do.

The busses arrived at the Sanatorium Kazakhstan to take us to the train station. The trainees loaded up our gear and then our counterparts. The trainees entered the bus one by one. I stalled. I stood outside the bus nearby John Drotos, not quite ready to board the vehicle. I stood by him, but I felt alone.

I can go home. I thought. *Right now, I can go home. Just tell Drotos the words. There's no shame in that...*

As the last trainees and their counterparts boarded the bus, I stood at the bus's entrance. After a moment that, in my mind, felt like an eternity, I stepped onto the bus.

Alone

It was a blustery and cool fall evening in *KIZ*. I walked home in the dimming light of day. Feral and domestic dogs alike barked and howled to each other in the distance. The instinctual ritual of these beasts echoed far and wide throughout the neighborhood. It had been a long day of training. Most of them were. Some of the other trainees and I went to a café to enjoy last minute beers and "American" time before our host families began calling for us to come home for dinner. It sometimes felt as if we were all in high school again with curfews. We knew our host families were just trying to keep us safe. No host family wanted to be the one responsible for losing its American.

I arrived at the front gate of my host family's house. *Creeeek!* I swung open the tall metal gate. Low and behold, I was greeted by my drunk neighbor standing in the yard. My host family never formally introduced him to me by his proper name, so I named him myself. He was Uncle Drunk, 300 pounds of inebriation. He stumbled around the yard while smoking a cigarette. The cigarette was to its last drag.

"Ehhh, *amerikanetsssss! Davayiiii poshli na khui!*" spurted the man with a deep laugh. "Huhuhu..."

Coughing followed his incomprehensible murmurs. He took a drag on his cigarette to clear his lungs. He flicked his neck as if he was scratching an itch on his Adam's apple. The last bit of cigarette embers rolled down his fishnet shirt.

"Ahhh, uhhh, ehhh, suka!"

I didn't understand his mumbling. I nodded to greet him.

As I started for the house's door, my cell phone began ringing. I stumbled through my pocket for my phone. I had bought the phone at the bazaar. It served as my only connection to the world outside of Kazakhstan. I looked at the incandescent glow of the screen. The number flashing was "unknown."

"Hello." I answered as I walked into the house.

"Tim…" It was my dad. "Where are you right now?"

"Uhhh, I just got home." I was confused by the question. "What's going on?"

Of course, he knows where I am, I thought. *I am here in Kazakhstan, and he is there in Nevada.*

"Tim," continued my dad, "we have some bad news. Your nana, she had a stroke…"

The conversation was short. I got off the phone with him. My stomach felt sick. My head pounded. My eyes welled with tears. There have only been a few times in my life when I felt utterly alone—where I felt this chill, a touch of the dark void and abyss of nothingness—and this phone call had been one of those moments. I was thousands of miles from home, and I could do nothing. I felt isolated, exhausted. I felt helpless. I felt totally and utterly alone.

Suddenly, the lights in the house flickered and went dark…

Power Outage

Power outages occasionally happened during my time in *KIZ*. Power outages and blackouts were just part of life in the village. It was just a norm for those who lived in Kazakhstan. Economic uncertainty and decaying infrastructure made for unreliable utilities.

Most of the times when we lost power, my host sister or host mom had been home and within seconds they acted. They were ready to offer up candles and matches. However, they were strangely absent on this night. Of all nights, they weren't there.

The house was pitch-black. I used the dull, incandescent glow of my cell phone's screen to break the darkness. It guided my path from my room down the hall.

"Hello?" I whispered. "Anyone here?"

I crept down the hall bumping into furniture. The dim glow of my phone led me to the door to the outside. I heard talking and laughing from outside, so I opened the door and went out to the patio. My host dad, Atasi, and Uncle Drunk were sitting at the table on the patio. Candles lit their faces with a glow. It was cool outside, but still warm enough to sit with a sweater. Despite the chill, Uncle Drunk continued to sport his fishnet shirt.

"*Timka*," called my host dad by the Kazakh name he had affectionately given me. "*Guten Abend*."

He pointed to the open seat on the bench next to Uncle Drunk. I took a seat, but I didn't say anything. My head was still whirling from the conversation with my dad. I sat in silence. Atasi and Uncle Drunk continued to converse.

Kazakh men do not cry. I thought. *Don't cry!*

Uncle Drunk turned to me to talk. He babbled on and on using incoherent words. I didn't understand him, but I wasn't really trying to understand. My mind felt clouded.

Atasi grabbed a shot glass and placed it in front of me. He had a vodka bottle in hand. Atasi filled up my glass. He filled two more shot glasses, one for Uncle Drunk and one for himself. I didn't want to drink. I felt horrible, and I knew alcohol would make it worse. Uncle Drunk grabbed his shot and took it down. Atasi followed. I acquiesced. Refusal to drink would have meant total, utter insult to the two.

"*Mobilnik*," exclaimed Uncle Drunk as he put one hand on my shoulder and extended the other out in front of me. "*Mobilnik*."

He wanted my cellphone. He wanted my lifeline to the outside world. He wanted the device that brought me small doses of freedom from Kazakhstan, but it was also the device that enslaved me to grief.

"*Davayiiii, Timmmkaaaa*," blurted the man. "*Mobilnik*."

His hand remained on my shoulder, but I didn't want to give my phone to this drunken fool. I looked at Atasi.

He gave me a nod of reassurance: *It'll be safe. It'll be okay.*

I took my cellphone from my pocket and handed it to Uncle Drunk. He glared and probed at the device. He swayed in his seat as if he was a blade of grass blowing in the wind. He was three sheets already. He pressed the keys, and he handed my phone back to me.

"*Moi nomer*," said the man proudly.

I looked at the screen to see that he had entered his telephone number. He meant for me to save his number.

He began to rattle on again. From what little I could understand, he said something about if I ever had trouble in *KIZ*, I was to call him. He would beat up any person needing a beating. Suddenly, Uncle Drunk stood up from the seat. He almost fell backwards in doing so.

"*Mafiya*," exclaimed Uncle Drunk. "*Ya mafiya*."

He pounded his chest.

Mafia? As in organized crime? I anxiously thought.

I didn't quite know how to reply. I was so exhausted at this point. I looked at Atasi to find some sort of acknowledgement of what I should say. He was no help. He smiled and stared up at Uncle Drunk. Uncle Drunk started to punch his fists into the air.

"Taekwondo, taekwondo," repeated Uncle Drunk while he chopped the air with his blade-like hands. "*Ya chempion!*"

He continued to kick, slice and karate chop the air. He continued to speak incompressible, incoherent words and phrases. What would have normally been a funny scene, was not.

This drunkard was annoying me. I decided that I wasn't in the mood for the charade, so I excused myself for bed.

A Dream

In the dark bedroom, alone now, I laid down on the hardwood floor. I stared at my phone. Its incandescent glow pierced the dark abyss. My fingers scrolled through my list of contacts.

Just one push of the button, just one phone call and I would be gone. I would be back home. With just one push of the button, all I would need to say is a few words—just a few words: *I want to go home*. I would be on the first flight from Kazakhstan. I would be back home to be with my family. I would be with her. I stared at the number for John Drotos. Just one push of the button to pull the trigger. Pull the trigger and Kazakhstan would be over. No more blackouts. No more drunks. I would be home, and I would never come back.

Other trainees have already ETed. I thought. *I wouldn't be the first. There's no shame in an early termination.*

Just pull the trigger. I stared for a long time. I laid there for a good long while. I couldn't tell how long for sure. Yet, something kept me from calling the Peace Corps staff. I don't know exactly what kept me from doing it, but I put the phone down. I got up from the floor, and I went to bed.

For hours, I laid awake in bed. I laid there in the dark, motionless. My mind felt numb. I finally fell asleep.

I dreamt, although the dream felt more like a recent memory. It was my last evening before I left for my "grand adventure" across the globe. I dreamt that I was at home in Nevada. I had said my goodbyes to friends and family, but this was the goodbye that pained me most of all. It was a farewell that would be my last with her.

As I dreamed, I opened the door of my grandmother's small house. I called her nana. I knew her house well. Much of the furniture and decor was a throwback to the 1970s and 80s. I had spent so much time there in my childhood and teenage years. I had spent so much time there with my grandparents, especially as they grew older and needed more help.

First, papa passed away, seven years prior.

My dream continued... I entered the room where my nana sat and watched television. This is where she had spent so much of her time since he passed away. She was in her eighties. I think she was tired of being alone without him. The whole family knew it.

Retirement. A move to Carson City from California. Countless rounds of golf. Children grown up. Grandchildren. Life had been good, but just like all things, time catches up with all of us. It had caught up with him. Time caught up with her.

In my dream, she sat in her chair watching television. Her body was failing her as she grew older, but she was still sharp and witty. She was wily too. I had always known her for her quick wit and humor. Even with a half century out West, she still spoke with a slight, Midwestern drawl.

"Tim, I'm proud of you. The Peace Corps, that is. It's somethin' to be respected. Somethin' I wish, I wish I could have traveled far away like that."

"But you've been to so many places." I reminded her.

She smiled, but I knew she masked her sadness.

"Kazakhstan," she continued, "I can't even imagine what that will be like. It'll be an adventure."

In fact, she had done some traveling, but that was many years before. In the 1970s, they visited Italy where papa had served in the War. Nana saw the places she had fantasized about visiting as a young girl. Rome. Athens. He had been her travel partner for all those years.

"I won't be visitin'," laughed nana. "Asia is too far for me."

"I will send pictures, and I will write."

"I won't be here when you return," interrupted nana. "Two years is a long time for an old lady like me."

At times, she could be pessimistic. She tried to soften her pessimism with a laugh.

"Nana, don't say that. You'll be here when I get back." I refused to acknowledge this inevitability. "Promise me!"

She couldn't make that promise.

In the back of our minds, we both knew that she was right. This moment would be our last together. We talked a bit longer. We had our last laugh. She loved to laugh. Then it was time for me to go. I gave her a kiss. She held back the tears as best she could. Tears welled in our eyes. And then I left...

Bedside Manner

Ring! Ring! Ring!
I jumped out of bed. I stumbled with my alarm clock. I hit the snooze button with no avail.

Ring! Ring! Ring!

I was dazed. My head pounded as if I had woken from a heavy night of drinking.

Ring! Ring! Ring!

I realized that it wasn't my alarm clock. It was my cell phone. I sat up in my bed, and I answered.

"Hello?"

"Tim," said the man's gruff voice on the other line. "This is Dr. Yuri." The Peace Corps' doctor had a thick accent. "I have not so good news. Your parents contacted Peace Corps headquarters in Vashington. Your grandmother had a stroke."

"Yes, I know." I said in a detached voice. "My parents were able to get through to me last night."

"Okay... ahh... good. You know about this then. Well, let me know if you need anything else. *Poka!*"

Click! The phone went dead. I looked at the clock. It was six in the morning. I laid back down in bed, staring at the ceiling.

Dva (Two, Together)

A rooster crowed. The sun began to rise. The early morning mist disappeared.

I dressed. I walked to school alone. I had scheduled to meet with my teacher, Muğalïma, for a review of Russian before our class started. The road to school was dusty and busy with cars and busses going to Almaty. Aside from traffic, I took little notice of my surroundings. I kept thinking and dwelling on the night before. I was tired. I was anxious. I felt so alone.

I walked through the school's front gate just as the bell rang. School children ran into the front door from the playground.

Muğalïma was waiting for me under the school's front awning. She stuck out from the crowd of rushing students. She was tall for a Kazakh woman.

"*Privet*," said Muğalïma with a smile. "*Kak dila?*"

"Okay... uhh..." I trailed off.

"Tim," started Muğalïma in English, "is something wrong?"

"Uhh, nothing, I mean... my nana, I mean my grandmaaa... she... shhheee..."—stuttering and quivering, trying my best to hold back the tears—"shhheee... she had a stroke."

She was caught off guard by my reply. Her dark eyebrows raised in astonishment.

"Well, I... uhh... I think... uhh... many people have strokes, and they recover," assured my teacher, futilely grasping at hope.

I don't think the Peace Corps had trained her on how to counsel trainees in this sort of thing, life's adversities and hardships that is. I mean, she was only twenty-two years old—my own age at the time.

"I don't think she will be okay. She is in a coma now."

Tears began rolling down my cheeks. I couldn't stop them.

Power Outages

All the night before, and so far this morning, I had forced back the tears. I felt so alone, and I was angry for that, but I couldn't hold back the tears any longer.

Muğalïma didn't quite know what to do or say. Like me, she was young and inexperienced in the ways of life. We both had little experience with death. Muğalïma put her hand on my shoulder. This small action felt like the right thing to do. It felt right for both of us.

"I'm sorry," said Muğalïma as she tried to console me. "Be strong for your grandmother."

We stood there for a moment in front of the school. I wiped away the tears, trying to get back my composure.

"Maybe you want to go home today?" asked Muğalïma.

No! I thought. *For what? To face my pain all alone.*

"No, no, it will be better if I am here. I need to stay busy."

"It takes courage to be here with me," replied Muğalïma. "I mean, it takes strength to talk to me about this. It shows me that you have strength to continue here. Time in the Peace Corps won't be easy. There will be difficulties."

"What do you mean?"

"Never mind, Tim. You will be a good volunteer. Just stay strong and have courage." Muğalïma smiled. "Let's go in and start our Russian lesson. Okay?"

Together, the two of us as *dva*, we walked through the front doors of the school.

Part II
A Novel Life,
Year One

Lesson 5
Cultural Integration

"It may be that the satisfaction I need depends on my going away, so that when I've gone and come back, I'll find it at home."

Rumi

Politics of a Bikini Contest

"*Nash volontur iz Korpusa Mira*, Meeesteeer Saaachleeend, Teeematiii Rooogeeerrr," shouted the host of the Miss Esil Region Beauty Pageant.

The tuxedoed host of the beauty pageant introduced me to the packed house in the auditorium of the *Dom Kultury*, the village's community center. I stood from my judge's seat, turned to the crowd of three hundred and gave an abrupt wave. It was a nervous wave. I was nervous as hell.

The crowd went up in a roar of applause and shouts of "Teeemati, Teeemati," another Kazakhstani name for me. Apparently, there was a famous rapper in Russia, Timati, who shared my

69

new namesake.[18]

I had only been in Yavlenka for four weeks, but the crowd was all mine. I had achieved celebrity status overnight, simply because I was American. Unfortunately, I couldn't relish the adoration. I hated being the center of attention of this big crowd, and my stomach sank deeper with each clap. I sat back down quickly, blushing.

I was the new toy in town. Everyone wanted to play with me. That was why I was granted the esteemed position of judge at the pageant, though I felt out of place for a judge. My hair was greasy and uncombed. I hadn't been able to wash it in over a week. I was the most underdressed of the seven judges. I was only wearing a sweater, slacks and a tie.

The rest of the six judges who sat at the long table with me wore sleek suits of satins and silks. They attempted to foppishly outdo each other in the size of their necktie knots and the pointedness of their shined shoes.

The first judge was an ethnic Russian, a businessman. He was the top supplier for sporting goods in Yavlenka and, coincidentally, farming equipment. He was asked to be on the panel of judges as an act of affirmative action—one Russian man representing the seventy percent of the village's population who were ethnic Russians. Yavlenka's Kazakh *akim* (mayor) and his police chief both graced us at the judges' table. They had never run in any election; yet, here they were a mayor and a police chief. Besides the *akim*, two other local politicians were present, both Kazakh. One was from *Nur Otan*, "Fatherland's Ray of Light," the party of Kazakhstan and its blessed and auspicious president, Nursultan A. Nazarbaev. The other politician was from a sister party of *Nur Otan*. His presence gave the appearance of political diversity, yet unity in Yavlenka. There was the

---

[18] Timur Yunusov (b. 1983), aka Timati, is a hip hop artist from Russia.

token Kazakh woman too. She ran a government department in the village. She happened to be the wife and boss of the organizer of the pageant, the director of the *Dom Kultury*, Abai. I affectionately knew Abai as Uncle Abai. I never quite knew if he was a real uncle or simply a family friend to my new host family, the Zheltoqsans.

"*Eto nashe zhyuri*," continued the host. "*Spasibo!*"

The audience clapped loudly while the pageant host finished introducing the judges. As he rushed off stage, the first contestant of the pageant suddenly rushed out from behind the stage curtains. A roar of applause went up in the auditorium as she strutted her stuff across the stage.

Rushed Away

Four weeks earlier there had been a less rowdy applause upon my arrival to Yavlenka. I arrived in Petropavlovsk, Petro for short, by a late-night train in the early part of November. Petro was the last train stop in northern Kazakhstan. The next stop, an hour down the line, was Russia.

The journey had been a long thirty-two hours from Almaty in the south. Aside from a few cities along the train route, there was not much to see between Almaty and Petro. At the lonely stops along the way, a Peace Corps volunteer would depart. He or she would wander off into the steppe to find a new life for the next two years.

The train slowly chugged through Petro. I was in a daze, but I woke up suddenly when the train jerked and jolted as it changed tracks and slowed. Late at night, it was too dark to see the city of two hundred thousand from my frosted window.

Four of us Kaz 19s had been assigned to the Petro area. Over the next two years, I would get to know these three other volunteers well, all the good and the not so good in each of them. Of course, they would get to know me in the same manner. They would become part of my family and support in Kazakhstan.

A Five Finger Feast

There was Dylan, or Deel as the locals called him. He was a fellow redheaded *ryzhiy* like me, but with a bit of a Southern twang. He was assigned to a secondary school in Petro. Deel was easy going and got along with everyone, mostly avoiding the inter-volunteer drama that plagued some in the Peace Corps. He would return to Kazakhstan a couple of years after his service ended as a married man, married to a local Kazakh girl. During training, Peace Corps staff warned us that a number of volunteers would find love in Kazakhstan.

Next up was Leo. He was going to teach at the local university. A chain smoker from the American Southwest, he was sometimes an outstanding guy and other times a trickster. He would be one of the few Peace Corps volunteers to extend for a third year stay in the country. Unfortunately, a libelous, Peace-Corps-bashing newspaper article published by a disgruntled student would cut his tenure short.

Then there was Rebecca from the Midwest. Opinionated, she made it known that she was a devout vegetarian. In a country of fifteen million staunch meat eaters, she was not going to bend the knee to the locals. I commend her for sticking to her convictions, but I still wonder how much she missed out by denying herself the simple delight of eating Kazakhstan's delicacy, sheep head. She was assigned to a suburb near Petro. In a vast country the size of Kazakhstan, her site was relatively close to mine in proximity. They were an hour apart.

As the train rolled into Petro, the four of us had already spent thirty-two hours together. This wouldn't be our last thirty-two, not at all. In these thirty-two hours, we saw the more unpleasant sides of each other. Farts. Pimples. Stinky breath. There was a lot to see in a human in a cramped, humid train ride. This was especially true when sleeping in a second-class *coupe*—a small five-foot-wide-by-six-foot-long four-person cabin. Four sleeping cots were bolted precariously onto the walls of the cabin.

Cultural Integration

The train was kept unreasonably hot. The windows were locked to prevent passengers from opening them since the locals believed only the worst maladies could be brought in by the autumn chill. We sweated profusely throughout the trip.

For the past few hours of the ride to Petro, the conversation between the four of us became stale. Besides us four, the last three Kaz 19s on the train departed in Kokshetau, a city four hours to the south of Petro. Ever since, the conversation between the Petro crew died out. However, with the imminent end of our journey, we began anxiously chatting with each other.

"What if your host fam isn't here again, Tim?" teased Leo.

Leo alluded to when I first arrived to *KIZ* for training. My host family neglected to pick me up on time.

This couldn't happen again. I thought. *Could it?*

I had chosen my new host family, a family of four, while on site visit in Yavlenka weeks prior. I was worried, though. I had sent text messages to my new host mother, but the messages went unanswered. It was an unsettling silence as I tried to coordinate transportation from the Petro train station to Yavlenka.

"What if you are stuck on the Petro streets?" teased Leo while he gave me a playful tap on the shoulder. "Or even worse, with Rebecca?"

He glanced at Rebecca to see if she responded, but she was too busy chatting with Dylan about her philosophy on vegetarianism. We had all heard her thoughts on the matter several times already. I ignored his remarks and stared outside.

The train hissed when the brakes were applied. We came to a complete stop at the train platform. Three volunteers, all wrapped up in winter jackets, waited for us on the platform. They were Kaz 18s going into their second year of service. Our local counterparts and host families waited with them. I was relieved to see Yekaterina Alekseyevna, my new counterpart, and her husband, Peter, standing and waiting amongst the group.

A Five Finger Feast

Yekaterina Alekseyevna and Peter were in their late forties, of Russian and Ukrainian heritage. They were a friendly couple, and I could tell that they loved each other dearly. Yekaterina Alekseyevna was a short and robust woman. She held herself well, and she always dressed in the latest Russian fashions. Peter was short as well, made plump from years of eating Yekaterina Alekseyevna's hearty butter-laden cooking. He had a genuine smile and a good laugh. He raised pigs and worked as a mail delivery man in Yavlenka. For the next two years, Yekaterina Alekseyevna would be my counterpart in Yavlenka. For two years, we would teach almost every English lesson together. She would adopt me as her American son during those years. We would often lesson plan together at her house, where she would give me cookies and *chai*.

The train finally chugged to a complete stop. A mad rush was made by the passengers in the *coupe* wagon. Suitcases and crates and boxes and bags made their way down to the station's platform. We exited the train past a well-dressed conductor. He nodded and smiled, flashing gold teeth. Hugs and handshakes went around in the small group of counterparts and volunteers.

The homecoming was brief. I would not see these other Americans for a long time.

I was quickly and anxiously rushed away by Yekaterina Alekseyevna and her man, Peter, to their old Lada sedan.[19] We rushed off through the dark, fro-

---

[19] Lada is a brand of cars built in the former Soviet Union and Russia.

zen city and out to the open highway in their car.

I was relieved to be on my final leg of the trip, but I was confused why my host family wasn't at the station to greet me.

"I am so excited to see my new family." I exclaimed to Yekaterina Alekseyevna. "Will we be going straight to their house tonight or will I be staying with you?"

Yekaterina Alekseyevna turned from the front seat to talk to me in the back.

"My dear Tim," started Yekaterina Alekseyevna.

She was one of the few locals who could pronounce my name correctly. She also spoke English with a British intonation.

"I have grave news for you," continued Yekaterina Alekseyevna with a worried look. "I received a phone call from your host mum."

"Uhh, what did she say?"

"I am very sorry, but they cannot have you to live with them," said Yekaterina Alekseyevna with a concerned tone.

"I don't understand. Wha... what happened? Why?"

I was flabbergasted. I had met the family during my site visit. They seemed like a good fit, and I was looking forward to living with them.

"I am not exactly sure. They say a family member, an aunt or uncle, she didn't say precisely whom, but someone is sick."

Yekaterina Alekseyevna took one pensive glance away while debating to tell me any more information.

She continued. "I must be honest to you. I think it has something to do with their relatives. To my mind, they have a nephew, or two, who works for the KNB. Do you know KNB? They are like Soviet KGB. You know, from the Soviet Union, KGB?"

"Yeah, I know of the KNB." I answered.

During training, Peace Corps had warned us about the KNB's interference with volunteers. Some in the Peace Corps would get to know the secret police of Kazakhstan well.

"To my mind, the KNB is what worries them. The KNB does not like foreigners. They worry that they… you may have trouble if you live with them, but Tim, let us not worry about KNB. You will not worry tonight."

"Well, I guess"—I tried to mask my unease since Yekaterina Alekseyevna's smile seemed reassuring—"if you say so."

"You know the saying *eto zhizn?*"

I nodded yes. It meant *c'est la vie.*

"You must adapt to our climate and to our manners. This is our national, what's the word, *Mentalität,*" said Yekaterina Alekseyevna, who was once a German teacher many years earlier. "I mean our national mentality."

"Well, where will I live now?"

"Tonight, you will live with me and my dear Peter," said Yekaterina Alekseyevna with a smile. "We are pleased to have you as our guest. Peter is excited. He is so fond of you already."

Peter glanced at me through the rearview mirror. With a smile he said something in Russian.

"Teem, *eto zhizn, i sve budet khorosho. Davay*! *Chai i banya*! *Sve normalno. Ladno?*"

I didn't understand a word of what he said, but it sounded encouraging. His smile was comforting.

"Okay." I answered.

Never Give *Dva*

The last contestant in the bikini round, a Russian teenager who I also happened to teach English to at the local school, rushed off the stage and the host of the pageant appeared from his hiding place behind the curtains. He had a surreal look for a Kazakh man. Perhaps it had been his uncanny smile with perfectly straight, white teeth.

"*Davay zhyuri,*" said the host. *Let's go jury!*

We held up our score placards to cast our votes. A possibility of five points could be given on a scale from one through five.

Cultural Integration

He listed off the scores for the bikini round: "*Chetyre, chetyre, pyat, tri, chetyre, pyat! A dva?*" *Four, four, five, three, four, five... and two...*

The host paused for a moment and looked at me confused. He quickly recovered, and the show continued on to the formal wear round of the pageant.

"Pssh, Teem," whispered Ksenia, "you cannot give *dva. Dva*, I mean a two, it is disrespect. No, no *dva*."

Ksenia was sitting behind me while she whispered in my ear. Ksenia was my Russian tutor. She was small and demure in look, but, nevertheless, strong-willed. She was also my most ambitious tenth grader, hence taking the American under her wing as a Russian pupil. She also happened to be my best English student. She was a perfect candidate to translate the pageant to me.

"Why?" I asked confused. "Why can't I give a two?"

We had been provided with five placards: *odin* (one), *dva* (two), *tri* (three), *chetyre* (four), *pyat* (five). There the numbers were laid out in front of each judge.

"Teem, two, it's"—Ksenia seemed to struggle for the right words, although her English was quite good for a sixteen-year-old—"*dva, eto nelzya. Dva* is forbidden."

"But I have five points available, so I gave a two."

"No *dva*," commanded Ksenia. "And also, no score of one!"

"She wasn't good, so I gave a *dva*."

It was already awkward enough to objectify a sixteen-year-old based on a bikini competition, especially one that I taught English to in school. No one else involved in the pageant seemed to have a problem with this, but I felt uncomfortable. My discomfort became more apparent with my lack of understanding around cultural norms of the grading system.

"You don't understand," said Ksenia critically, and she attempted to explain. "In Kazakhstan, *naprimer*, for example"— once more she struggled for the right words, yet, determined to explain—"in Kazakhstan, in a school that is, a teacher can give a five and four, and sometimes three, but no two, and never one."

"But why?" I suppose I was being obtuse.

"Let me explain you. Two doesn't show respect. It, it…"

Ksenia lost me in the logic and the Soviet mentality of the argument when the host came back on stage. The first contestant in the formal wear portion of the show had just finished her round on stage. I quickly grabbed my placards. I wasn't sure what score to give since I hadn't even paid attention to the contestant's performance.

"*Pyat, chetyre, chetyre, chetyre, pyat, chetyre*," called out the host as he went down the row of judges. "*Pyat! Spasibo* Meester Sachlend! *Spasibo!*"

He shouted my name extra loud for the five I gave to the contestant. I could tell in his tone that he was telling me my upstart, silly shenanigans would be no more. This *dva*-wielding American was put into his place. The host continued to speak after our scores had been tallied, but I didn't understand him and Ksenia was taking too long to translate. Suddenly, though, the other judges rose to their feet, and Uncle Abai began leading them out of the auditorium.

"Teem, go," motioned Ksenia, pushing me to follow.

I rushed out of the auditorium with the other judges.

"To appear"

Peter pushed the gas pedal down and the car careened along the highway at eighty miles per hour. The Lada rolled with the uneven asphalt. It undulated up and down, rising and falling like a boat cresting waves. The car sped fast through a dark landscape. Nothing appeared to be out there in the black.

"*Yavlyatsya*," spouted Yekaterina Alekseyevna.

"What?"

I was in another world, lost in my thoughts, looking out of the window into the dark nothingness of northern Kazakhstan.

Cultural Integration

"*Yavlyatsya*. It means 'to appear' in Russian," clarified Yekaterina Alekseyevna. "To my mind, this is how our dear Yavlenka came to have its namesake."

"*Yavlyatsya*." I was intrigued. "What's the story there?"

"It is said," started Yekaterina Alekseyevna, "that Yavlenka appeared out of nowhere. At least, that's how the story is told. One winter's night Yavlenka appeared out of thin air, but I do not know the details very well."

"Tell me more about Yavlenka."

I knew almost nothing about the place I would spend two years of my life.

"Yavlenka is a nice village, nicer than most in Kazakhstan. Clean," emphasized Yekaterina Alekseyevna as if she was proud of that fact. "Much farming here. Oh, and it is situated above the Ishim River. You know our Ishim? It is a lovely place, Yavlenka."

"How many people live in Yavlenka?" I asked.

Yekaterina Alekseyevna said something in Russian to Peter. He said a few words back as if to clarify a factoid about the village, and she turned to me.

"To my mind, six thousand or seven. We are Russian village."

As an ethnic Russian woman in an independent Kazakhstan, she seemed proud of her heritage. At the same time, she seemed insecure about her statement.

"Old village, one hundred and thirty years! To my mind, the year eighteen hundred and seventy-five is when it 'appeared.' You know we are in *Siber*?"

"Siberia?"

I acted as if I was astonished by her *non sequitur*, but I had been made well aware of this fact during training by my host mom in *KIZ*.

'*Yavlenka, it is in Siberia.*' I could hear Äje's laugh ringing in my head. '*Aww, it is so cold there. It snows there as we speak.*'

"*Da, da*," answered Yekaterina Alekseyevna, "everything you see outside, it is *Siber*-ia."

I glanced outside into *Siber*-ia, and I saw nothing but dark. It was too dark to distinguish much except snow on the ground and the moon above. Siberia was dark. The land seemed to sleep, cold and soundless. Even just thinking about the enormity of Siberia perplexed me. Beyond my view of dark nothingness, lay frozen swamps and marshes, birch-tree and pine forests. This is how Siberia was for hundreds, if not thousands of miles, stretching from Yavlenka in the southernmost part to the Arctic Sea in the far north. Then it stretched across the rest of eastern Russia with steppe, tundra and taiga—and barely a person to be found in between.

I was jolted out of my thoughts when, unexpectedly, with one quick jerk, Peter made the Lada take a sharp right-hand turn off the highway. The tires screeched. We sped past what looked like a grove of trees, and suddenly a cityscape began to form. A small quiet town appeared from behind a shroud of trees. Homes and hovels, shops and offices, they appeared out of nothing. A town square, a park, a mosque, a church, a hospital, a stadium, a school, a bazaar and some cafes, a police station, a granary, and even a billboard of President Nursultan A. Nazarbaev, they all suddenly appeared before me from the dark, Siberian landscape. Packs of feral dogs appeared, roaming the streets. Horses and cows, chickens and turkeys, small herds of

sheep and some goats all seemed to "appear" before me. They were, by now, asleep on soft, comfy beds of hay in their barns and stables. Six thousand or so ethnic Russians and Kazakhs, a few Armeni-

ans, some Ukrainians and Tatars, and a few Volga Germans—
they laid in warm beds in this sleeping land.

Let Us Drink

I arrived in a small conference room in the back of the *Dom Kultury*. The judges needed to make our final decision. Who would be crowned this year's pageant queen? Ksenia followed me to help translate. The door was closed tightly behind us in the cramped room. The other six judges stood around the table in the middle of the room reviewing points. Chatter went back and forth, but I didn't understand much of what was being said. They didn't seem to care too much about my opinion.

Ksenia translated: "Okay, they say there are two winners."

"A tie?" I asked.

"*Da*, a tie. Now we must make one *chempion*."

It turned out that the tie was between two Kazakh girls. One attended the bigger school in town, the Russian-language school where I worked, School № 1, Timofey Pozolotin. The other girl was Kazakh also, but she attended the smaller and more exclusive school in Yavlenka, the Kazakh-language school.

"How is the tie going to be broken?" I asked Ksenia as she listened diligently to the debate between the other judges.

The talk between the judges continued for a long while before Ksenia responded to my question.

"*Nu*, it seems we will take vote."

The judges went around stating who they wanted to see crowned winner. Four votes, including mine, were cast for the candidate from the Russian-language school. Two had been cast for the other girl. It was as if grassroots democracy unfolded right before my eyes. These were small steps towards the democratization of Kazakhstan.

Uncle Abai began to set shot glasses on the table and pour vodka. He was ready to celebrate the decision.

However, there was one vote to be cast, the *akim*'s, although his vote wouldn't matter in swaying the outcome at this point. The score was four to two, after all. Nevertheless, he still needed to vote since he was the *akim*. He began to speak a few words in Kazakh but soon turned to Russian. I didn't understand exactly what he had said, but whatever was spoken was done in a calm, pensive manner.

When he finished, three judges looked disgruntled at hearing his words and so was Ksenia.

"Teem," shouted Ksenia, "the *akim* has voted. The girl from Kazakh school is winner."

"She doesn't have the votes, though. It's four to three, right?"

"*Da*, but he is *akim*. He is boss."

With Ksenia's words, Uncle Abai had already put a glass of vodka into the judges' hands. Judges still looked stunned by the usurping of democracy. The egalitarian enthusiasm that existed in the room just moments before faded quickly.

"*Druzya*," shouted Uncle Abai.

He began to give a toast to the competition. He thanked the judges, and he toasted the soon-to-be-crowned queen, the girl from the Kazakh-language school.

We all drank the shot of vodka to seal the scurrilous deal, and we were ushered back out to the stage. It was decided that each judge would give a small speech. I was told that I would give mine in English and Ksenia would translate to the audience. I wasn't looking forward to the spotlight, but it was too late. We walked into the auditorium.

As we walked towards the stage, someone jumped onto my back. It was an ambush. My new host brother, Ağasi, jumped from behind me. Ağasi was a sixteen-year-old, short with a buzzed head. The Kazakh boy was excited to find out what the decision was. He grabbed at me as if I was a toy that could be handled roughly.

Cultural Integration

New Toy

"Timati! Timati! You sleep?" shouted Ağasi as he busted into my bedroom.

I was startled and woke from an afternoon nap on the couch. My bedroom had been set up in the Zheltoqsan family's only spare room in the house, their living room. It was freezing in the house, so I slept under thick blankets and a sleeping bag.

The Zheltoqsans were my new host family. They were a Kazakh family of five, two parents and three teenage children. They took me in after my plans to live with my original host family fell through.

I hadn't even been in Yavlenka for twenty-four hours, but Ağasi took it upon himself to show me my new surroundings. I got dressed in long johns, two sweaters and anything else that could keep me warm. It was cold in the November chill, and though it was only three in the afternoon, the sun was setting quickly into the horizon. Ağasi and I went towards the door to put on our boots.

"Timati," began Ağasi, "we go Dosim house. You know Dosim? He my frrrend."

Ağasi, I soon learned, was a gregarious teenager, and he always had a crowd of followers.

We left the house. Rex, the Zheltoqsan's dog, ran over to us. Rex was a short-haired mutt with a hunter's demeanor. This very intelligent dog protected my host family and their homestead at Four Sovietskaya Street from the village's feral beasts and wandering drunks alike.

"Rex like you," declared Ağasi. "Rex police dog. My faahterrr took him from police."

My new host father was Äke. Äke was a retired cop from the Yavlenka police force. Because of this, the family had a certain clout within Yavlenkan society.

We left the house at Four Sovietskaya Street. We walked the once-muddy, now-frozen road. Icy snow crunched underfoot.

"Timati! You know Adriana Lima?" asked Ağasi.

He was a funny boy. He loved to quiz me on pop culture, and he was obsessed with supermodel Adriana Lima.

"She sooopermodel." He answered his own question before I could respond. "She from *Brazilia*. I love Adriana. Ahh... she foootur *zhena*!"

"*Zhena*? Your wife?" I asked to clarify.

"*Da*, Timati, my wifff! You know girls love me," continued Ağasi. "I pimp boy at school! All girls want me."

The bragging of his sexual prowess continued while we walked down the road. We eventually arrived at Dosim's house. It was a small house with white plastered walls and baby blue window shutters. We knocked on the door, and Dosim quickly opened it. Dosim was a Kazakh boy, the same age as Ağasi. However, while Ağasi had a youthful-look to him, Dosim looked older. He had a thin line across his upper lip. He was trying to grow a mustache on his pimpled face.

"Timati," said Ağasi, "dis Dosim. Dosim, dis Timati, my new *brat*—my braahterrr."

"Pleez you meet," struggled Dosim. "You... *chai* want?"

As good manners dictated, muddy shoes were kicked off and lined against the wall next to the door. It was rude to wear one's shoes inside. We sat inside Dosim's kitchen, staring awkwardly at each other, sipping tea while Ağasi rattled on about his romantic liaisons and his undying love for Adriana Lima.

"Timati," interrupted Dosim. "You... ahhh... see wwwillage Yavlenka, now?"

"*Da*." I responded. My Russian vocabulary was obviously

growing more extensive every day.

"*U menya mashina*," said Dosim.

"Timati," interrupted Ağasi, "Dosim, he hafff cool car! We cool boyz!"

They both seemed proud of this status emblem, the car.

We finished our tea and went towards the door, stumbling over each other as we put on our boots. We ran outside to his garage. Dosim opened the garage door by hand, and inside was a brand-new Mercedes-Benz.

"Didn't expect to see a car like this." I muttered.

"Moment, pleez," said Dosim as he opened the car door.

He needed to warm up the car's engine in the freezing temperatures. After several minutes of waiting in the cold garage, Dosim beckoned us to join him in the car. A part of me felt as if Dosim had never driven a car before. Perhaps we were stealing his dad's new car—Dosim so desperate to impress the new American. I didn't ask questions. We left the garage, and we drove to the "wwwillage" center.

Even though the sun was finally setting beneath the frozen world of Yavlenka, the center of the village was buzzing about with people in warm *dublenki* jackets and big fur hats. They were going about buying groceries in the small shops called *magaziny*. Many people were leaving work for the day. Yavlenka was the region's government center, so many people worked in local governmental offices.

We parked the car near the town mosque. A large park and the *Dom Kultury* sat next to it.

"Timati, we go to *Dom Kultury*," commanded Ağasi. "We show you *musey*... ahh... museum and liiibraaary... You see Uncle Abai here."

We walked through the park, where the trees were frozen. A large monument to those Yavlenkans who had fallen in the Great Patriotic War (WWII) stood quietly in the faint twilight sun. A

Superman-like statue stood over a list of names carved on the monument. It was long and extensive. The names frozen in stone attested to only a small fraction of the half a million Kazakh-stanis who lost their lives during the Second World War. Communist leader and founder of the Soviet Union, Vladimir Lenin, stood here in the park too. His granite façade was crumbling. Graffiti was painted at the base.

The *Dom Kultury* was a large two-story building, built of grey bricks. We walked into the main doors, and we went directly to Uncle Abai's office.

Although he was wrapping up with work for the day, he took us on a tour. We went upstairs to the museum. It was small, but it was full of artifacts, giving middle-of-nowhere Yavlenka a sense of its own place in the world. The tour of the museum was quick. The museum itself consisted of two rooms and a closet converted into a mock yurt. The larger of the rooms was dedicated to those of Yavlenka who fought and died in WWII, particularly to the war hero whom School № 1, Timofey Pozolotin, was named.

Cultural Integration

At the end of the museum tour, Uncle Abai grabbed a giant book from the curator's office. It was a registry of visitors. He proudly showed me the signatures and pictures of a group of English tourists and a professor from Florida who had visited Yavlenka in 1999. It seemed they had been the last foreigners to come through Yavlenka. That was eight years prior.

"Timati, we do *fotografiya* fooor book," stated Ağasi as he positioned me in the mock yurt. "You our new *geroy*… ahh… hero, like Timofey Pozoltin, so we need *foto*!"

While Timofey Pozolotin lost his life for commanding a tank regiment against Nazi Germany, I was a "hero" for simply being an American in Yavlenka. This still didn't stop Uncle Abai from taking a polaroid of me. With one click, my likeness was captured for the posterity of Yavlenka. I signed the registry book as the Englishmen and university professor had done eight years before. Ağasi and Dosim wanted to sign it as well.

We said our farewells to Uncle Abai. Ağasi rushed us to the next stop on the village tour.

"Timati, we go *magazin* now," directed Ağasi. "My mutter need *khleb*… ahh… bread. Need fooor supper."

We walked through the cold air from the *Dom Kultury* to a large *magazin* (shop) on the main plaza in Yavlenka. We walked in through the doors, and my glasses instantly frosted over when they hit the warm air inside.

"Follow me," commanded Ağasi.

I stumbled blindly through the store. When my glasses finally defrosted, I could see that the shop was spacious. The food and the goods were kept under glass countertops or up on high shelves behind the counters where the women grocers stood at attention. Bread and beer, shampoo and detergent, VHS tapes and useless trinkets—the *magazin* was a consumer's delight of housewares, alcohol and outdated movies from the West.

The grocers seemed to know Ağasi, and they gave him fond

smiles as we passed. Ağasi knew many people around the store. He was a very extroverted and likable guy.

Ağasi stopped to greet an elderly Russian man with a large fur hat and a sunken grimace. Ağasi shook his hand to pay respect, and he spouted off some unintelligible words to the man.

"*Amerikanets*, ehh?" asked the Russian man curiously.

The old man had lived most of his life under the Soviet regime, but now he was face-to-face with the former enemy, an American. *How odd history must have felt to him...* The man extended his hand to me. He did not crack a smile or even a smirk, but he wanted to shake my hand. I grabbed his hand in return, smiling. He continued to frown as he disgruntledly said something to Ağasi. The man looked very disgusted as he turned and walked away, unimpressed by this new shiny American.

"Timati," began Ağasi, "he *zloy*. Ahh... he angry. He mad. You make him mad."

"But how?" I asked, confused. "What did I do wrong?"

"No... ahh... *perchatki*."

"*Perchatki*?" I was lost on the word and my cultural *faux pas*. He grabbed my hands and took off my gloves.

"*Perchatki*!" exclaimed Ağasi. "No gloves. It bad, bad luck wit glove and say 'hello'."

"Oh, I can't shake hands with my gloves on?"

"*Da*, no *perchatki*. No shake hand."

I would later learn that the custom of taking off one's gloves while shaking hands came from ancient tradition when Kazakh warriors greeted each other on the lawless steppe. As an act of fidelity to show they weren't hiding weapons in their gloves, warriors would take off their gloves to greet each other.

There would be many more embarrassing, cross-cultural *faux pas* to come in my time in Kazakhstan. This new toy would commit oh-so-many more.

Cultural Integration

An Angry Father

The speeches and awards finished up. The judges were beginning to take pictures with the contestants as the crowd vacated the auditorium. I was so relieved. I was done with the toughest part of the evening, an unprepared speech in front of the large crowd. The speech was stale and unimpressive, but Ksenia hovered nearby. She offered a translation, I assumed, that would've put the nineteenth-century Russian poet Alexander Pushkin to shame.

"Meester Sachlend," yelled a feminine voice.

I turned to see who it was. It was the girl I had unwisely given the score of *dva* (two) during the bikini round.

"Pleez, you *fotografiya* with me?"

She didn't seem to hold my scoring gaffe against me. I was relieved. She just wanted to take a photo with the new shiny toy, the American.

Her father, a grimy-looking man, had a camera in hand. The girl and I stood next to each other, ready to take the picture.

"Timati! Say cheeeez!" commanded the father as he pointed the ancient film camera at us.

The camera flashed. I began to walk away. The father followed me from behind.

"Timati," yelled the man. "*Dva? Pochemu dva?*"

Dva! All I needed to hear was the word *dva*, the number two, but I knew enough already. The father was upset over his daughter's score. It was time to be held accountable for my misguided, culturally insensitive scoring.

I turned to see the man angrily gripping his camera with crushing force. He began to rant and rave. With each new word, his face became a tinge redder and his voice a tone louder. The dad continued grilling me in Russian with many words that I didn't understand. He was beginning to wave his hands furiously about as he yelled in intangible Russian. The camera was about to fling off into space like a miniature Sputnik with every wave and motion.[20]

I was trapped.

Ağasi suddenly came out of nowhere. He said something to the man as he ushered me away.

"Timati, we go now," blurted Ağasi.

He grabbed me by the arm. We walked out of the *Dom Kultury*, escaping this angry man.

"Timati, I got yooor back," smiled Ağasi. "You my *brat*! You my braahterrr!"

'*I got yooor back.*' It seemed like my back was thoroughly covered here in Yavlenka. These people in Yavlenka had all appeared in my life as if overnight—*yavlyatsya* as Yekaterina Alekseyevna would put it. Ağasi. Ksenia. Yekaterina Alekseyevna. They were all willing to help this new American adjust to his strange new life. The thought was comforting to think that they all *got* my back.

Ağasi and I walked through the frosty dark night back home at Four Sovietskaya Street.

---

[20] Sputnik 1 was the first satellite in outer space. It was launched by the USSR in 1957.

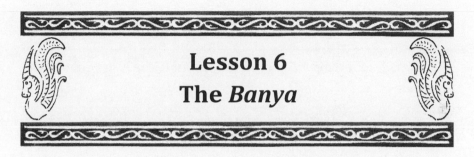

Lesson 6
The *Banya*

"The banya *is like the Russian's second mother."*

Alexander Pushkin

Fire

I opened the door. Heat blasted into my face with a swoosh and sudden maddening rush of hot air. My eyes began to water and swell with tears. The room was dark, yet, blinding with scorching heat. On one side of the door, the warm, humid temperatures were comfortable. On the other side was scorching heat. It was burning fire. Unbearable heat was the only clear sensation existing beyond the door. Sight was blurred. Touch and taste became painfully numb. Smell was staunched. Even sound was muffled and muted.

I stood in the doorway, heat blasting the front of my body, feeling naked and exposed. I was, after all, stripped down to nothing and in the buff. There was nothing to hide the blemishes, pimples and imperfections that God gave me. Sweat voraciously oozed and seeped from my pores—dripping down my face and down my neck, my chest and my belly, and down to my shriveled *khui*. The sweat trickled down my legs and feet to the grated floor below.

There was no turning back from the monstrous heat pulsating from the small room, this furnace, this nuclear reactor. I was committed. My host father, Äke, stood awkwardly behind me, naked. He was waiting to enter the small room, if only I would step in through the door and into the heat.

"Meeery Hristmas, Teemati," croaked Äke with a diabolical laugh. He had a distinctively raspy, Kermit-the-Frog-like voice. "*Davay*! *Banya*!"

With his sinister smile and his words of encouragement, I forced myself into the hellish heat.

Ice

When I exited the front door of my house at Four Sovietskaya Street, I woke suddenly from a sleepy stupor. The cold hit me harder than I thought it would. It was an awful cold, made worse by the black darkness of the morning sky.

The locals in Yavlenka called this freeze the *moroz*, the frost. When it came, it was strangely beautiful. At the same time, it was frightening, painful and suffocating. It numbed every sensation. Eyes glazed over. Nostrils dripped and then froze. Ears, fingers, toes and other appendages numbed to the feeling of painful nothingness.

The *moroz* crept in slowly, starting in late September as the mercury dropped. First came *nul* (zero degrees Celsius), then *minus pyat* (minus five), then *minus desyat* (minus ten), then *minus dvadtsat* (minus twenty). When it jumped to thirty or forty below Celsius, the world stopped frozen.

Today was Christmas, and the temperature hit minus thirty-six degrees Celsius.

The *Banya*

"Merry Christmas." I sarcastically murmured to myself.

My words froze to my scarf. I gasped the frozen air for a breath. I coughed. It was difficult to take in small breaths in the extreme cold.

On this Christmas Day, *Dyed Moroz*, the Russian version of Santa Claus, brought me a wonderful gift of unbearable cold. It was a little trick to rub in the fact that it was my first Christmas away from my family back in Nevada. Instead of celebrating Christmas, I headed for work at School № 1, Timofey Pozolotin.

The Kazakhs being Muslim by association didn't celebrate Christmas, while the Russian Orthodox Church held the holiday on January 7. Most people, though, adhered to Soviet atheistic sentimentalities. Most holidays had an air of secularism, but with less of the American consumerism.

I continued to walk in the morning dark down the frozen road towards work. The world outside was silent, except for the crunching of ice crystals under foot. *Crunch, crunch, crunch, crunch...* It was a short walk from my host family's house to

school. It was eight in the morning, but the sun would not rise for two or three more hours.

While the cold could be excruciating and pervasive, it was strangely beautiful to walk through on these *moroz* winter days—as long as I could get past the fact that my hands and feet were frozen. The frost brought a pleasant, calm beauty to the village. Frost clung to all the trees and fences. It made everything glisten in sheer whiteness under the streetlamps. When the sun eventually rose, everything in Yavlenka and the countryside shined in pure white. The frost reflected all the rich, empyrean colors of the Siberian sky. Siberia, in these ephemeral bits and pieces of time, was remarkably the most exotic and beautiful place on earth.

'Wait until the fierce buran (blizzard) comes in January and lasts into March, sometimes April.' I could hear the locals tell me. *'Then try to appreciate winter with snow piling up ten feet high and wind blowing down everything in its path.'*

The blizzards would come later. For now, cold temperatures aside, I marveled at winter's beauty.

My frozen feet and hands, and the icicles hanging from my scarf, quickly brought me back into reality from my daydreaming. I walked briskly to keep warm. Parts of my body froze; I sweated in others. Underneath the layers and layers of clothes, I was oily and greasy. I felt disgusting. I hadn't showered or washed myself properly in over a week, maybe two. In this frozen land, indoor plumbing was few and far between, and there was little I could do about getting a proper bath.

I continued along the icy road to the school, trying to forget that I felt cold and stiff, oily and greasy. Down the frozen path leading into the schoolyard, I saw glowing and emanating lights beyond the trees piercing the dark world.

School № 1, Timofey Pozolotin, emanated with flashing colored lights. This was unexpected. The school was an unimpressive large Soviet-built building, but it appeared as if someone had decked the grey structure in bright lights for Christmas. The lights weren't for Christmas, though. They were put up to ring in the New Year that would be upon us in just a few days.

The school's warm glow welcomed me, and I walked up to the big blue doors of building. I reached for the door handle. It was ice-cold and hard to get a good grip. I pulled the heavy door to open it. The frost made it stick. My glasses instantly frosted over in a whoosh of warm air. I felt heat rush behind me, escaping into the cold world outside. I walked through, and the door slammed shut.

I went straight to my classroom to unpack. It didn't take long before I was defrosted, and blood was pumping back into my limbs and appendages. I would soon be celebrating Christmas Day by teaching Kazakhstani children how to say "Hello, my name is..." and other useful English phrases.

Quack

Although it was only mid-afternoon, the sun was beginning to set over the long flat horizon of Siberia. I had just arrived back home from work. I walked through the door of Four Sovietskaya Street from outside. I took off my coat, boots and the rest of my layers of winter clothes, and I made my way to the kitchen.

My host mother, Anasi, and her eldest daughter, Ülkenapa, were there cooking a late lunch.

"Hellooo, Timati!" said Ülkenapa.

She was seventeen years old. Her round face was always smiling and welcoming.

"*Privet*." I replied. *Hi.*

"Pleeez sit dowwwunnn!"

She pointed to the bench and table that sat in one corner of the cramped tiny kitchen.

I sat on the cushioned bench, looking around the small room. It was packed full of things. In one corner, the barely running refrigerator stood. It smelled stale when opened. In another corner, a gas stove sat. It was rusted and dented. The one window in the room was frozen over with a thick sheet of ice.

The house was cold from an afternoon of no heating. It was time to flip on the "thermostat," so Ülkenapa fidgeted with the *pyechka* (wood-fired stove) in one corner of the kitchen. A bucket of black coal and a pile of chopped wood lay next to the black rusty contraption.

Anasi served me a cup of tea as I sat.

Anasi was in her early forties. She colored her dark hair a reddish color, probably to hide the streaks of grey that came with middle age. She never said much of anything to me, and most of the time she looked unhappy. Maybe it was the cold, dark winters that got her down, or maybe it was just the way she was. Whether sad or happy, she was a decent cook.

As I sat, my host brother, Ağasi, and his father, Äke, burst in through the front door of the house from outside. Their faces were red from the cold. Ağasi was wearing a beat-up *dublenka* (jacket). Äke wore the same, but he also wore a funny fur hat on his head. The hat was called a *shapka*, and large fur flaps hung down over Äke's ears.

"Timati," shouted Ağasi, "Merry Chrisssmas!"

Ağasi was a small boy, barely a teenager of sixteen, but he was louder and more robust than others his age. His presence crowded the kitchen.

"*Spasibo* and Merry Christmas." I thanked him.

"Faahterrr and I, we *ubili*... ahh... we keeell *gusi*," interjected Ağasi with a smile. "Tonight, mama make good supper, Chrisssmas supper, wit *gusi*. You know *gusi*? Dey say *'ga-ga-ga'*?"

"Kill *gusi*? *'Ga-ga-ga'*?" I was confused. "I don't understand."

"Yesss, Timati, *'ga-ga-ga' gusi*! It like… ahh… burd wit looong neck, like ducky. We kill to eat! You know *gusi* say *'ga-ga-ga'*? Dey taste so goood!"

"Oh, geese!" I laughed. "They say *'honk-honk'* in English."

"No, Timati, *gusi* say *'ga-ga-ga'*," insisted Ağasi.

"Teemati," interrupted Äke as he walked into the kitchen.

I could see where Ağasi's small stature came from. Äke was thin and no taller than five-foot-five. Father and son now stood side by side in the already crowded kitchen.

"*'Ga-ga-ga'*, *'ga-ga-ga'*! No, no *'hooonk-hooonk'*!" shouted my host father. "*'Ga-ga-ga'*, *'ga-ga-ga'*!"

Äke flapped his arms as if he were flying away like a goose. He insisted that my English translation of geese honking was incorrect. Geese say *"ga-ga-ga."*

"Teematl!" continued Äke. *"Banya, banya!"*

Äke changed the motions of his hands from flapping to a soaping and lathering motion of his body.

"Banya, banya!" repeated Äke.

"My faahterrr say tonight befooor supper we make *banya*!" interpreted Ağasi. "We go poooplic *banya*! It vary nice! It *klasno*! Vary gangsta der!"

My ears piqued with curiosity and my heart began to pump faster with Ağasi's announcement of our evening at the *banya*. The *banya* was exactly what I needed for a Christmas present. I was quickly learning how great a Russian *banya* was, especially when showering and cleaning myself was becoming ever more difficult with the drop in temperatures outside.

The *banya* is a type of sauna or steam room. In most *banya* there is a large *pyechka* that heats pots of water. The water makes steam, and the combination of extreme heat and high humidity makes the body sweat profusely. Sweat and oil, and all the other junk that clogs the skin's pores, oozes out. A week's worth of filth, sweat, stink and everything gross encrusted in the skin is flushed down the *banya* drain. The feeling you get by using the *banya* is like running fifteen miles, but at the same time, it is like taking some euphoric-inducing drug. The Kazakh-stanis swore by its curative properties and the *banya*'s ability to purge the body of toxins. In my opinion, whether it cured the body of maladies or not, it was one of the most refreshing experiences ever devised. In the dead of winter, when there were deathly cold temperatures outside, the *banya* was simply a reprieve of fresh air.

"*Davay, davay*! Five minooot, pleez!" shouted Äke. He tapped his fingers on his wrist, motioning me to get ready.

I had lived with the Zheltoqsans long enough now to realize that Äke was not the most patient of men. He was a military man, a veteran of the Soviet's war in Afghanistan in the 1980s and a former police officer in Yavlenka. He demanded military speed and quickness, so I rushed to my room to grab a towel, flip flops and shampoo.

When I returned to the entryway of the house with my *banya* gear in hand, the rest of the family had dispersed from the kitchen, except for Äke. He was doing a strange thing to his nose. He was rubbing it with a yellow goo.

Since I had arrived at the Zheltoqsans in Yavlenka, I started to learn how Äke was not only a man of military action, but he was also one of the most interesting and somewhat unusual men I'd ever met. Unlike his son, Ağasi, who was chatty with no limit, Äke wasn't much for words. Perhaps it was better to say he was stoic. This philosophizing outlook, combined with being a recent pensioner in his late forties, added to his ponderings. He had a lot of time on his hands to think and tinker and plan. He seemed like he was a man afflicted with an existential crisis. He was intelligent, but the man was bored, and he seemed a little depressed. He was stressed because he had nothing to do all day but milk cows and tend sheep.

When I had first arrived in Yavlenka, he asked me to have my parents in America mail hair-growth formula from the States to help fix his "hair loss." He claimed his stress was making him lose his hair. According to him, America had "superior hair-growth technologies." At least, that was how I understood his choice of Russian: "Rogaine! Rogaine! *Luchshaya tekhnologiya*!"

Since most of the conversations between us were performed more through hand signals and motions, rather than actual tangible and intelligible words, I could never be quite sure what our conversations were really about. Nevertheless, when we did talk, when we truly broke through to each other, our conversations were, at the very least, unique.

I learned that he had some unusual ideas not only about his hair loss, but about his health in general. He had recently gotten "sick" just as the *moroz* really began to set in upon Yavlenka. It was a sickness accompanied neither by cough nor sneeze. It was an insidious sickness with no fever, dizziness, nausea, vomiting or diarrhea. He was sick, though. I could tell this for sure. He was fatigued and unwell. Some in Kazakhstan took pepper-laced vodka shots to combat such a sickness. Äke was above this form of relief. To fight this sickness, he took these strange injections, a favorite prescription given by his local practitioner. Sugar water? Placebo? Something else? He possessed a small medical case, and he took one injection a day for several days during the infliction. He claimed they gave him strength as he huffed and puffed, pounding his chest like a mighty silverback gorilla.

This time, though, when I saw Äke in the kitchen, there were no injections involved. He was doing something strange with his nose. It looked as if he was rubbing it with something unfamiliar, a sort of strange gooey substance. I peeked into the kitchen to get a better look.

"Teemati," acknowledged Äke with his croaky and hoarse voice. "*Davay, davay!*" *Come on, come on!*

He held his hand out for me to examine what he was rubbing on his nose. It was yellow and slimy. It took me a second to figure out what it was, until I took a deep whiff. The substance resonated the uniquely pungent smell of mutton. It was a piece of animal fat, coagulated and congealed.

"*Baran*," smiled Äke. *Sheep.*

His nose glistened, oily with smeared sheep fat.

"*Pochemu*?" I asked why he was using this treatment.

"*Gute Gesundheit*! Meee havvv *gute zdorove*... ahh... *gute* heeelth *für moroz*," answered Äke in a mishmash of languages.

He implied that this technique was good to improve health and fight off the *moroz*. He pounded his chest in his gorilla-like manner and took in a deep breath through his nose. He held out his hand to me again as if to offer me a try.

"No, thank you." I didn't bother saying it in Russian since the conversation was lost and beyond understanding for both of us.

Real Medicine

Äke and I ran outside to the family's Volkswagen Golf, where Ağasi was already warming up the car's engine. We began for the village's public *banya*.

"Timati, you know faahterrr rich man?" exclaimed Ağasi randomly while we drove the village's bumpy roads. "He *bogatye*! He rich man! He hafff dis cool car, and he hafff *mnogo baran*... ahh... many sheep!"

It had been in this same, small vehicle a few weeks prior that Äke and Ağasi had taken me for a road trip to buy sheep from a neighboring village. It was a strange scene to see Äke wrestle with a sheep and throw it into the back trunk of the small Golf.

"Yesss, he verrry rich man," said Ağasi proudly.

I played dumb and acted as if I hadn't realized the Zheltoqsan family was well-off according to average Kazakhstani standards.

The *Banya*

"We at veeellage *banya*," shouted Ağasi. "We rich boyz!"

We pulled into the *banya* parking lot. The public *banya* was on the outskirts of Yavlenka. It was housed in what looked like it had once been an old barn. In a village where most people didn't have running water, and some didn't even have their own place to bathe, the public *banya* was essential. Well, it was quite essential for those who could afford the luxury.

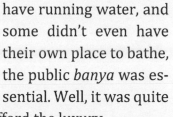

The necessity of the public *banya* was still strange to me. I had observed many houses in Yavlenka had once been equipped with the fixtures necessary for indoor plumbing: toilets, sinks, even baths and showers. However, the key components to make them functional (e.g. plumbing) disappeared over the years.

Oh, the good ole' days of the USSR! That was how the locals explained away my inquiries about these now-useless fixtures. Many villagers, especially so in the Russified north of Kazakhstan, would reminisce of their fond memories of the days before *Perestroika* (Soviet economic restructuring) and Kazakhstani independence. Villagers claimed that many people in Yavlenka, at one time, even had heating pumped into their homes from centralized power plants. The villagers blamed the last Soviet leader, Mikhail Gorbachev, and his economic reforms for their plumbing woes. They still curse his name to this very day.

"Do you know of *Perestroika*?" My teaching counterpart, Yekaterina Alekseyevna, would frequently ask me. "Oh, it was so awful. That awful Gorbachev! There was never heat nor light nor water. Overnight things fell apart in our *dear Soviet Union!*" Eventually, her conversation would return to the once-glorious dairy of Yavlenka. "Its products had been known throughout the Soviet Union, until *Perestroika*. *Perestroika* ruined our village's pride, the dairy!"

Not only ruining the once-glorious dairy of the village, the collapse of the Soviet Union also destroyed the village's infrastructure for indoor plumbing.

We entered the *banya* from the cold outside. My glasses fogged over instantly in the humid interior. An elderly woman sat inside a small kiosk collecting money.

"*Dvesti pyatdesyat,*" said the Russian woman with a smirk.

I pulled out my money to pay her. I handed her the ₸250 entrance fee—roughly two dollars, chump change in America, but a steep fee for many in Kazakhstan. I made my way into the changing room.

Inside the small dressing room, I placed my things into a cubby hole and slowly began to undress. Ağasi and Äke had no qualms when stripping off their clothes, but to me this didn't come so naturally. It seemed that my American Puritanical roots were getting in the way of a speedy disrobing. The Zheltoqsan men, now completely naked, entered through the door of the main washing area of the *banya*. I slipped on my flip flops, and I hesitantly followed into the room, exposed and naked.

The air was thick inside this room. The room was comfortably hot and humid. My nose was hit with the distinctive smell of damp wood, eucalyptus scent and soap. The large room was walled with wooden panels. The tiled floor was slippery with water and soap splattered on it. The tiles slanted toward the center of the room to drain water. A cold and hot water faucet stood in one corner of the room. Several waist-high benches were in the center of the room. A closed door lay on the opposite end from the entrance.

We were the only people in the *banya*. This made it easier for me to be there in the nude. I followed Äke and Ağasi's lead in *banya* etiquette and procedures. There seemed to be a process to the *banya*:

1) Grab a handheld,
rubber tub piled up
in the corner of the room;
2) At the faucet, fill the
tub up with hot water;
3) Dump the bucket-load
of water over the body;
4) Refill the tub with hot water from the faucet;
5) Lather up with soap and shampoo;
6) Dump water once more over the head and body;
7) Repeat steps two through six several times…

"Teemati!" began Äke, "*davay,
davay, paritsya!*"

He grabbed a bundle of
dry birch-tree branches
that lay on one of the wet
wood benches.

Ağasi interjected: "My
faahterrr want you *paritsya*.
You know what is *paritsya*?"

"No." I shrugged ignorant of
this "*paritsya*" word.

"Yesss, *paritsya*. It… ahh… it *nastoyaschoye
lekarstvo*… ahh… trooo medaseeena… ahh… vary
good medicine."

I was still confused.

"You like *paritsya*. Good fooor *serdtse*… ahh… heart, good
fooor heart. Faahterrr hit you wit *venik*."

Ağasi slapped his chest as he said this "*venik*" word.

"Hit?" I blurted out in confusion.

Äke began pushing me towards the damp, turgid door that lay in the corner of the *banya*.

I grabbed the door handle to pull it open. It was swollen and stuck. I pulled again, harder this time. It opened with a jerk. I stood at the doorway for a moment as extreme heat blasted the front of my body.

"Meeery Hristmas, Teemati," shouted Äke. "*Davay! Banya!*"

We passed through the door. It slammed shut behind us.

The heat in this dark room was unbearable.

A rusty metal furnace sat in the corner of the room. It roared with immense energy, emitting a fusion of scorching heat. A cauldron of boiling water was on top of the furnace. Two tiers of wood benches were mounted up against the wall opposite the stove. I cautiously sat on the top level. The bench sizzled my buttocks when I sat down.

Äke grabbed a ladle floating in the cauldron. He scooped boiling water, and he poured it onto the furnace's metal surface. The water hit the heated surface and instantly evaporated in a quick *hiss*. The room became *even* hotter than before.

"*Zharko, zharko!*" shouted Äke. *Hot, hot!*

Äke's voice was muffled by sizzles, spits, hisses and sputters—the sounds of unbearable heat. The air was so thick. My head felt so heavy. At the same time, I felt woozy and lightheaded. I tried to breathe in and out, in and out. *Slowly… Slowly…* This simple task was too difficult. My breathing picked up speed, and I began panting.

"*Paritsya*," shouted Äke.

Äke commanded me to lie down on the hot bench. He held the bundle of birch-tree branches. This, I assumed, was the *venik* that Ağasi had warned me about. I was wary of what was to come with this *paritsya* and *venik*, but like so many other things in Kazakhstan, there was no use in fighting it. *When in Rome...*

I laid on my back on the bench. I covered my face with my right hand, and I cupped my privates with my left. My back burned from the hot damp wood surface of the bench.

"*Gute Gesundheit,*" laughed Äke, reminding me that this was for my health. "Harrrt! Blooood! Gooood!"

He pounded the place on his chest where his heart was.

If this was his attempt to calm me before he would begin whipping me with the *venik*, it didn't do much good. My heart was already racing with every pump of blood.

It's good for my health, I reminded myself. *'Gute Gesundheit!'*

Äke took the *venik,* and he began tapping my chest with the dry branches slowly and softly.

The leaves rustled: *Sheesh... Sheesh... Sheesh...*

This isn't so bad. I thought.

Äke stopped his initial tapping for a second. I peeked over to see what he was doing. He was dipping the *venik* into the cauldron of boiling water on top of the furnace.

Whopppsssssssshhhhhh! The thrashing came in a swift wet crack and whip of heat. Leaves and hot water flew everywhere. From head to toe, my body was thoroughly whipped by the *venik. Whopppssssssshhhhhh! Whopppssssssshhhhhh!*

The sensation was horrendous. It was torture. The thrashing movement of air made everything feel hotter in the room.

Äke commanded me to flip over and lie on my stomach. It was time to use the *venik* on my back.

As I turned over, I continued to cup my privates to protect

them from the hot bench. My face smashed into the hot bench. I braced for the flogging of birch-tree branches.

Whopppsssssshhhhhh! Whopppsssssshhhhhh!

The thrashing ended shortly after it began. Äke tapped my shoulder motioning me to stand up. Leaves stuck to my body.

It was now my turn to return this "favor" to Äke. I grabbed the *venik* from his hand and dipped it into the boiling water. Instead of lying down on the hot bench, he stood upright and rigid in the middle of the room ready for the punishment.

Right as I readied the *venik* for my first strike, Äke motioned me to pause. With the ladle, he scooped water from the cauldron, and he dumped water onto the hot metal surface of the furnace.

Hsssssssssssss... Water sizzled and evaporated instantly into white steam. The mercury in the room rose several degrees.

Äke motioned for me to begin the *paritsya*. Giving the *paritsya* was even more of a workout for me than receiving the treatment. I panted, and I sweated profusely while I hit my host father with the *venik*.

After a minute or two—time was hard to perceive in this room—I stopped hitting Äke. We had both taken all we could from the heat and the *venik* whipping. We ran out the door.

In the main room of the *banya*, Äke picked up a round washing tub. He went to the faucet and filled it up with cold water. He then proceeded to dump it over his head.

"Ahh... GOOOOD!" sighed Äke as steam came off his body.

I followed my host father's lead. The water that came from the faucet was ice-cold. I dumped it over my overheated body without question and hesitation. The feeling was refreshing but, at the same time, quite unpleasant.

"Enjoy the bath!"

Next Äke took a small plastic scrubber, and handed it to me. It looked like a sponge, but it wasn't soft.

The *Banya*

"*Davay, davay,*" commanded Äke, and he mimed for me to scrub his back with the sponge.

I looked at him with disgust, but Äke didn't notice.

First the venik and paritsya, and now this. I thought. *How does one refuse such wonderful invitations?*

There I was, in Kazakhstan, naked and exposed, exfoliating the back of a forty-something man with an insistent personality. My life had reached a point of no return, all thanks to the simple task of cleaning oneself.

As I scrubbed Äke's back, two Kazakh strangers entered the main room of the *banya*. They were large burly men, each with a well-endowed beer gut. They looked no older than thirty. One man wore a funny felt hat and gloves, and he began taking the *venik* to himself, thrashing furiously in the middle of the room. Ağasi began talking to the other man.

"Timati," interrupted Ağasi.

I was still scrubbing his father's back.

"Dees men, dey policeman. Dey no see Amerikan befooor. I tell dem you cool boy. Now dey want you *paritsya.*"

"But I just *paritsya.*" I said with concern since I really didn't want to *paritsya* again.

"Teemati," shouted Äke, "*davay, davay, paritsya! Posle banyi vodka i pivo! Ladno?*"

"Yesss, Timati," affirmed Ağasi, "you *paritsya* again wit dis man. It feel good. Afer *banya*, you and faahterrr drink vodka and beer, and we make Chrissmas party wit family. Mama cook *gusi*, '*ga-ga-ga*' *gusi*, not 'hooonk-hooonk' *gusi*!"

As Ağasi and Äke spoke to me about our post-*banya* plans, one of the large husky men had already begun to suit me up with all the proper *paritsya* gear. He handed me the *venik* and the sweaty gloves he had been wearing. He put his felt hat on my head. It was laced with sweat and soapy water. He then motioned me over to the door of the small sauna room without saying a word. His face was serious, almost a grin. He opened the door, and a rush of hot air and steam escaped.

I looked back at Äke and Ağasi.

"*S legkim parom*," said the duo in unison. *Enjoy the bath!*

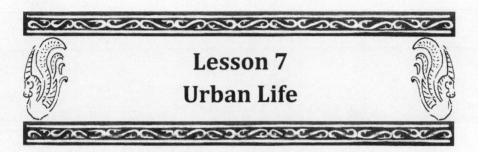

Lesson 7
Urban Life

"My master and his friends continued on the shore till I was almost out of sight; and I often heard the sorrel nag (who always loved me) crying out, 'Hnuy illa nyha, majah Yahoo;' 'Take care of thyself, gentle Yahoo'.*"*

From Gulliver's
Travels *by*
Jonathan Swift

Official Business

Kumshat: "Hello! How are you?"

Nastya: "I am fine, thank you. How are you?"

Kumshat: "I am fine too, thank you. What is your name?"

Nastya: "My name is Nastya. What is your name?"

Kumshat: "My name is Kumshat."

A Five Finger Feast

The monotony of teaching basic English was beginning to set in by my fourth month in Yavlenka. Most of my students, whether fourth graders or seniors in their final year of school, could barely put together an English sentence. They could barely understand a word I spoke.

My students' problems in English were complicated ones, and not necessarily faults of their own. Even though the astute president of Kazakhstan himself declared English-language education a priority for all students to learn, English in Kazakhstan, particularly in rural areas, lagged. Not enough time, teachers and resources were dedicated to this bold endeavor. Teaching methodologies could also be ancient, austere and lackluster. Soviet methods of rote repetition were still the norm. There would be a lot of work ahead at School № 1, Timofey Pozolotin.

Even with this challenge, I still grew restless to speak "real" English, not the basic English I spoke in my lessons with my students. While the English teachers at my school spoke English good enough to converse beyond rudimentary topics, even they gave me glazed-over looks when I caught them with a word or phrase they didn't recognize. If I spoke too fast, they looked at me like deer in the headlights.

I was beginning to feel desperate for "real" English. The only people within hundreds of miles of Yavlenka who could give me the reprieve I sought were the other volunteers in the "big" city nearby, Petropavlovsk.

For the first few months after arriving in Yavlenka, I came into Petro infrequently, and I saw the other Americans who lived there even less. In the beginning of my time in Yavlenka, I found it too difficult to navigate to the city without the help of the Zheltoqsans or my counterpart, Yekaterina Alekseyevna. Also, the Peace Corps' rules and regulations prevented me from leaving my site too much, except when I was drawn to the city for official work-related reasons.

Urban Life

It was sometime around my twenty-third birthday in February, and the icy miserable *buran* (blizzard) that followed, that sparked a more frequent venturing into Petro. The dark winter and the loneliness of the village was beginning to take its toll. My "official" excuse for a weekend in the city was to help with an English club run out of the American Corner, a State Department-sponsored library. On the second and fourth Saturdays of the month I began making the two-hour trek into the city to help with the volunteer-led club.

Pig in a Blanket

It was March now, but it was still freezing temperatures outside. Winter lingered. It refused to unclench its grip on the world outside. It tried to hold on as long as it could.

I woke early this Saturday so that I could catch an early bus to Petro. No one else in the Zheltoqsan household had woken yet. This meant the fire in the *pyechka* hadn't been set, and it was near freezing throughout the house. I quickly dressed, grabbed a quick snack in the kitchen and made my way to my jacket and boots at the door.

I hated these cheap Chinese-made boots. I had bought them at the bazaar during training in the south. They pinched my feet and cut off the circulation to my toes. I tried to wear tennis shoes with warm socks to get through the winter, but my host mother, Anasi, made a hissy fit. There was something in her psyche that prevented comfort from overcoming custom. I wore these awful, dreaded boots to avoid her chastising.

After I put on the boots and my jacket, I opened the door and stepped out onto the front porch. I tripped. I looked down to double check if I had tied my boots. I had. I tripped over a chunk of meat lying frozen on the porch. It was a frozen goose. Around Christmas two months before, my host father and host brother had butchered a gaggle of geese. Anasi kept the slaughtered flock on the porch, our freezer. It was a practical solution to limited space in our refrigerator.

I continued on my way, opening the door to the porch and walking to the front gate of Four Sovietskaya Street. Sovietskaya Street was frozen. By now, old snow had been compressed into sheets of ice. The walk to the bus station was a short but slippery one. From Sovietskaya Street, I took a quick right and then left over a large rusty pipe that ran parallel to the main road. This took me into the hospital's yard, which connected me to the commercial center of Yavlenka. Not too many people were out in the village center this early on a Saturday morning. Leaving the main square through a short alley by the village nightclub, the path took me to the main road that ran through town. The bus station lay on the busy drag. As I left the alley, I saw a bus full of people pull away, heading for Petro.

"Damn, I missed it." I muttered through my frozen scarf.

I had started to figure out the bus "schedule" that departed from Yavlenka's small station. Even with this knowledge, I found the busses and the large passenger vans called *marshrutka* came and went according to their own timetable. I didn't know how long I would have to wait for the next bus to arrive.

I entered the door of the station. The window of the door was frozen over with a thick layer of ice. The inside of the building was long, cavernous and cold. The walls were bland, and the floor was made of cracked tiles. Narrow benches lined the walls, but they were empty. At the end of the hall was a ticket window, and a room branched off into a small café. The food tasted mediocre at best.

I walked up to the ticket window. It was empty.

"Hello?" I said into the void behind the glass.

No one responded.

"Hello! Someone is here." I repeated. "I am here."

No one responded.

I turned from the window and walked to a bench. I sat... and sat… and sat some more. No one came to tend the ticket window.

After sitting for a long while, I heard a noise from the café. A plump middle-aged woman walked out of the café. She didn't look like the typical Russian, and she didn't look like a Kazakh. She was dark and tan. Perhaps Armenian? Several Armenian families lived in the village.

"*Amerikanets*?" asked the woman shrilly, acknowledging that I was the American.

"*Da*." I replied.

"Petro?" clarified the Armenian.

"*Da*."

"*Nu, marshrutka*," said the woman speedily, and she pointed to the door that led outside. "*Idti*!" Go!

I was confused. I often was. Nevertheless, I walked to the door and opened it.

Lo and behold, outside, sitting in the potholed parking lot was a white van idling. It was covered in icy mud. The exhaust pipe pumped out thick white smoke dissipating quickly into the freezing air. A burly wrinkle-faced man was leaning against it, smoking a cigarette.

I approached, trying not to slip on the ice underfoot.

"*Zdravstvuyte*!" I greeted him with a newfound chirpiness.

He nodded. He looked at me with suspicion.

"Umm, Petro?" I knew he was going to the city, but I figured I would ask, just in case.

"*Da*," replied the driver, countenance never changing.

"*Skolko stoit*?" I asked how much the ride would cost since the faster vans usually cost more than the busses.

"*Trista*," blew the man with a puff of cigarette smoke.

I coughed from the smoke. I slipped him Т300, the equivalent of two and a half dollars.

He slid open the van's side door, and I stepped up into the vehicle. I found a seat in the empty van; there was no seat belt. I waited in the cold *marshrutka*.

My boots pinched my toes. I was beginning to lose feeling in my right foot. I continued to wait in the idling van. My mind wandered through the mundane of the moment.

Unexpectedly, the van's door slid open with a whoosh of cold air. *Kah thunk!* A white rice sack slammed onto the van's floor. It was stuffed with something heavy and solid. It was clearly not rice. A young Russian man pushed the sack the rest of the way into the van. He jumped on board, slamming the door shut.

Our driver took a final drag on his cigarette. He loaded himself into the seat and released the parking brake.

Vvvrooommm... We were off for the city. We sped through Yavlenka, turning on the main highway.

I sat in silence in the cold vehicle. The noise of the air rushing against the speeding van and the engine loudly clanging muffled my thoughts. I began fixating on the strange decorations the driver had placed in his *marshrutka*. Shiny CDs, the type of CDs used for storing data or playing music, hung from the rearview mirror. They were strung to a string, dangling with no purpose but to shine and reflect. A small intricately painted picture of the Mother Mary and her baby Jesus sat up front next to the driver's stick shift.

The rice sack began to roll around the dirty floor of the *marshrutka*, but the young man who carried it didn't seem to care.

We passed areas of land with few people to inhabit it. The land was mostly left for fields and forests, a few lakes and grassy marshes. The Ishim River snaked alongside the highway. A few very, very, very small villages lay a mile or two off the main highway. Chirikovka. Rassvet. Krasnaya Gorka. They were blips along the frozen landscape.

The sack began to roll even more as the van swayed up and down the undulating highway. It had probably been years, maybe even since Soviet times since the road had been repaved. The highway bumped and rolled like a lake picking up waves on windy day, jostling and rough at times. This flowed all the way to the city.

In the suburb of Bishkul, we passed through a police checkpoint. The driver slowed to a snail's pace here. Policemen with large-brimmed hats and crisp uniforms sat in a tower-like building monitoring traffic. Some officers were walking in the middle of the road, among the slow-moving traffic, whistling and flagging down vehicles. Their job was to pull over cars and busses to hand out large fines to unregistered vehicles. Some locals once told me that these police also checked for—and occasionally, from what the locals alluded to, planted on unsuspecting drivers—illegal contraband, like drugs and moonshine. A small bribe, "insurance" as the locals called it, to the officers could sway them to look the other way to most infractions. We passed through successfully and picked up speed. The rice sack began rolling around the van floor again.

The road to the city turned at the police checkpoint through marshland. Petro lay above the wetlands on a plateau. Entering the city from this direction, took us past a large Russian cemetery. Headstones and massive crosses dotted the gradual hill going up to the city.

We passed by Petro's many *dacha*. These small cabins, some shacks, were the revered and blissful summer retreats of Russian society. Many citizens from the city came out to spend summers playing in their "countryside," cultivating garden paradises in their *dacha*. Much of the

urban folks' fruits and vegetables were grown at the *dacha*. Now, at winter's end, the *dacha* territory lay cold and dormant with no sign of life in the bleak landscape.

We hit a pothole, and the sack bounced and rolled into my right foot. My foot was numb from my boots, but I could still feel how heavy the sack was. I looked down. Blood seeped through the rice sack lining, rubbing against my cheaply made boots. I retracted my foot.

What the hell? I thought. *Blood?*

The owner of the sack paid no notice.

It then dawned on me. Inside the sack was a large dead animal, a fat pig likely. The man was probably taking it to market, slightly marinated and tenderized by the rolling of the road and the dirty wet floor of the *marshrutka*.

An Apartment

Most busses and *marshrutka* stopped at the Petro train station on the southern edge of the city. From here, passengers from the outlying villages had a few options to further their journey by:

1) Escaping Kazakhstan on a train east or west into Russia;
2) Going eight hours south to the capital Astana, and then twenty-four more hours onto the metropolis of Almaty;[21]
3) Heading into Petro by means of city bus, taxi or foot.

Of option three, I usually chose by foot. Walking had been my only form of exercise during the winter months. Exercise, in the American sense of working out, just wasn't easy to come by in the village—especially during the many cold and snowy days.

When the van let me off at the train station, I began walking briskly toward the center of the city. I was heading to meet Jack-

---

[21] Nur-Sultan (fmr. Astana) is the capital of Kazakhstan (pop. 1,000,000).

son, a volunteer who taught English at Petro's tech school.

I didn't know Jackson as well as I knew some of the other volunteers, like Dylan and Leo, who also lived in the city. Dylan and Leo, Kaz 19s, still lived with host families. Jackson, a Kaz 18 in his second year of service, had just moved out of his host family's house and into an apartment all to himself. He would let me crash there occasionally.

Petro was set up in a grid of streets, perfectly designed by Moscow bureaucrats during the Soviet days. Despite this easy-to-use grid, I tended to take shortcuts bisecting the large blocks.

My shortcuts took me through the muddy and frozen court-yards and back alleys of the tall concrete apartment complexes that dominated the cityscape. Clothes lines and satellite dishes hung above from apartment balconies. In between the prefabricated blocks of drab concrete, were small cottages. Some were kept up pristinely in wood-carved, ornate and brightly colored fashions dictated by Russian tradition. Others were decrepit and falling down. These one-storied homes rose from trash heaps that littered the mud. I walked past the cottages. Electrical wires were strung like a web above, running from here to there, from house to house.

I eventually made my way to Internatsionalnaya Street, one of the main drags in Petro. It was almost noon. The sun broke through the mostly overcast sky, though it was still frigid. The sidewalk, especially where traffic was heaviest, was covered in thick layers of ice. It was slippery, slick and perilous. I continued along Internatsionalnaya Street. The street was long, and many people were shuffling about with some going to the bazaar or the many *magazin* shops on the street. Others were running to and from work. Even on this Saturday, school children and college students were just now leaving their studies and heading home. Sunday would be their only day of rest.

After walking for nearly forty minutes from the station, I arrived at Jackson's apartment building. Jackson lived far down Internatsionalnaya at the intersection of Pushkina Street, a road named after Alexander Pushkin, a Russian poet.

Aside from an old Soviet-era mural of Lenin that still loomed on the apartment's façade, the streetside of the building was mostly obscured by twisting branches of overgrown trees.

I went around to the inner courtyard. It was large, rectangular, flanked by three-storied apartments on each side. A rusty playground sat frozen and unused in the middle of the courtyard. Water and gas pipes stretched across the area, some giving off steam in the cold air. They were large and raised off the ground, most were wrapped in plaster and fiberglass. The metal door of Jackson's stairwell was wide open, unwelcoming and dark. A staircase of polished concrete went up into the building. I entered. Jackson lived on the second floor.

I began walking up. I looked down and noticed syringes and needles were shoved up where the stairs met the wall. Heroin was a growing problem in Kazakhstan. The ancient Silk Road of spices and silks had given way to trafficking illicit drugs from Afghanistan and human cargo, such as prostitutes from Kyrgyzstan and migrant workers from Tajikistan.[22]

When I reached the second floor, I turned right and went to Jackson's door. The door was covered in a leathery cushioned material. Maybe this was to keep out the cold. I buzzed his doorbell. *Bzzzzzz... Bzzzzzz...* I waited a moment, and I pressed it again. *Bzzzzzz...*

A number of locks were twisted and turned on the other side. With a blast of warm air, Jackson, a young guy slightly older and shorter than myself, stood in athletic shorts and a sweatshirt with the words "North Face."

"What's up, dude?" These were the first words of "real" English I had heard in almost three weeks.

I walked in and took off my dirty boots as was the tradition when entering a local's home. Volunteers had adopted the custom, even when visiting other Americans in Kazakhstan.

"Can I shower?" I asked since I hadn't washed in over a week.

"Yeah, man. Go for it," replied Jackson nonchalantly.

The bathroom was like most in these Soviet-built apartments—small, crammed full with a toilet that broke often, a sink that over flowed, a rack to dry clothes, rubber bins to wash laundry, and a shower and tub. The bathroom was thoroughly Soviet in design, although Jackson had given his own American touches to the room.

---

[22] Kyrgyzstan and Tajikistan are former Soviet Republics located to the south of Kazakhstan.

A Five Finger Feast

For starters, in most apartments one would find a trashcan filled with toilet paper. This small cylinder was reserved for soiled toilet paper. Toilet paper wreaked havoc on the old pipes in these apartments. Despite this, Jackson thought the practice disgusting, so I happily flushed my used toilet paper.

I turned on the shower faucet and let it run. Jackson's heating was connected to a centralized system that was pumped in from the pipes that lay strewn across the courtyard outside. This gave the heating and water situation a certain mysteriousness, but even more so, an annoying uncertainty. Sometimes too hot and sometimes too cold, in Kazakhstan one learned to live without certain luxuries. I continued to let the water run. The water temperatures varied back and forth from freezing to scorching hot. I had learned the hard way in previous showerings to run the water for a while until the temperatures leveled out before jumping in. The water was finally adequate, perfect for Kazakhstani standards, so I stripped down and jumped in.

The shower was blissful, and I took it all in. The week's worth of grime and grit, oils and grease washed away, spinning down into the drain.

When I finished up, I found Jackson busily working in the kitchen. The kitchen was like the bathroom, small and cramped. The refrigerator was ancient and hummed loudly, emitting freon. The stove had pots and pans piled on it. Jackson truly lived a bachelor's lifestyle. A small table sat under a frozen window.

"Yo, Tim," said Jackson, "I'm makin' PB and J. You want one?"

"Of course! How could I resist?"

Peanut butter, an American invention, was a luxury in Kazakhstan. Jackson had it sent over by his family in the US.

"Cool, dude. By the way, we need to get ready to go soon. Just got a text from Dylan. We are going to meet him at his place on the way to the American Corner."

I knew what this meant. If Dylan's host mother, Natasha, was home when we went to pick him up, our timing would be thrown off. Natasha, like most locals, required guests, even if for a moment, to sit down and have tea with her.

Yahoo

Night fell.

After the English club, we spent a long-time eating food and drinking beer at Café Döner with the other volunteers. The café had been a longtime staple for volunteers in Petro since 1999. Since the café was owned by a friendly and service-oriented Turkish family, the café seemed like a "Westernized" attempt at bringing Americanized fast food to Kazakhstan. Asides from the Turkish döner kebabs, the café attempted hamburgers, hot dogs and pizza. The atmosphere of the place verged on Chuck E. Cheese's, even with cartoon mouse characters painted on the walls and a playpen filled with plastic balls for children.

We were here with our Peace Corps groupies. The groupies were local friends who spoke English. They seemed to befriend the volunteers in each new group of volunteer arrivals. Dylan had already become more than friends with one of them.

It had been a long day as we finished our last beers. It was already midnight. I was tired. Café Döner closed up shop, and Jackson and I said our farewells to the other volunteers and groupies. We were finally heading back to his apartment.

The busy streets of the daytime's urban life had faded. Most people in the city had made their way to warm homes and beds. Not even the ubiquitous drunks and feral dogs of Petro seemed to be out in the frozen night. The city was motionless. Icy streets glistened under the incandescent, yellow glow of streetlamps.

We neared Jackson's apartment at the intersection of Internatsionalnaya and Pushkina. As we crossed Pushkina Street, a Lada sedan crept up to the traffic light and stopped opposite of us. It idled in the quiet night, waiting for the light to change to green. Another car, another sedan, quickly came down the road from behind. The brakes of the car screeched as it approached the red light.

Smack! Jackson and I jumped in surprise. It appeared as if the sedan slid on a patch of ice, hitting the back bumper of the idling Lada. The Lada's bumper now hung on the ground.

Is that driver drunk? I thought.

The stoplight turned green, but the cars didn't move forward. Their exhaust plumed in the cold air.

Two tall men eventually emerged from the Lada that had been hit. They both walked right up to the driver's side of the car that hit them. The man inside quickly jostled to lock his vehicle's door. He was too late. The men opened the driver's door. They pulled the man out of his seat. He was small and demure. One of the men threw him to the icy road. The other hit him with a loud *whack!*

Jackson and I decided it would be prudent to walk as quickly as possible into the shadows of his apartment building nearby. We watched from there.

The two men took a few shots at the poor guy as if he was a rice sack filled with meat. I was now familiar with what rice sacks filled with meat looked like, after all. The man being attacked tried to get up off the ground. He fell back down on the slippery ice.

The traffic light turned red.

The two men then turned back to their car. They had gotten their fix of "justice." This was their own form of a cruel and twisted car insurance policy. They got back into their Lada and sped right through the red light.

They honked their car horn as they shouted out their windows at us: *"Idi naaaa khuiiiiiii!"*

Their tires screeched as they sped down the icy road. Their bumper hung down, rattling on Pushkina Street.

We continued to watch from the shadows. We were flabbergasted and stunned at what we had just witnessed.

The man who had been attacked slowly picked himself off the ground. He rolled into his car with a slump. He turned right onto Internatsionalnaya Street, somehow managing to drive his car away.

"What the Hell?" shouted Jackson angrily as we turned towards his apartment. "What the *hell* was that? I hate this country and these goddamn"—it was clear that Jackson had pent up anger as he let out a roar that echoed off the apartment buildings towering over us—"bastards! Savages! This whole country is bullshit! If that was me, I would have gone after the bastards! I am so tired of this goddamn place, with its idiotic people, its shitty food, shitty schools, its thugs, its shitty cops, its corrupt politicians. It's corrupt! It's crooked! I hate how no one smiles. I hate Kazakhstan! Can't wait to go back to America!"

The usually calm Jackson had snapped.

We continued into his building. Jackson was still angry when we got up to his apartment. He went straight to his room, closing his door behind him, not saying as much as "goodnight."

After brushing my teeth in the bathroom, I set sheets on the sofa in the living room. I turned off the lights and laid myself on the sofa. I couldn't sleep, though. The car scene kept racing through my brain.

Idi naaaa khuiiiiiii. This simple Russian epithet rang inside my head. The sound of the crash, the yelling of the men, the violence in their actions, they all kept repeating through my head. I didn't want to admit this to Jackson, but the incident was, in the very least, exciting! The monotony of daily life had turned into seconds of excitement, despite a man being pounded into the asphalt. In those few moments, Kazakhstan, for me, had been like the Wild West. It had been exciting, rough, chaotic.

Jackson's reaction etched into my brain too. He seemed to have had a momentary break. The pressure of Kazakhstan was finally getting to him.

Who am I to judge? I thought while I laid on the couch.

We, as in the volunteers, would all have our brief moments like these in Kazakhstan. Blips and moments of frustration with the culture or the cold or the combination of the two. Most of what we would do in this country of our volunteer service would be boring and monotonous work, even frustrating at times. There would be many hours and days ahead filled with boredom during my two years of service.

But there would also be these small bits and pieces of excitement—the passionate, unadulterated thrill of Kazakhstan.

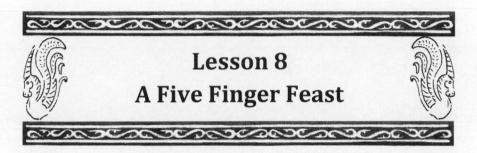

Lesson 8
A Five Finger Feast

"There was a table set out under a tree in front of the house, and the March Hare and the Hatter were having tea at it. Dormouse was sitting between them, fast asleep, and the other two were using it as a cushion, resting their elbows on it, and talking over its head. 'Very uncomfortable for the Dormouse,' thought Alice; 'only, as it's asleep, I suppose it doesn't mind'."

From Alice's
Adventures in
Wonderland
by Lewis Carroll

"Drink me..."

*H*e *flicked his neck! This means one thing in the sign language of Kazakhstan,* I anxiously thought to myself. *It's time to drink... as if I hadn't already had enough. Can I keep up at this mad, frantic pace?*

125

My palms were sweaty; my head was dizzy.

He flicked his neck again.

Well, I suppose, if he insists.

My inhibitions had been greatly reduced to zero.

"Timati," egged on Uncle Ağayindi. "*Chut-chut vodka...*" *Only a little bit of vodka!*

He held out his hand pinching the air to assure me that the vodka shots would be little small baby ones. Uncle Ağayindi was family, after all. I had to trust him. He was my host mother's little brother, my host uncle. Oddly for an uncle he was my same age, twenty-three.

"*Chut-chut?*" I replied, pinching the air to emphasize the *chut* in *chut-chut*.

I could barely handle even one *chut* more of vodka. Anything more than a *chut* would certainly kill me.

"*Chut-chut,*" assured Uncle Ağayindi again.

He smiled. He flicked his neck once more.

I had learned that flicking or tapping the neck, the infamous *shchelchok po sheye*, meant "time to get drunk." The legend goes something like this... During the reign of tsar Peter the Great, a carpenter or shipbuilder—the exacts were lost on me after copious amounts of vodka—was rewarded for his service to the tsar with the gift of the ultimate bar tab. He was tattooed on the neck with the tsar's royal insignia. With this marking, all the man simply needed to do was flick or tap his neck, showing the tattoo in any tavern in the empire, and he would be given a free drink. Naturally, he had many drinking buddies.

I had found my drinking buddy in the form of Uncle Ağayindi. He flicked his neck again.

It's rude to decline the invite, I thought.

It was true. Refusing a drink was a great insult in the hybrid culture of northern Kazakhstan, a place where Russian and Kazakh culture met.

"*Nein* much, much vodka," said Uncle Ağayindi grinning.

He held up two shot glasses and an unopened bottle of vodka. It was Status Vodka, gold cap. High standards as far as vodka went in Kazakhstan. It was ₸300 in stores, a liter of premium vodka for less than three dollars.

"*Kak voda!*" affirmed Uncle Ağayindi. *Just like water.*

The rest of the guests at the dinner party had already vacated the living room where we now sat. The whole party had dined and wined earlier for a grand feast in this room. Most of the men, aside from Uncle Ağayindi and me, were now outside smoking their post-dinner cigarettes. The women were in the kitchen washing dishes.

"Just you and me, Uncle Ağayindi." I told my host uncle.

He didn't understand me. Instead of answering, he began pouring the vodka shots.

A logical person would have backed off this cliff. Of course, I was far beyond logic and reason by this point in the night.

"Bring it on! *Insha'Allah!*" I said with a flick of my neck.

And down the rabbit hole I went.

The First Beautiful Day

April 12 was the first warm day I had seen in Yavlenka since arriving in November. For months, the village had been covered in a thick white coat of snow and ice. For months, the oppressive winter had ravaged the spirit of Yavlenka and its people. Mother Nature was neither loving nor nurturing as she rained down icy terror on the landscape.

I woke around nine on this Saturday morning and decided to take a much-needed walk. Though it was still cool out, I put on shorts, a t-shirt and a hoodie—very un-Kazakhstani in fashion. I didn't care; I needed to celebrate the warmth. I made my way to the kitchen, where I found my youngest host sister, Qoyan.

Qoyan was in the seventh grade. She was tall for her age, but thin and scrawny. She was sprawled out on the kitchen floor, scrubbing with a wet rag.

"Good morning, Timati," said Qoyan with a smile.

"Morning!" I replied. "What are you doing? Cleaning up so early in the morning?"

She looked at me with a blank stare.

I repeated my questions in Russian.

"I don't know," replied Qoyan as she shrugged her shoulders.

She went back to work scrubbing the floors. I grabbed a breakfast snack of bread and butter from the kitchen table, and I made my way to the door to begin my morning walk.

For simply meandering around and exploring the village, many Yavlenkans thought me strange, others an American spy. Nevertheless, I enjoyed taking walks around the village. It helped with the boredom of village life. And with the relentless assault of arctic ice and wind subsiding, I took this opportunity on a warm Saturday to get outside and enjoy the outdoors. Unfortunately, the warm temperatures had melted the winter's snow into a lovely quagmire of mud.

I walked carefully around the puddles, and I made my way down the mud road. My house at Four Sovietskaya Street was a short walk to the Ishim River. Yavlenka was situated on a plateau above the river. I went to the edge of the plateau, and I stood looking over the river.

Millennia of erosion had carved out a small ravine where the river flowed northward toward Petro and into Russia. Today, the once-frozen waters of the Ishim were finally flowing, turgid and spilling over the river's banks. The river flowed to the tune of spring. For every bird's chirp, the river gurgled. For every feral dog's bark, the river spluttered.

I continued along the road that looped around the village along the plateau's edge.

The air was beginning to feel alive, energized. The big thaw finally allowed the aroma of spring to fill the air, a strange mixture of blossoming flowers and smoke. In the distance, past the Ishim, I saw fields smoldering. They were on fire. With spring's arrival, I had learned that farmers burned and scorched their fallow fields to prepare the soil for the bounty of summer's short life. It also made the village smell like a campfire, a small price to pay for the warmth of springtime.

The leaves of the many birch trees surrounding the village had yet to bud, but the branches of these white-bark trees vibrated with bountiful energy waiting to be released. The grass was still yellowish brown and thawing, but I could feel the vivid greens that would burst forth soon.

'*Nature's first green is gold,*' I thought to myself.[23]

The atmosphere of this nice April day was one of relief and exhilaration. It was like that feeling when you hold your breath underwater for a long time and finally come up for air. The entire world around me was finally taking that deep breath. Life and all the vibrancy of spring were filling its lungs.

I took a deep breath. I coughed from the smoke.

A horse trotted down the dirt road towards me. It pulled a wagon with a youthful Russian boy on it.

"*Zdravstvuyte* Meester Sachlend," shouted the boy.

It was one of my seventh-grade students, Losha. His smile was a breath of fresh air in a land of toothless grimaces and frozen glares.

I eventually wandered back to the homestead.

"Hellooo!" shouted Ülkenapa, smiling. "Goood mooorning!"

My seventeen-year-old host sister, Ülkenapa, was in front sweeping the dirt path leading to Four Sovietskaya Street.

"Hi!" I replied as I walked through the fence's gate. "What's up, homie?"

I made it a goal to teach my host siblings English colloquial-

---

[23] From "Nothing Gold Can Stay" by Robert Frost (1923).

isms and slang.

"Whaaa?" She was a bit befuddled. "Oh, yes! Waaatttsssup! I kleeen! Today we make parteee. Now it *subbotnik*."

I had learned that a *subbotnik* was a type of "spring cleaning." Several days of school had been canceled to allow students to partake in a village-wide *subbotnik*. Somehow this form of child labor was legal in Kazakhstan.

I grabbed another broom, and I began helping Ülkenapa sweep the path.

"Today parteee for Qoyan! We have frrrend and famaaaly."

"Oh, yeah?" I inquired. "Why is there a party for Qoyan?"

"Qoyan have happy buuurfday," informed Ülkenapa. "She now thirteen years!"

Qoyan had acted so nonchalant earlier. I would have never known it was her birthday.

"Alsooo, today *Dyen Kosmonavtiki*! Me so happy! Today goood day for parteee!"

Today was turning out to be a good day. Not only was it *Dyen Kosmonavtiki* or Day of the Cosmonauts, a surreal leftover of a Soviet holiday, but it was warm outside. More importantly, and to my surprise, it was Qoyan's thirteenth birthday. For Kazakhs, the thirteenth year was one of the most important birthday celebrations, like a sweet sixteen of sorts or a *quinceñera* back in the States.

I finished helping Ülkenapa, and I headed around the back of the house. Along the way I smelled thick heavy smoke, like a barbecue mixed with melting plastic. I followed the wafting billows of smoke.

At the end of my nostril-led

search, I found Äke and Ağasi working vigorously away. My host brother, Ağasi, was tending a smoldering pile of burning trash and leaves as part of his *subbotnik* duties. His father, Äke, on the other hand, had set up a small fire and a cauldron with boiling water and mutton.

"What up?" shouted Ağasi. "Where you go dis morning?"

"I went for a walk." I replied. "Today is so beautiful!"

"Yesss, toooday vary, vary lovely! And toooday goood supper foooor Qoyan's burtday."

"*Beshbarmak*," interrupted Äke with a stern, yet welcoming smile on his face, "*für hozyayka. Beshbarmak!*"

His raspy, high-pitched voice resonated like a frog croaking. Äke pointed to his cauldron of boiling mutton.

"My faahterrr say make tasty dish," said Ağasi. "It foooor our *hozyayka... ahh...* hostess, Qoyan. It *beshbarmak*! I know you vary much like *beshbarmak*!"

I looked down into the boiling stew. Water and melted fat glistened in the sun. Long strings of intestines floated around in the boiling water. A sheep's head bobbed up and down while Äke stirred the concoction with a pole. The head was bloated like a leathery balloon. The eyes were swollen shut, and its tongue stuck out of its mouth. The mixture looked anything but appetizing.

Family Recipes

"*Priyatnogo appetita!*" Anasi announced *bon appétit!* With a confident smile, my host mother plopped a giant dish of *beshbarmak* on each of the two *dastarkhan* (round short-legged tables). She was dressed in her finest clothes. In fact, everyone at the party was dressed up nicely. The tables had been set up in the biggest room in the house, the room where I slept, the living room. The two tables were packed with dishes and glasses and piles of food—a meal of grand proportions where the hosts had put all their sweat and blood, their pride and honor into making sure their hospitality was well given and, likewise, well received. The two *dastarkhan* were set up with a cornucopia of Russian and Central-Asian dishes. Colorful mayonnaise-laden carrot, beet and eggplant salads dotted the large tables in small bowls. Dishes of pickles and pickled tomatoes sat before us. Open-faced sandwiches called *buterbrod* were slathered with mayonnaise and topped with *shproti* (canned sardines). *Manti* (steamed meat-filled dumplings) sat on dishes smothered in oil and sprinkled with dill. Doughnut-like fried goodness was strewn across the two tables. These delicious things were called *bauyrsakh*.

One *dastarkhan* was placed farthest away from the door, in the most secure, warmest and most comfortable part of the living room as tradition dictated for its most respected and honored guest. In Kazakh culture, this guest tended to be the eldest male. The men congregated at this table. Most men sat on the floor, though some sat at the couch adjacent to the table. They towered above the other guests. There were six of us men: my host father and his older brother, the *akim* (mayor) of the small village of Presnovka; the family friends, Uncle Abai and Spartan; Uncle Ağayindi and me. Uncle Ağayindi and I were the youngest at the men's *dastarkhan*. The rest of the men were forty or fifty years plus.

The women sat separately at the other *dastarkhan* as tradition dictated. Three women sat crowded around the short table: Anasi; Uncle Abai's wife; and Anasi's friend who lived up the street. In Kazakh, her friend's name meant "Pure Water."

The teenagers of the house and the guests' children had all removed themselves from the living room. They sat in the kitchen, away from the adults' sight, although ready to serve at their parents' guttural beacon.

The men sat quietly and stoically at their table, spouting off an occasional Kazakh word or two. The women, on the other hand, rattled on to each other. Everyone tried to speak in Kazakh at first, though eventually the unintelligible chatter turned into Russian. This allowed me to understand some conversation.

While many Kazakhs in the north of the country claimed they spoke Kazakh, their grandparents' language was still alien to them. Most felt more comfortable speaking in the *lingua franca* of the former Soviet Union, the language they learned in school and spoke at workplaces, Russian.

While everyone started grabbing at the *beshbarmak* from the center dish at each table, Uncle Abai's wife asked me a question from the women's table.

"Timati! Try *our* national dish Kazakhstan, *beshbarmak*?" asked the rotund woman.

This was a question, or a derivative of, that I had been asked over and over in my time in Kazakhstan. It was the first question

Kazakhs asked me when I met them. For the new Kazakh nation, *beshbarmak* was the pride and joy of Kazakhstan. The Kazakhs linked it to the nation's long-ago nomadic past when they rode free on the steppe, herding their animals from pasture to pasture and living an idyllic warrior lifestyle. Of course, this was more a romanticized past than an actual truth. The dish came about from the semi-nomadic lifestyle of the Kazakhs who were forced to settle down by the Soviets eighty or ninety years ago. This was when the steppe began to be farmed and Russian diets were introduced. It was also never noted by my Kazakh hosts that the dish was also a national bestseller in Kazakhstan's small neighbor to the south, Kyrgyzstan.

"Yes, I have had *your beshbarmak*," I replied.

"What think *our beshbarmak*?" She asked again.

The question was loaded. It was always loaded, so I stated the politically correct answer.

"*Beshbarmak* is the most deliciously dynamic and tasty dish ever devised by human beings!"

A lie, for sure, but answering otherwise, would mean becoming an epicurean pariah in the eyes of my Kazakh hosts. In truth, *beshbarmak*—which I didn't mind eating, and I enjoyed when it was made fresh—probably wouldn't win over too many food connoisseurs. The dish's taste tended to be slightly bland, with hints of gluten and oily goodness. The best way to describe it was mutton stew with noodles.

In a nutshell, *beshbarmak* consisted of large flat glutenous noodles mixed with tender boiled meat, usually mutton or horse meat, but poultry and beef were sometimes substituted. Onions, dill and potatoes were added for flavor and substance. Sometimes a sheep head was thrown in, but that was more of a gimmick than a staple to the dish. If horse meat was used—which Kazakhs prided themselves as horse eaters, and they fondly claimed horse flesh was the purest of meats—it usually came in the form of horse sausage. The large noodles tended to be slimy and goopy, but when made fresh, they were rather tasty and agreeable.

Beshbarmak was a vegetarian's nightmare. In fact, vegetarianism was such an alien and sacrilegious concept to the Kazakhs that to be vegetarian was to be antagonistic to the fundamentals of the national culture and psyche. Volunteers who came to the country as vegetarians tended to starve until they converted and embraced *beshbarmak*.

Though simple in its taste and ingredients, it was not so simple in process. The dish was time consuming, and it took hours to make. Throughout the day, the family had taken great efforts to make the meal for the party.

Asides from the process of slaughtering and skinning the sheep the day before, Anasi and Ülkenapa had taken vinegar to clean the intestines out. Afterwards, the guts were thrown into a boiling cauldron with a sheep head and other fatty, meaty parts of the animal.

While Äke supervised the cooking process of stirring the brew and watching the flames, waiting for the flesh to be nice and tender, Anasi and Ülkenapa had prepared the dough. They rolled out feet upon feet of noodles that would go into the stew. Once the meat was just about ready, they threw the noodles into the boiling mixture.

Voila! Time to eat! And time for a toast!

As everyone was beginning to chow down into the meal, Äke quickly sprang up and made the first toast.

"Qoyan!" called my host father.

The birthday girl came running into the living room from the kitchen, hopping like a bunny rabbit.

"Qoyan, *moya devochka, lublu tebya...*" *My girl, I love you...*

He switched to Kazakh for the toast. I didn't understand.

Ching! Ching! Clink! Clank! Clink! Clank!

It was simple and quick and down the vodka went. Everyone grabbed for a chaser. A glob of *beshbarmak*. A slimy pickle.

A Counting Lesson

"Timati," began Äke's brother, the auspicious *akim* of Presnovka, "ahh... *beshbarmak*!"

The *akim* pointed to the *beshbarmak*. He then picked at the fatty meat and began cutting it up into smaller pieces. As the eldest and most venerated man at the party, it was his job to cut up the meat in the *beshbarmak*. Tradition dictated it. He paused. Then he dropped the knife into the dish. He held up his right hand, palm towards me. His greasy fingers were spread apart.

In his Kazakh tongue, he counted on each finger: "*bir, yeki, ush, tört, bes.*"

The men fixated on his hand, all nodding in agreement.

"*Bir, yeki, ush, tört, bes,*" repeated the *akim*.

"*Bir, yeki, ush, tört, bes,*" repeated the men in unison.

"*Bir!*" The *akim* pointed to his small, wrinkled pinkie. *One!*

The rest of the men nodded.

"*Yeki!*" wheezed the man, a smoker most of his life.

He wiggled his ring finger.

"*Yeki!*" yelled Spartan and Uncle Abai in unison. *Two!*

"*Ush!*" The head honcho *akim* pointed to his fat middle finger, flipping me off unconsciously.

Äke interjected in his best attempt at English: "Timati, thoreeee, thoreeee!"

"*Tört!*" continued the *akim*,

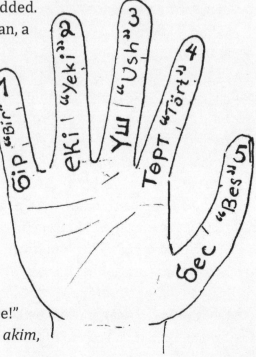

pointing to his index finger. *Four*!

Finally, he came to the thumb.

"*Bes*! Ahh... *beshbarmak*! Fivefff feeengerrr!" shouted the *akim* while he wiggled five fingers in front of my face.

Beshbarmak! A five-finger feast!

From the table's central dish of *beshbarmak*, the boiled sheep head that topped the mutton and noodles glowered at the *akim* with an angry frown. The eyelids had been boiled shut. The flesh was tightly wrapped around the skull, leathery and wrinkled. The front teeth poked out of its grin, bucktoothed and goofy. The tongue stuck out of the mouth, grey and shriveled.

The *akim* grabbed the head. He began cutting up the boiled head, divvying up the choice parts of the face and head to the men at the *dastarkhan*. An ear went to Uncle Abai. Younger than his friends at the table, it was as if his older friends were saying he needed to listen to them, his elders. The eyes went to Spartan so he, as a close family friend, could help protect the Zheltoqsan family. The brain went to Äke to give him knowledge and wisdom. The tongue went to Uncle Ağayindi so that he could speak his words truer.

As an afterthought, the *akim* passed some scraps of the head to the women at their table. They gnawed at the upper palate and jaw.

A piece of the cheek went to me, though the meaning of its significance was lost in translation.

"*Davay*, Timati!" said the *akim*. "*Kushay*!" Eat!

I grabbed the leathery piece of goopy meat with my *bes* (five) fingers. I stared at it for a moment. Grease and juices from the flesh dripped between my fingers.

"*Kushay*!" repeated the *akim*.

It would be rude not to eat the piece of flesh. With one quick gulp, I swallowed the slimy cheek. It tasted bland and flavorless, rather unappetizing. It slithered down my throat.

A Five Finger Feast

Rules of Conduct

There seemed to be rules and order to this strange meal. I had to take careful steps to be vigilant so as not to offend my hospitable hosts and their guests. I tried my best to follow five simple rules to this five-finger feast.

Rule № 1: First, before the eating and drinking commence, make sure you wash your hands. At a Kazakh meal, forks are hard to come by. The hand becomes the utensil. Thus, the hand must be clean. I had learned this the hard way. Once, at a previous dinner, I offended my host mother by not washing my hands before eating. Anasi was mortified.

Rule № 2: Remember, never drink alone! Drinking alone means you've got a drinking problem. Alcohol is poured to all people present at a party, because to share a drink with someone is to ask him or her to become a friend. This sometimes means sharing your heart and soul with one another. The more you drink, the closer you will become with your drinking partner. A subsection to Rule № 2: It is better to have a reason to drink. Any day will suffice. Any day can become a holiday, anniversary, festival or birthday to celebrate.

Rule № 3: Stick to one variety of alcohol. The more you mix, the worse you will feel the next morning. Remember, though, when a bottle of alcohol is opened, it must be drunk until gone. A shot glass must be drunk to the bottom. There are few minor notes to Rule № 3. You are not allowed to pour your drink into someone else's. This will take away your "happiness." Do not fill a glass being held in the air. This makes a mess. Do not pour a drink when the wrist is turned up. It shows disrespect to the person being served.

A couple exception clauses exist for Rule № 2 and Rule № 3. Typically, women can opt out of drinking vodka or other hard liquor, particularly if they are pregnant or elderly. They have the option to drink wine or even juice in most situations. Practicing

Muslims are also exempt from Rule № 2 and Rule № 3 since Islam prohibits alcohol consumption.

Rule № 4: For every shot, eat a snack or nibble of food. This is the chaser and will prevent excessive inebriation. After all, the purpose of drinking is to be social—becoming inebriated is only a side effect. Becoming visibly intoxicated, otherwise known as making-an-ass-of-oneself, is discouraged. Although, the exception is if a person is late to the feast, the latecomer must catch up and drink a full glass of vodka—a type of "penalty."

Rule № 5: Don't interrupt a toast! Toasting is a great equalizer among men and women. Toasts must be long, wordy and poetic. Everyone will eventually get his or her turn at toasting. The more guests, the more toasts! If the person giving the toast is incomprehensible and mumbling, allow him or her to do so. And remember, once you pick up your glass for a toast, it cannot be put down until the toast is done and the shot is drunk.

Additionally, to Rule № 5, the first three toasts seem to have a theme. The first toast is taken for the "occasion," or "to the person being celebrated," or "to the meeting of friends," etc. *Mezhdu pervoy i vtroy pererivchek ne bolshoi! Between the first toast and the second shot of vodka, there is no break*. The second toast is taken "to friendship" (*za druzhbu*). The third toast is "to love" (*za lubovyu*). In Kazakh, this is *makhabbat ishu*. If no women are present for the third toast, the men should tap the corner of the table with their glasses rather than with each other before drinking. If the table is round, like many *dastarkhan* are, well, I hope there are women present.

A Toast from the Heart

"*Mezhdu pervoy i vtroy pererivchek ne bolshoi!*" shouted the exuberant Äke.

It was a rule, after all, that there is no break between the first and the second shots.

Äke beckoned Qoyan to receive her toast: "*Idi syuda!*"

The birthday girl re-entered the living room. She had been hanging out in the kitchen with the other kids eating. She looked embarrassed as she inched slowly into the room. The murmur of the guests quieted down. (Remember, Rule № 5: never interrupt or talk over the toaster.)

"Spartan!" said my host father while he spurted off some Kazakh words to the tallest Kazakh man in the room. "*Tost!*" commanded Äke to his friend.

Spartan was half-German, half-Russian, and of course, he was pure Kazakh—at least, in heart and soul. Somewhere along the ancestral lines, this forty-year-old man could claim a tiny percentage of Kazakh ancestry, though he didn't look the part. He was a friendly man, with a good demeanor and a happy go lucky attitude.

His toast, being the second toast of the night, was supposed to be to *za druzhbu*, to friendship or some sort of derivative. Spartan stood up from his seat on the couch. He towered high above the *dastarkhan* and the other guests sitting on the ground. His smile disappeared.

"*Tovarishchi i nasha* Qoyan," started Spartan. *Comrades and our Qoyan...* "*U menya yest zhelanie kupit dom, no ne sredstvom...*" *I have the desire to buy a house, but not the means. I could buy a goat, but I do not have the desire to do so. Let us drink so that our means and our desires coincide.* "*Za druzhbu!*"

His audience clapped and the men nodded in agreement. I clapped with them.

Wait! An epiphany hit me. *I heard that toast before.*

Although inspiring in tone and execution, Spartan had plagiarized. This was common practice in Kazakhstan. Even with my limited Russian, I recognized the quote. It was from a 1960s comedy called *Kavkazskaya plennitsa, ili Novye priklyucheniya Shurika* (*Kidnapping, Caucasian Style*). The Soviet-era movie had been aired on the local television a few nights before the party.

But who cares? I thought as I came to terms with vodka helping to grease my inhibitions. '*Let us drink so that our means and our desires coincide!*' To friendship!

Spartan sat down and wiped a tear from his cheek. Aside from being a poet, it was clear that Spartan was already drunk.

The alcohol was beginning to take its intended effects on the group, connecting their souls to each other. The toast was for the birthday girl, just as much as it was for his old friends sitting around the *dastarkhan*. It was for the dreams they all shared, perhaps never quite having met.

Toasting was a way for the hybrid Kazakh-Russian culture of northern Kazakhstan and its people to express themselves freely with one another. It connected people through the cold of the winter and the void of existence. And in a part of the world where talking freely wasn't encouraged and could send you to jail, or worse, a toast was amnesty for men and women. In the toast, they could say what they wanted and express themselves without the fear of reprimand or reproach.

More drinks and toasts and smile and sentimentalities went around.

The mass of *beshbarmak* in the table's center dish whittled down.

A banjo-like instrument called a *dombra* came out. Music began.

Uncle Abai and Spartan each took a *dombra* in hand. *Ding, ding, ding... Dong, dong, dong...* The two men tuned their instruments as they warmed up. Then they began as if they had played the songs together a thousand times before.

141

The music was simple, yet enchanting—strangely haunting. It was the music of a vast and lonely steppe, the land their ancestors rode. The duo sang songs of sons lost to war or famine, songs of daughters stolen by disease or by enemy alike. The music resonated a folkish twang, but beautiful like a symphony in every note they plucked. They sang songs of friendships and love, a romanticized time from a bygone past, both Soviet and Kazakh—a time that may have never even been. But that didn't matter to the group at that moment. To them these songs were *their* reality. The soul of the Kazakh people came out as the music continued, and Uncle Abai and Spartan played into the long night.

Prayer to *Allah*

Once the music died down and everyone had his or her chance to become a poet of sorts, spilling out their soul to Qoyan and company in a toast, it was time to move on to the next portion of the evening's activities. Thankfully, by this point, this didn't include more *beshbarmak* or booze. Everyone was stuffed to the seams with mutton and vodka.

First, to redeem our souls for our gluttony and to find forgiveness for our debaucheries and sins. It is, after all, prohibited by Islam to consume alcohol, so we needed to say grace.

Äke took it upon himself to lead our group in prayer. Äke stood up as he called in the kids from the kitchen. Qoyan, Ağasi and Ülkenapa shuffled in. Uncle Abai's two teenagers followed. Äke then squatted on the floor. He swayed at first from the alcohol, but he somehow gained his composure. He held his palms together, facing up close to his mouth. Everyone followed in the same manner. Being raised a good Lutheran, I sat with my hands clenched and my head bowed in the Christian manner, respectful of my Muslim friends.

"*Al humdu lil Allahil lazi at'amanaa wasaqaana waja'alana minal muslimeen,*" whispered Äke in a quiet voice. *Thank you, oh*

Allah for feeding us and making us amongst the believers...

For a man who rarely attended mosque, Äke did a fine job in the matter of piety on this night.

"*Allah rakhmet,*" followed everyone in unison as they put their palms to their faces and brushed them downwards over their eyes and to their mouths.

A Mad Tea Party

With our bout of piety over, it was time to move on to the final scheduled segment of the evening festivities.

Anasi spat out a few words in Kazakh and the tables were cleared of dishes and plates by the kids. With a few more Kazakh words, Qoyan and the children were sent back to the kitchen. Tea kettles, jars of buttery cream, small bowls used as cups called *chashki* and handfuls of wrapped candy and trays of cookies returned.

Qoyan, in particular, looked weighed down as she balanced the steaming tea kettle. It was a stressful ordeal to be a birthday girl in the Zheltoqsan household.

Candy was thrown onto the tabletop while tea with milk was poured for each guest around the *dastarkhan*. We began sipping tea and eating the treats.

Makhabbat ishu as the third toast goes, always to love.

"Timati," spurted Anasi's friend, the woman named Pure Water in Kazakh.

She interrupted me while I chewed on a cookie and drank tea. She had been silent for most of the evening, but as the night went on and the libations went around, she began getting louder and more boisterous with the other guests.

"Timati, *za lubovyu*," shouted Pure Water from across the room. "*Makhabbat ishu!*"

She held up her cup of tea to me, and then she scooted over to the men's *dastarkhan*, breaking rank from the women. She held out her *chashki* to cheers with mine.

A Five Finger Feast

Clunk! Clunk! Splat! Our teacups met. Hot tea with cream frothed over the edges and onto the floor.

Pure Water was a pudgy woman. In Kazakh culture, this was a sign of a good housewife. It meant she was a good cook, and her family could afford to eat and drink well. Her hair was dyed blonde, attesting to the Russification of northern Kazakhstan.

Pure Water scooted closer to me, forgetting personal boundaries. I could smell her breath, fresh with vodka.

"Chto vash znak, Timati?" asked the woman. *What's your...?*

"Znak? Uhh, snack?" I responded with confusion.

"Da, znak," replied Pure Water.

She grabbed my left hand with some force, and she flipped it so my palm faced up. She started pointing to its lines and crevasses. She was mumbling incoherently. I realized she was reading my palm and telling me my fortune.

I had already learned in my few months in Kazakhstan that astrology, superstitions and horoscopes ruled many people's lives in this part of the world. Don't whistle in the house, unless you want to lose all your money. The "evil eye" is omnipotent and all pervasive. Sitting at the corner of the table for a girl meant she won't have babies. Sitting on dirt or ground outside for a man caused infertility. Although to combat this, eating meat could give men virility. One cannot pass an object to another person when there was a doorway in between them. Breezes through an open window caused all sorts of maladies. The list went on and on...

"Eta liniya..." *This line means...* Pure Water continued saying things that I really didn't understand while she gazed intently at my palm. The fortune teller paused and turned back to my face, inching ever closer.

"Govorite po-kazakhski?" asked the inebriated Pure Water. Her breath reeked of vodka when she asked me this commonly asked non sequitur. *Do you speak Kazakh?*

Beshbarmak

Like the *beshbarmak* question, this was another question Kazakhs loved to ask me. The answer was clearly no, since I barely spoke the *lingua franca*, Russian.

In fact, in the north of Kazakhstan speaking Kazakh got you almost nowhere since the majority of the people in the north were Russian. Also, the ethnic Kazakhs there were rusified to their core.

While I was engaged with the fortune teller, I noticed Anasi taking pictures of the guests with my digital camera. My camera was new technology in Kazakhstan and a novelty for the family. They used it just as much as I did.

"Timati," repeated Pure Water, bringing me back to her attention. "*Govorite po-kazakhski?*" *Do you speak Kazakh?*

She spat as she spoke. Her mouth was full of globs of candy and cookie matter.

Like the *beshbarmak* question, I had the answer to this question down solidly.

"*Men Kazakhsha suylemeymen.*" I responded.

"*Molodyets*, Timati!" exclaimed Pure Water, and she began clapping in delight. *Good job!*

Others around the table began to take notice of her clapping and our odd conversation. They inquired about the commotion. The other guests asked me to repeat my answer about my professed Kazakh-speaking abilities.

"*Men Kazakhsha suylemeymen.*" I said again.

The partygoers clapped in unison. They acted as if I was a fluent and native speaker of their Kazakh tongue. I smiled to myself, foolishly proud of my Kazakh abilities.

It didn't take much skill to say in the Kazakh language that I didn't speak Kazakh: *Men Ka-zakh-sha suy-le-mey-men*.

The fortuneteller grabbed my hand again, twisting it awkwardly towards her pudgy stomach. Pure Water continued reading my palm in her lap. She mumbled to herself in some

145

hybrid language, part Russian and part drool, part Kazakh and part drunk.

This line says you will find happiness, and this one says you will have much love with one of our beautiful young Kazakh girls, etc., etc., etc...

Anasi took note of our intimate proximity. With camera in hand, she commanded us to scoot closer to each other.

"*Foto! Foto!*" shouted my host mother. "*Davay!*"

"*Foto!* Timati! *Foto!*" demanded Pure Water.

She pulled me in even closer. My whole body was forced forward, and my face smashed into her breasts.

"*Potseluy! Potseluy!*" repeated Anasi with a word in Russian that I hadn't heard before.

"Wha... What?" I was confused.

"*Potseluy!*" repeated Anasi again as she puckered her lips and began kissing the air.

Potseluy? Kiss! Oh, no, I gasped to myself. *Resist!*

"*Davay!* Timati! *Davay! Potseluy!*" said Anasi again.

"*Nyet, nyet!*"

I didn't want to kiss Pure Water, even though I could see Pure Water so desperately wanted to kiss this gangly intoxicated American. Anasi positioned the camera ready for the shot. Her finger slowly pushed down the button of the camera.

"*Potseluy!*" commanded Anasi to Pure Water.

Snap! Just as the flash went off Pure Water grabbed my head. *Mwahhhh!* With great force and passionate fervor, she gave me a watery, vodka-laced kiss with her sloppy, drooling lips smashing into mine. Like *beshbarmak*, it was the bland, oily taste of Kazakh hospitality.

Down the Rabbit Hole

The other guests laughed with glee and delight in seeing the kiss and the messy aftermath. Pure Water turned on me the instant her lips left mine and the camera was put away.

"Timati! *Nyet!*" shouted Pure Water. "*Ya zamuzhem*! *Ya zamuzhem*! *Ya zamuzhem*!*" repeated the now-angered woman, stating that she was married.

She pushed me away from her, and I fell into the *dastarkhan*. The fortune teller got up and left the room in a drunken huff and angry stupor.

The rest of the guests slowly got up and left too, snickering and laughing at what they had just witnessed.

The festivities were winding down. The men went to smoke outside. The women went to help the children clean the dishes in the kitchen as tradition dictated.

It came down to just Uncle Ağayindi and me left in the living room. We sat on the ground at one of the short tables with our bottle of Status Vodka, gold cap. A flick of the neck, a pour of a shot and down the hatch the vodka went. Another flick of the neck and Uncle Ağayindi poured another shot. All caution was thrown to the wind.

"*Davay! Brüderschaft!*" commanded Uncle Ağayindi.

"What is a *brüderschaft?*" I asked in a blur of hazy confusion.

"*Kommen* tooo meee," motioned Uncle Ağayindi. "Weee cooonnect heart to heart... like *brüder!*" *Like brothers!*

He reached over to where I sat, and he grabbed my right arm. He wrapped his right arm around mine almost as in the shape as a pretzel hugs itself.

"*Davay!* Ahh... weee *trinken gut* vodka like theees way," struggled my host uncle in a weird mismatch of Russian, German and English.

Uncle Ağayindi reached for the vodka shots with his left hand while we were still entwined with our right arms in this awkward *brüderschaft* hug. He handed a shot glass to my right hand, and then he grabbed his own glass with his right hand.

With this strange, tangled embrace, he began a toast: "To my *brat*... uhh... *brüder*... uhh... brother! *Davay, brüderschaft!*"

A Five Finger Feast

We took our shots in unison with a tangled mess of arms, the strange custom of the *brüderschaft*. With this shot of vodka down, and *down, down, down the rabbit hole I fell.*

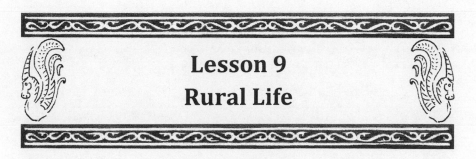

Lesson 9
Rural Life

Genghis Khan

"**Y**ou know my faahterrr he *soldat* in War Afghan?" asked Ağasi to me while we walked down the dusty road from our house at Four Sovietskaya Street.

"Soldier?" I acted as if I hadn't heard Ağasi's story before, but Ağasi had explained this fact to me on several occasions.

"*Da*, he was smart and... ahh... bravvv *soldat*," continued my host brother proudly.

My host father, Äke, had served in the Soviet Union's ill-fated war in Afghanistan in the 1980s. Unlike the Great Patriotic War (WWII), which Victory Day (*Dyen Pobedy*) had just been celebrated on May 9, there were no memorials in the village to those who had served or fallen in Afghanistan. It was a forgotten war to many, except for Ağasi.

Bark! Ağasi's dog Rex was faithfully following behind, chasing stray dogs and keeping the village's many packs of feral dogs at bay.

A Five Finger Feast

Like my host father, Rex was retired police. He was a former police dog, an intelligent German Shepherd, but mostly a mutt.

We were all walking down the long, straight dirt road as it headed to the far edge of Yavlenka. It was that time of the evening when we needed to bring the family cow home from the pastures that lay just beyond the village's boundary. The family cow, Adriana Lima, named after the Brazilian supermodel who Ağasi loved so dearly, had been led out early in the morning to the pasture to feast on spring's bounty. Adriana Lima was coming home to rest in the barn for the night.

Even by eight o'clock in the evening, it was still daylight out. The sun was just beginning to descend on the flat Siberian horizon with the sky turning from blue to yellow, then becoming orange, then red. The sunsets in May! They were a spectacle granted only to the sparse population of the northern latitudes. Siberia was spectacular in mid-May with the days becoming longer and warmer. Perhaps this was God's way of repaying them for the tough winters they suffered.

Ağasi continued to proudly talk: "Yesss, my faahterrr bravvv soldurrr. He... ahh... warrior. You know we sons of Chingeskhan? He great warrior! You know Chingeskhan?"

"Chin-ges-khan?" I asked.

"*Da*, Chingeskhan," replied Ağasi. "He Mongol warrior-king."

"Genghis Khan?"

I swatted at a small mosquito before it could land on my leg. Mosquitoes were becoming more frequent in the evening hours as temperatures slowly gave way to summer.

"Yesss, Chingeskhan. Dat what I say you, Chingeskhan."

"Yeah, I know of Genghis Khan."

Of course, I knew of the Mongol warlord that smashed his way out of Central Asia during the Middle Ages. Genghis Khan and his descendants conquered the world from China to Poland, raping and pillaging every bit of civilization in between.

Rural Life

"*Nu*, we his sons. All Kazakh his sons."

Ağasi was on to something. According to researchers, millions of people from Tamerlane to Akbar the Great and many more across Central Asia, India, China and Siberia share the same Y chromosome.[24] They descended from a single patriarch who lived hundreds of years ago. *Chingeskhan?*

Potato

Ağasi and I continued down the dusty road, heading towards the family's cow. It was as if the Pied Piper was whistling, and groups of teens and young boys began to join our walk out of the village. From every other house we passed, more and more children joined the walk to the edge of town. The teenagers and young boys who joined us all gawked at me in a strange look of admiration and novelty. They whispered to each other about me and giggled—being the only American in Yavlenka made me a small celebrity. The luxury of anonymity was gone for me here in the village.

As we walked toward Adriana Lima, we passed by the small houses and cottages of Yavlenka. Some homes had been built in the gingerbread-house fashion prominent in Russia and Siberia. These homes had been painted with bright colors and decorated with intricate carvings and trim. Other houses were plain, made of grey Soviet-style cinder blocks. Some homes were well kept and others were dumps, a small number even decrepit and falling down.

Russians and Kazakhs, young and old, were out in almost every yard. They were toiling away digging and planting. With the warming temperatures, it was finally time to plant the backyard garden, and more importantly, it was time to plant the staple crop of potatoes.

The potato was a necessity of survival. Some used them to

---

[24] Timur (1336-1405), aka Tamerlane, conquered Central Asia. Akbar the Great (1542-1605) was a Mughal Emperor in India (1556-1605).

"Potatoes for Sale"

feed the family and survive the country's cruel winters, while a few villagers used the potato to survive financial uncertainty that plagued the post-Soviet economy. In a country prone to inflation and unstable food prices, the potato and backyard farms helped to prevent a family from breaking the bank. "Breaking the bank" might not be the most appropriate term to use since most people in Kazakhstan didn't trust, let alone even have, bank accounts. Most money was kept under the mattress.

Some of the luckier and more entrepreneurial-minded families, like my host family, were good at making an extra *tenge* (₸) or two from their hard labors. A fruitful garden, a productive brood of hens or a milk-producing cow, like Adriana Lima, could bring good money to a family's income, helping to subsidize meager monthly salaries of $200 to $300.

In the days of the former Soviet Union, these small money-making activities would have been frowned upon, if not even punished by the state. Nevertheless, since the days of *Perestroika*, in the new capitalist-oriented Kazakhstan, the extra money helped families inch closer to an Americanized consumerist dream. This was an auspicious status that had been denied to them for so long under communism. Like Americans, Kazakhstanis were beginning to dream now of a modern consumer lifestyle of Coca-Cola, Motorola, Ford and Microsoft. For better or worse, the dream of buying new televisions or new refrigerators or brand-new cars was becoming a reality.

Rural Life

We continued along, walking past the small farms and people plowing and digging in their yards. A group of men in mud-
clad pants stood next to a plow stuck in the hard soil. They were
taking a break to drink soda. A hunched-over *babushka* wrapped
up in a shawl pulled a horse as it tilled and plowed through the
ground. Music blasted from her cell phone. The song was "I
Kissed a Girl" by Katy Perry, a recent invasive Americanism.
These people were peasants in the twenty-first century, simple
and plain, dreaming of gadgets and modern consumer goods.
They were all becoming acolytes of a new age of techno-fueled
and cellophane-wrapped consumerism.

Gay

"You know dis, Timati?" blurted Ağasi. "When she say, 'she
kiss gurl, she like it,' she *lesbiyanka*?"

"Are you talking about the Katy Perry song?" I asked. "She's
a lesbian?"

"Da, she kiss gurl, she like it. Dis vary hot!" Ağasi enthusiastically exclaimed. "I love kiss gurl. Gurl love Ağasi!"

We continued along the dirt road toward Adriana Lima. We
were approaching the edge of the village, past this point we
would finally reach the pasture and the place where we would
meet our cow.

Ağasi began blasting the Katy Perry song from his cell phone,
as he hummed along. Next in his music queue was a Tupac song,
the beats of globalization, from LA to Yavlenka.

A tall dark-haired boy ran up from behind Ağasi and slapped
him in the ear. Ağasi cringed. It was Aram, the village bully. The
Armyanin (Armenian) was also one of my soon-to-be-graduated
eleventh-grade students, although he barely did any work in
class. Aram wrapped his arm around Ağasi's neck, jerking him
closer to him. Rex growled at Aram, but the Armenian didn't
flinch. Aram whispered something into Ağasi's ear, and he gave
me a little devious smirk. Ağasi nodded and turned to me.

153

"Timati," started Ağasi, "Aram want to say you... ahh... you know in Kazakhstan we no hafff... ahh... gay people?"

"No gay peepeel," repeated Aram.

"Oh, yeah?" I acted as if I was shocked by the statement. "And how do you know that?"

Ağasi turned to translate my question to Aram.

"We know. It trooff," responded Aram. His English was abysmal. "No gay!"

Ağasi interrupted: "Yesss, Aram say trooo. *Nu*, maybe here in Yavlenka no gay boyz. Petro, I don't think hafff. Maybe Astana or Almaty hafff gay people."

"I don't think so. I bet there is someone in Yavlenka and Petro who is gay, and I bet you know them too."

"Nooo, Timati," replied Ağasi. "No hafff gay boyz here."

Aram butted in. "No gay!" His words came out forceful and violent. "We kill gay!"

"Yesss, dis trooo. If gay man lifff in Kazakhstan, people... ahh... hooort and keeell him."

In Yavlenka, there were very few, if no, openly gay people. That was certainly made clear by Ağasi. Yavlenka was far from cosmopolitan, plus they had bullies like Aram to fear, so they kept their lives and secrets to themselves. Those in the LGBTQ community in Kazakhstan had to keep their orientations and identities to themselves for fear of being harassed and harmed by hate and ugly *machismo*. Some, in the bigger cities, lived double lives. Acting straight, sometimes even marrying the opposite sex, but secretly going out to the limited number of gay and lesbian bars and clubs.

The Peace Corps warned the volunteers, gay and straight, to be careful opening up to the locals about the topic, especially in the rural areas. Most LGBTQ volunteers kept their orientation a secret from even their closest local friends and host families in Kazakhstan. Even for volunteers who strayed just a bit from what was perceived as the norm, the macho male figure for men or the good housewife figure for women, there was always that chance of getting beat up by a group of drunks.

Cowboy

Tupac's song finished by the time we shook off Aram from our heals and we made it to the village pasture. The pasture was far and wide, stretching from the village's edge to a forest a mile or two away in the distance. The pasture was used not only for the cows, but it doubled up as a dumping ground for garbage. Piles of smashed plastic bottles, broken electronics, rusty tin cans and used toilet paper strewed the field. This trash was the price of consumer modernity.

The herd of cows came slowly back towards the village. Cow bells clanged louder as they approached. Two men on horseback rode along passing through the herd, poking and prodding the cows, steering them towards home. The groups of kids and teen-agers waited patiently for the cows to approach.

As the cows came closer, the kids went into the herd, iden-tifying which ones belonged to their family by the brand marks on their hind legs, or a special collar with a cowbell, or simply by the pattern of their cow's hide. One by one, the kids rounded up their cows and began taking them home.

Rex ran after the cows, sniffing and biting at their ankles.

Ağasi and I waited for Adriana Lima to come. We waited as cows and people passed us back into the village, but none of the cows that went by looked familiar.

"Timati," exclaimed Ağasi, "I no see Adriana Lima!"

"You know what she looks like more than I do." I wasn't sure what to tell him.

Ağasi didn't hear what I said. Instead, he ran off into the herd looking for Adriana Lima. He ran from cow to cow. I followed behind him.

"Timati! I no see!"

Ağasi ran up to one of the cowboys sitting on his horse. The grey-haired man had a wrinkled face. His thick grey mustache covered his frown. His long leather jacket was covered in dust, torn along the edges. His head was capped with a fedora.

"*Nyet korovy!*" shouted Ağasi to the man, explaining that he couldn't find Adriana Lima.

"*Kak familiya?*" asked the cowboy for Ağasi's surname.

The man's raspy, gruff voice was that of a heavy smoker. I noticed a flask of vodka hung from his saddle bag.

"Zheltoqsan!" replied Ağasi.

With this information the cowboy rode around looking for Adriana Lima. For several minutes, the cowboy went round and round, weaving in and out of the herd, searching for the cow, Adriana Lima.

"Where Adriana Lima? If no find"—Ağasi's face looked worried as if he knew his impending doom—"Mama and Papa keeeell me!"

Ağasi continued to search frantically while I watched with dismay. The cowboy returned. His wrinkled face was unchanged from before.

"Zheltoqsan!" shouted the man to Ağasi. "*Nyet korovy!*"

"Timati, we no hafff Adriana Lima," said Ağasi when he turned to me. "Mama and Papa keeell me…"

Cattle Rustling

The last few cows were rounded up by their owners. We stood, stupefied, futilely staring out into the pasture for a non-existent Adriana Lima. It was beginning to finally get dark outside, so we began back towards home.

We continued home in silence for a long while down the road towards Four Sovietskaya Street. Ağasi's earlier mood of play-fulness and pride, now turned sullen. Ağasi moped. We both knew what awaited him at home for losing the family cow. He was on death row.

Rural Life

Along the path home, we passed a small shop. The words МАГАЗИН (*MAGAZIN*) were painted above its door in red letters. The shop was attached to a colorfully-painted gingerbread-looking house.

I decided, in this moment of gloom, to cheer up Ağasi by getting him a soda. It was an act of kindness, a "last meal," before his impending execution at home.

"Ağasi, come with me." I led him over to the door of the *magazin*. "Wait here."

I entered the small shop, leaving Ağasi outside as he sulked. The inside of the store smelled dusty. A long counter split the room in half. The clerk, a Russian woman in her late forties with maroon-colored hair, stood ready at the counter. There wasn't very much choice of things to purchase, typical for most small shops. Aside from the ubiquitous white bread that was lined up on the counter, the store had a small selection of candy and cookies, soaps and detergent, a freezer filled with sausages and *pelmeni*, a variety of vodka options, a few pirated DVDs and VHS, and a refrigerator with soda and beer. All the goods in the store were on display behind the glass counter. Unlike in America, where one could freely go down aisles to pick out items, in Kazakhstan, customers had to ask the clerk for permission to purchase. All products, no matter how big or small or how cheap or expensive, were kept behind the lock and key of the counter. It made things, to say the least, tricky for a foreigner who didn't speak Russian very well.

Luckily, I was just getting a soda, easy enough. I approached the counter.

"*Zdravstvuyte!*" I greeted the clerk.

"*Zdravstvuyte,*" replied the woman as she patted down her maroon-colored hair.

"Coca-Cola." I smiled and handed her ₸100 ($0.75).

The clerk reached into the refrigerator, and she pulled out a bottle. She handed me the soda.

I took the bottle of soda and quickly exited the shop. Rex was waiting for me outside, but Ağasi was no longer there.

This is weird. I thought. *Where's Ağasi?*

I began down the road towards the house, thinking I would find Ağasi along the way. I walked and walked, block after block, and still there was no sign of Ağasi. The sun had finally set when the last sliver of light disappeared behind the long Siberian horizon. The mosquitoes had buzzed off to sleep. I opened the Coca-Cola and drank it down to the halfway mark, leaving the rest for Ağasi.

As I began to approach the final block before arriving at the house at Four Sovietskaya Street, I heard loud arguing. It was Ağasi. He was standing under a streetlamp arguing with a young boy. Lo and behold, there was Adriana Lima with the boy.

By the time I reached Ağasi, the shouting had ended, and Ağasi had wrestled the reins of Adriana Lima from the young boy. The boy was not much older than ten or eleven. I recognized him. He was Aram's younger brother. Rex ran up to Ağasi and the boy. He barked at the young kid. The boy ran off down the dark road.

"Timati," began Ağasi, "I hafff Adriana Lima! Dat was braahterrr Aram. He take Adriana Lima, but I... ahh... more strong and more *umnyy*... ahh... cleeevar! I take back!"

I gave Ağasi the Coke bottle. He drank down the liquid with one victorious gulp.

We continued towards home, dragging Adriana Lima behind. Her cow bell rang as she mooed. We arrived at the house at Four Sovietskaya Street, and we walked Adriana Lima through the gate into the farmyard. Ağasi opened the barn door. *Smash!* The wind blew the door back as it opened with force. Ağasi flipped on a switch and a dim light bulb flickered on.

To our surprise, there was another cow in the barn. It was

Adriana Lima! Ağasi did not say a word. He walked into the barn to inspect the cow. He looked it up and down, checking the cow's markings and its collar.

"*O bozhe moy,*" exclaimed Ağasi in disbelief. "Timati, dis trooo Adriana Lima! *Frack! Frack! Frack! Papa keeell me! Mama keeell me! Aram keeell me!*"

The real Adriana Lima must have wandered home on her own. We somehow missed her.

"Well, let's just go back and return the cow to the Armenian boy." I said, a simple idea.

"Yesss! We do dis fast! Befooor Aram know!"

Village Justice

We locked the barn back up and began leading the Adriana Lima imposter back toward the spot where Ağasi had taken the cow from the boy. It was too late. Just as we walked out from the gate onto the street, we could see a group of five Armenians approaching. It was Aram, his young brother and three older Armenian men. One carried a pitchfork. They were here to take back their cow and, from the looks on their faces, to kill Ağasi.

They began shouting and yelling. I didn't understand much of what they said in their thickly accented Russian. Ağasi looked scared, and it seemed like he was doing his best to give back their cow, but it seemed that this was not good enough. Rex was barking and growling at the men.

With all the commotion happening in front of Four Soviet-skaya Street, the front porch light turned on. The door opened. *Creek... Smash!* It was Äke. He was half dressed in camouflage pants, a white undershirt and a dirty fur hat. The flaps of the hat hung over his ears. He did not look very happy. I heard the house door open again. *Creek...* My host mother, Anasi, poked her head out the door. She retracted it quickly once she saw the group of angry men.

Äke interrupted the argument.

I didn't understand much of what was exchanged or what words were being said, but I could tell nobody was happy. I backed away a couple feet, not really knowing what to say or do. I decided to observe, at a very safe distance.

The arguing went on and on, until suddenly a car sped from around the corner of the dirt road. It was a police car. It flashed its lights as it stopped just short of slamming into the group. It kicked up dirt into our faces. Anasi must have called the police. To her, the house had, after all, been besieged by a mob.

The policeman got out of the vehicle. He was a Kazakh man with a pencil-thin mustache, dressed in a crisply ironed dark-blue uniform. His name on his badge read "Chingeskhan." As he approached the group, he put on a larger-than-life brimmed hat with the insignia pinned to the front, symbolizing the authority bestowed to him by the Republic of Kazakhstan.

Everyone in the group stopped arguing. They all went around shaking the police officer's hand. When the officer shook Äke's hand it seemed as if they were old work buddies. Äke was a retired cop. They gave each other friendly smiles and patted each other on the back. I stood back and kept my distance.

Once handshakes had gone around, the officer started interrogating the Armenians. The Armenians began shouting and ferociously talking with their hands. The officer stopped them right away. He would not permit shouting in his presence.

Each side presented their case to the policeman and vented their grievances. After several minutes of negotiations, the reins of the imposter Adriana Lima were handed to the Armenians. In exchange, the eldest of the Armenians took a wad of cash from his pocket and handed it to the officer.

I was confused. Was this a "fine" for starting the small riot or was it a bribe to keep themselves out of jail? This was justice in the village.

Everyone shook hands once again. The Armenians walked back home leading their cow away. Äke invited the police officer inside to have tea, and the two went in through the front door. *Creek... Smash!* Rex ran into the farmyard where he usually slept at night. Ağasi approached me with a smile of relief.

"We *udachnyy*... ahh... we lucky. Dis policeman was *soldat* wit my faahterrr! Dey fight in War Afghan. Dis why we win wit family Aram! Kazakh boyz win! Chingeskhan boyz win!"

I didn't care who "won." I was just glad no one got hurt and the true Adriana Lima had been found.

The next day was gorgeous. It was warm and sunny. One wouldn't have thought the drama from the night before had actually transpired.

I came home from work and entered the yard at Four Soviet-skaya Street through the front gate. I heard a noise coming from the side of the house. *Thump! Crack! Thump! Crack!* It was the noise of chopping wood. I walked towards the noise.

Ağasi stood among a pile of wood, some chopped in half and others still awaiting their fate.

"Timati! I cut wood. You see?" shouted Ağasi. "I strong boy! I strong *soldat* like faahterrr!"

His mood was back to his happy-go-lucky self.

"*Da*! Like Genghis Khan." I replied.

"Yesss! Chingeskhan boy! Timati, look me cut wood. Dis my *nakazanie*... ahh... pooonishmant fooor last night fight."

Ağasi smiled at me. He turned back to the axe and wood, and he continued to serve out his sentence. *Thump! Crack! Thump! Crack! Thump! Crack!*

With the swing of his axe, village justice was being served. Everything seemed to have come full circle here in the village. Adriana Lima had been recovered, and more importantly, no one had been hurt in the process.

Life in Kazakhstan could only get better from here. Indeed, with summer just around the corner, life wasn't so bad in Yavlenka and Kazakhstan.

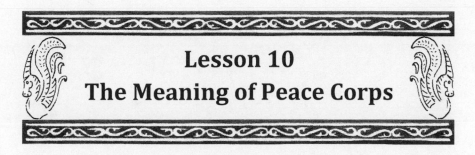

Lesson 10
The Meaning of Peace Corps

"Though this be madnesse, yet there is method in't."

*Polonius in Act II,
Scene II of* Hamlet
by W. Shakespeare

A Letter to Fifth Graders

May 2008
Dear Mrs. Braun's Fifth Grade Class,

First, I want to thank you for your wonderful letters. I read each one of them, and it was fun hearing about your lives in Carson City. I enjoyed seeing the drawings of your class too. Today, schools all over Kazakhstan are out for summer. This is a national holiday in Kazakhstan called *Posledniy Zvonok* or Last Bell.[25] I hope you all enjoyed writing back-and-forth with your

---

[25] *Posledniy Zvonok* or Last Bell (May 25) is the final day of the school year in Kazakhstan. It acts as a graduation for eleventh graders.

pen pals from my seventh-grade class. In your letters, many of you asked very interesting questions. I've tried to answer them.

How do your students dress?

Posledniy Zvonok was finally upon me. The past seven months of working at School № 1, Timofey Pozolotin, had sped by quickly. Now, it was my last day before school was out for the summer. Hundreds in the village gathered in front of the drab-looking school on a cold and windy May morning to celebrate the end of the school year. Although the temperatures had risen greatly since the beginning of spring, northern Kazakhstan in May was frequented by rainy, overcast and chilly days. The festivities on *Posledniy Zvonok* were no exception to the rule.

Students who had entered school eleven years prior were now seventeen and finishing their final year of grade-school education. The students graduating on *Posledniy Zvonok* had survived the byzantine system of Kazakhstani education. Some worked hard to get to *Posledniy Zvonok*. Others simply bought their *diplom* from their teachers or a governing *zavuch* (dean).

At least, the students who bribed their way to *Posledniy Zvo-*

nok had been clever, and economically well-off, enough to not have been filtered out of the school system by state testing in the eighth grade. Many of the students who were deemed "not-so-exceptional" were often forced out of school at the age of fourteen or fifteen. These students were handed off to "colleges" (trade schools), never technically "failing" school. In a country with a ninety-nine percent literacy rate, officially, no student ever failed in Kazakhstan.

Aside from the faults of the Kazakhstani education system, I still felt proud for the twenty-two graduates who gathered for their *Posledniy Zvonok*. I had taught most of them a thing or two about the English language that I hoped would stick with them. Maybe I had instilled a desire to continue their English education as they headed to universities in Kazakhstan or Russia.

As crowds gathered, Timofey Pozolotin, the WWII hero, looked over the crowd from his stone edifice, standing tall in front of the school. The twenty-two graduates came out from the school's front doors, marching in pairs. They lined up in the playground. I stood next to my counterpart, Yekaterina Alekseyevna, and her homeroom class of sixth graders. Other younger students followed the lead of their teachers, looking on towards their graduates.

The graduates were so proud, and they were all dressed up in the finest suits for the young men. For the young ladies, well, they were clad in the unique-look of

French maid outfits.

The French maid costume was a custom I never quite got used to, even after several months of life in Kazakhstan. The traditional school garb for girls was reminiscent of black-and-white French maid outfits. Like teenagers throughout the world, many of these "French maids" tested the limits of their outfits. While a part of Russian and Kazakh culture was conservative in attitude, dress and thought, some women in Kazakhstan pushed the limits of how scantily clad they could dress.

Drrriiiing! The school's bell rang, the "last bell." Music with shrill trumpets and horns began blaring and blasting from speakers hidden near the school building.

A deep Kazakh voice began singing: "*Altin kun aspana, altin dan dalasa, erliktin dastanu, elime qarasa...*"

The national anthem of Kazakhstan was now a familiar tune for me, although not for the rest of the world. Years later the fictitious theme song from the mockingly cruel but funny film, *Borat: Cultural Learnings of America for Make Benefit Glorious Nation of Kazakhstan* would mistakenly be played at a sporting event in Kuwait. This was in lieu of Kazakhstan's real anthem, *Menin Qazaqstanim*.

As the music of the anthem blasted, one of my seventh graders, a yellow-haired Russian boy named Losha, began marching out into the crowd. He carried the sky-blue banner of *glorious nation of Kazakhstan*. A golden eagle flew under the sun in the middle of the banner as it waved in the wind. He marched in a goose-step

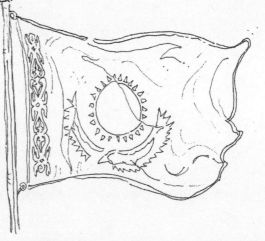

manner, reminiscent of a Nuremberg rally. Although his moves were militaristic, he sported a baby-blue tracksuit with the word "*Қазақстан*" printed in yellow on the back. He marched force-fully before the crowd until the anthem ended.

The director of the school, a tall and strong-looking Kazakh woman named Bastygy Mektepovna, approached the podium up front. Her four administrator *zavuch*—all of which were middle-aged women, two Russian and two Kazakh—stood behind her.

Bastygy Mektepovna spoke to the crowd: "*Dorogie druzya…*"

What kind of holidays do you celebrate?

"*D*orogie druzya," started Bastygy Mektepovna. *Dear friends…*

She commanded the room while addressing the ten men sitting in front of her. She held a bottle of vodka as she talked.

"*Segodnya vash dyen…*" *Today is your day. It's a day to honor the men who have served and protected us from danger. I congratulate you! Now drink!*

She spoke as if she was reading a cheesy Hallmark card, calm and composed. I was lost in most of the translation after "*dorogie druzya*."

Despite this fact, I raised my glass with the other men in the room. A few drips of clear liquid frothed over the brim onto my fingers. *Clink! Clink! Clink!* We went around tapping our glasses with each other, and down the vodka went.

It didn't seem to faze anyone in the room, especially our school director, that we were all getting drunk in the school cafeteria. I just went along like a sheep following the herd, not wanting to offend anyone with my American manners.

Drinking with this group of men, after all, was my attempt to reach a sense of "community integration," a fancy Peace Corps term for "fitting in." During training five months prior, the Peace Corps drilled "community integration" into our trainee heads over and over. Today gave me the perfect opportunity to practice "community integration."

It was February 23, Day of the Soviet Army and Fleet, now called Day of the Defenders. The holiday had its roots in the drafting of soldiers into the Red Army during the Russian Revolution. However, after the Second World War, the holiday took on its modern form as a sort of Fathers' Day.

The ten men who worked in the school, me being the tenth, were summoned to the cafeteria by the school's Party Planning Committee. Students were eating lunch in the cafeteria when we arrived for our party, but they were shooed away by the Committee members.

Most of the men gathered in the room were repairmen and janitors who worked the night shift at school. Only three of us in the cafeteria were teachers: Leonid Ilyich, a PE teacher; Nikita Sergeyevich, military sciences; and me, Timati Kurtovich, English. I had played basketball in the school's gym a few times with Leonid Ilyich, but Nikita Sergeyevich never spoke to me until this day. The other men gathered here were more like Nikita Sergeyevich. When they saw me in the halls, they nervously ignored me, perhaps not knowing what to say to the foreigner working in their building. One man, Vladimir Vladimirovich, was the exception to the rule. He was the night watchman. His job was to stay at school on weekends and nights to keep the school's furnace running during the harsh winter months. Whenever I went to campus during off hours to lesson plan or use the internet, he was there. A very strange man, I never knew if he was drunk or just crazy. Maybe it was the school that drove him to hit the bottle and slowly lose his sanity over time.

Locals said the school was haunted, built in the 1970s on what was a cemetery. The building had several leftover murals and paintings from its Soviet days. These scenes depicted a perfect Soviet utopia of scientists and farmers, but also a dystopia of armies and missiles. The murals were eerie when left alone in the dark and drafty hallways.

Drrriiiing! The school's bell rang, reminding me that students were attending class. The school's director and the members of the Party Planning Committee left the room to continue working the school day. The men were left to our own devices.

I didn't really understand much of the conversation between the men, but that didn't really matter since there wasn't really much talk once the women left. Most of these men were solemn men with stoic faces.

To break the ice, we drank a few shots until libations and words flowed smoothly. Shot after shot of vodka went round. Each man, in turn, toasted the group.

Eventually, it was time for my toast. I stood up from my seat with shot glass in hand. I was never good at toasts; however, I had been waiting for the perfect moment to give this particular one. It was a perfect toast for the holiday, the Day of the Soviet Army and Fleet.

I said something like this in Russian: "Many years ago the Soviet Union and America were enemies, but today Kazakhstan and America no longer need to fear each other, because we have found a new friendship. Let's drink to this international friendship! *Za druzhbu mezhdu narodami!*"

After I gave the toast, I could hear the crickets in the room. The men looked at me in silence, not drinking.

Did I say something wrong? I thought to myself.

Maybe my toast sounded more like this to them: "Many year Soviet-USA no like. Today we friend. Drink!"

That would have been understandable enough, right? Maybe it was that my Russian was unintelligible. Or maybe, on the other hand, the men were so moved by my eloquent words that they were overcome by pathos. Or maybe they were already so drunk they just couldn't speak.

After a moment of silence, Nikita Sergeyevich stood up tall, reached across the table to cheers me.

"*Molodyets*! *Güt* job," Nikita Sergeyevich said, smiling.

"Good toast," echoed around as the rest followed suit; nodding and cheering went around the table between the men.

We continued to drink like old *tovarishchi* (comrades). I felt like I had become one with the men of School № 1, Timofey Pozolotin. I had become a man among Siberian men.

Do you have a girlfriend?

"**M**eester Sachlend, I troo man now," proclaimed Losha as he entered my classroom during the passing bell. "I have love! I love Aloondra!"

Losha was a short blonde Russian boy of thirteen. His face and height made him look much younger than his age. Losha was the class clown in my seventh-grade English class.

"You are a real man? In love, really? When did this happen?"

"Aloondra my gurlfurend in Amereekah," said Losha. "*Ya znayu, chto eto pravda!*"

"Losha, use English!"

It took effort to keep my students from speaking Russian in English class. It wasn't easy fostering an English-only classroom, especially when most of my students could hardly say "My name is ____" in English. Plus, aside from Yekaterina Alekseyevna, the other two English teachers at School № 1, Timofey Pozolotin, struggled with their own English abilities.

"It troo! I love Aloondra! When we make letter to Amereekah?" asked the spirited Losha.

I could see he wasn't joking. I could see in his face the excitement at the thought of his American girlfriend.

For the past couple of months, my seventh graders had been writing letters to pen pals in my hometown of Carson City, Nevada. The pen pal project helped foster relevance for English-language learning for my students. What's the saying? You can lead a horse to water, but you can't force it to drink. Well, the pen pal project would be salt in the oats for my seventh graders. I had found a willing teacher to take on the project, Mrs. Braun and her fifth-grade class. Every couple of weeks, we would send and receive letters.

Losha was paired with Alondra, an eleven-year-old girl. Losha wasn't a student who excelled in his English studies. Yet, it seemed that the pen pal project had captured his short attention span. Even so, I didn't think Losha would build up a love affair in his head with these brief letters:

"My name is Losha! What is your name? I am 13 years old. I am from Yavlenka. Yavlenka is nice and it has green summers. What is your nature like in America? My hobbies are football and volleyball. I go to school in class 7[a]. We like our Kazakhstan! Sincerely, Losha."

And here's the spark that ignited the flame:

"Dear Losha, My name is Alondra. In Nevada we have hot summers and cold winters. It's not very green here. We live in a desert. I like football just like you do. In the U.S.A., football can start very young and it is called pee wee football, and then can go through college and even adult football. When does football season start there? Someday, I wish to go to college in California. I heard that one of the foods you eat is sheep head. What is done with the rest of the sheep? Does the wool get used? Is the rest of the sheep eaten too? We have lamb chops here, and leg of lamb. Bye, Alondra"

The letters went back and forth for several weeks. *Dear Alondra... Dear Losha...* They were the most rudimentary and simple letters. *What is your favorite sport? I like football... How many siblings do you have? I have two sisters...*

I was confused on how Losha had built up his love for this girl, Alondra, in his head. They were star-crossed lovers, though I doubt Alondra thought of their relationship as such. After all, he was here in Yavlenka, eight thousand miles from Carson City. He was thirteen; she was eleven. I didn't have the heart to tell Losha about the impending doom of his love.

Over a week passed before it was time to receive our next batch of letters from Nevada.

I went to collect the mail from the post office. The local post office was across the playground from the school. The line was short. Although only a few *babushka* were in the queue, the wait would still be long. After waiting in the small room for half an hour, I finally made it up to the counter. An unsmiling woman greeted me. I told her I had a packet waiting. She left the counter for the backroom. She returned five minutes later with a packet in hand. Continuing to frown, she handed it to me, and I signed the paperwork. *Sign here, there, here and there, and sign here...* The packet from Mrs. Braun's class was finally mine.

I returned to my classroom and opened the packet. A note fell out indicating that the packet had been searched and inspected by KazPost and various governmental agencies— most notably the National Committee of Safety, acronym КНБ (KNB), aka the secret police.

A few photographs were in the packet from the fifth graders. Each of my seventh-grade students had a letter addressed to them, except one was missing. It was Alondra's. I pulled out a letter from Mrs. Braun:

"Dear Tim, I am really sorry but Alondra moved. Please, tell Losha I will find a new pen pal for him. Yours, Irene."

The next day I had the letters ready to hand out to class. Before the bell rang, I pulled Losha into the hall.

"Meester Sachlend, I so happy for Aloondra letter," said Losha with a smile on his face.

"Losha, umm"—I started, but didn't really know how to proceed—"I am sorry, but Alondra did not write you a letter."

He looked at me with a big grin on his face. He didn't understand a single word I said.

"Umm... Alondra, uhh..."

How can I explain this? It'll break his heart. I thought.

"Alondra moved away and no longer can write to you."

He continued to look at me with a big smile on his face. It almost seemed cruel to tell him the truth. In this exact moment, ignorance was truly bliss.

I switched to Russian and explained to him what happened.

Drrriiiing! The bell rang. His smile disappeared, and we rushed into the classroom. I went up to the front of the classroom to begin the lesson. Losha went to his seat and sat quietly. He wasn't his usual clowning self. Not once did he interrupt class for a laugh. *Drrriiiing!* The bell rang. Class was over. Students left for the next class. Losha approached me.

"Meester Sachlend," he started, "it okay. Aloondra was gurlfurend, now no gurlfurend. I okay. I troo man."

He seemed to have come to terms with the reality of his short-lived affair with this faraway American girl.

"You are a true man." I affirmed to Losha. "There are plenty of fish in the sea."

He sighed. "*Eto zhizn*..." exclaimed Losha. *C'lest la vie...*

Do you wear a funny fur hat?

Losha smiled at me in a mischievous manner. We weren't in the classroom anymore, so I had little authority over him.

And he knew it. I had just bumped into the Losha on my afternoon walk home from work.

"Meester Sachland!" shouted Losha from across the frozen snow-covered road. "Thiiiss soommer? Where you hat? Where you *shapka*? *Bez shapki?" Without a hat?*

He was bundled up from head to toe in layers of warm clothing, although it wasn't "too" cold outside.

After a long and brutal winter, temperatures had finally reached, what I considered, "warm" and reasonable. The temps were now around the freezing point. I was hoping the *shapka* (hat) issue would be over by now as I quickly ran home after a long day's work. Yet, Losha reminded me that it wasn't.

Yes, it was colder than I anticipated, and my ears were a bit chilled because they were left bare without the protection of a hat to cover them. Part of me was wishing I had a hat to cover them up, but I was too stubborn. I was also too cheap to buy the ostentatious fur hats that local men and women wore through the winter months.

For weeks, if not months, I had felt the need to shed my knitted *shapka* and get some desperately needed fresh air. I was tired of wearing my grimy hat, and today was the first "warm" day of the year. As a result of this Siberian "heat wave," I needed to celebrate the warmth, relatively speaking, by shedding the chains of winter misery.

When I woke up this morning and went to work, it had been only a degree or two below freezing. It was weird to think that minus one degree Celsius was a "warm" day in the middle of March, but for northern Kazakhstan in the winter, these temperatures were tropical.

Of course, my host mother had been horrified when I had left the house after breakfast without wearing a hat.

"Timati! *Shapka*?" shouted Anasi as she chastised me for my lack of headgear.

I acted as if I didn't understand her. I continued for the door.

"Where you *shapka*?" chimed in my host brother, Ağasi.

"I don't need it." I responded confidently. "It's warm today!"

"No, Timati! Dis bad! *Bez*... ahh... witout hat bad fooor healt; bad fooor head," explained Ağasi. "Much sickaness! You need wear *shapka*."

I didn't care to listen to Ağasi or Anasi. My Kazakhstani education was full of people of every age, friends and strangers alike, telling me what I should or shouldn't do. Months of this had begun to wear on my nerves.

"It will be okay!" I told Ağasi and Anasi as I ran out the door before they could reply. "My health is strong, and I will survive a little cold!"

Outside was colder than I expected, but I forced myself to keep walking, without a hat—*bez shapki*. Mind over matter.

I arrived at school. My ears were frozen and red. When I walked into my classroom, *bez shapki*, on that "warm" Kazakhstani morning, Yekaterina Alekseyevna looked at me with much dismay and horror.

"Tim, where is your winter cap?" demanded Yekaterina Alekseyevna sternly.

My glasses were still fogged from coming into the warm school from the cold outside.

"Umm... I forgot it." I played dumb.

Yekaterina Alekseyevna, who acted more as a mother figure than a colleague, went on warning me of what might happen if I did not wear a *shapka* outside in the cold temperatures. The common cold. Bird flu. The plague. They were on the long list of maladies that she warned me of.

I explained to her how it was so nice and warm outside today. A *shapka* would only hinder my happiness.

She rolled her eyes and chuckled. She described to me the concoction for treating the impending illness that awaited me:

pickle juice mixed with soda water, a splash of vodka and a dash of pepper.

Drrriiiing! The school bell rang and classes began promptly at 8:30 a.m. Yekaterina Alekseyevna and I taught all of our classes together. We taught one period after the other, grades four through eleven. The classroom was still cold, even with the school's heating system working at full capacity. Most of my students kept their jackets on to keep warm.

Throughout our day of teaching English vocabulary and reading simple English stories, I anxiously glanced out at the classroom windows. I daydreamed of warmer temperatures and an end to winter. The windows were frosted over with a thick sheet of ice.

Drrriiiing! Classes ended, and I started on my way home. I made my way out the front door of school, where I was stopped. Even as I rushed to get home for lunch, my *shapka* dilemma would continue.

"Timati!" The noise rang like a shrill pitch.

It was the Key Lady. She was a middle-aged woman whose sole job, as far as I could tell, was to sit at the front entrance of school and watch over the door with the school's master key-chain of ancient skeleton keys. The keys were placed in the middle of the desk in front of her. She was accompanied by the school's three cleaning ladies. These women cleaned the school continuously throughout the day with a strange substance that smelled more like gasoline than any proper cleaning agent.

"*Shapka?*" inquired the Key Lady.

I made a futile attempt to explain why I did not wear my *shapka* today. After ten minutes of clumsy wrangling through the Russian language, I convinced her there was nothing to worry about. My health would be just fine walking outside without a *shapka*.

I escaped, and I walked briskly back to my house. It was cold outside. There I was back to Losha...

"Meester Sachland, Meester Sachland! Thiiiss soommer? Where you hat? Where you *shapka*? *Bez shapki?*"

"You know Losha?" I decided to just give up since there was no way of winning this argument with the whole village. "I don't know where my *shapka* is, and I don't care!"

He didn't understand what I said. He still stood there smiling.

I picked up a piece of snow, pressed it together into a ball and tossed it up into the air. Up, up, up it went. It arched, and then down, down, down it came back. It landed squarely on my head. Icy snow crystals splattered and flaked into my hair. A shiver went down my spine.

Losha looked confused, but after a moment passed, he began laughing hysterically.

I bid him *adieu* as I skipped home down the road to the beat of Losha's chuckle... *Bez shapki*.

Why do you want to live in Kazakhstan?

Laughter. My sixth-grade class had been laughing at me hysterically. I had just finished giving instructions for a writing practice for them to do in their journals. Something I said set the classroom off in hysterical laughter.

Teaching wasn't as easy as I had thought it would be when I first signed up for the Peace Corps. I frequently had to remind myself to "go with the flow" and not worry.

As they laughed, I began to blush, and I tried to laugh it off with my students. My ego was shattered. My ego was often shattered time and again in Kazakhstan.

Usually, if students got off task like this, Yekaterina Alekseyevna would quickly react with a terse Soviet-style reprimand. But Yekaterina Alekseyevna was absent.

She had stepped outside the classroom to talk with our school director. I didn't know why Bastygy Mektepovna was here to talk to her, interrupting the middle of our lesson. I just went with the flow.

Don't worry. I thought. *Go with the flow.*

Interruptions were common at School № 1, Timofey Pozolotin. The school nurse needed to give vaccinations to students in the middle of my lesson. The teacher next door needed to publicly berate a student for his or her behavior from the previous class period. The circus was in town, so a clown needed to perform a magic trick to promote the show. It had all happened before. I found it was best to just go with the flow. It was best not to raise too many questions.

My class was still laughing.

I tried to get their attention back by using elementary commands in my broken Russian. That made things worse.

They continued to laugh.

I had realized that most people thought I spoke Russian strangely. Of course, most Kazakhstanis had never heard a real foreigner speak Russian, so I was their only basis of judgment. I probably sounded like a toddler speaking Russian.

My students continued to snicker, even as they began writing in their journals. They finally piped up once Yekaterina Alekseyevna came back into the classroom. My counterpart ruled the classroom with an iron fist—a very Stalinist approach.

At the end of the class period, Yekaterina Alekseyevna gave out marks and recorded them in her grade book.

The process would have been illegal in the United States, but teachers in Kazakhstan were accustomed to giving out grades to students publicly for all classmates to hear. It was a Soviet way of public conformity. Teachers shamed the "naughty" students, usually the students who needed the teacher's help the most. They rewarded the brown nosers, whether they deserved it or not. The grades were far from objective, although no one ever got less than a three (the equivalent of a C grade). Ones and twos (F and D grades) reflected poorly on the teacher. It was all very archaic in thought and deed.

Since the students were a bit wound up still from the class period's interruption, Yekaterina Alekseyevna gave out mostly three grades. A couple fours went to the kowtowers.

Drrriiiing! The bell rang and the students rushed out of class. Students for our next class period walked into the classroom.

"Tim, our next class is canceled"—stated Yekaterina Alekseyevna, but class cancellations were endemic, so I wasn't surprised—"since we have a meeting with the director."

"Meeting? Why?" I asked Yekaterina Alekseyevna, intrigued.

In my six months at School № 1, Timofey Pozolotin, I had personally talked with the director two times: the day I visited Yavlenka during training, and the day I officially started work in November. She rarely acknowledged my existence.

"I am not sure. She mentioned, to my mind, something about the regional educational department," replied Yekaterina Alekseyevna curtly.

"The regional education department?"

"Yes, our regional educational department," stated Yekaterina Alekseyevna matter-of-factly.

"I am confused."

"I am too," laughed Yekaterina Alekseyevna nervously.

Yekaterina Alekseyevna ushered the new students entering the classroom to go back out the door. Where would they go during the canceled class period? I wasn't sure.

We headed down to the director's office on the first floor. Her secretary, a short redheaded woman sat at a small desk in the office. The secretary commanded us to take a seat on two rickety chairs leaning against the wall. She knocked on Bastygy Mektepovna's door and cracked it open. A terse conversation was exchanged between the two, and the secretary closed the door. She assured us it would only be a few minutes.

I noticed the secretary's desk looked straight out of the

1950s. A giant, ancient dial phone and typewriter sat idle on the desk. Kazakhstan's auspicious president (for life), Nursultan A. Nazarbaev, glared down on us from high above on the wall. His countenance was a serious, presidential one with no smile.

A few minutes turned into fifteen, and then into thirty as we waited.

Eventually, our director, Bastygy Mektepovna, swung open her door and commanded us to enter, without a semblance of a smirk. She commanded us to sit down in the chairs in front of her desk.

Her office was unimpressive. Another portrait of Nursultan A. Nazarbaev hung on the wall, though in a slightly different pose than the picture above her secretary's desk. This one made the president's features reflect a look of power and omnipotence. A small desk separated Bastygy Mektepovna from her visitors. It was mostly cleared of papers and any remnants of actual work. An ancient-looking computer monitor sat on her desk, looking as if it had never been turned on. A miniature sky-blue and yellow flag of Kazakhstan stood upright on her desk.

Bastygy Mektepovna spoke too quickly in Russian for me to keep up. I simply sat and nodded my head in agreement. I looked over to Yekaterina Alekseyevna. She was doing just as I was. We were both bobblehead dolls, head nodding and pretending to listen to every word of the director.

After a few minutes, the director stopped talking and Yekaterina Alekseyevna picked up with her translation of what had transpired: "Bastygy Mektepovna, our school's director, has asked you, Tim, to accompany her to meet with the director of the regional educational offices. Her name is Nadezhda Konstantinovna." She paused for a moment. "Will you go?"

I didn't have much of a choice in the matter.

"Uhh... yes. I guess so?" I replied.

"Excellent! I will go with you too to help translate," responded Yekaterina Alekseyevna. "But I must tell you neither I nor Bastygy Mektepovna know of why the director of the regional educational department wants to meet."

We left Bastygy Mektepovna's office and made our way to the exit.

Drrriiiing! As we exited the school, the bell rang. One class over and another class period would soon begin. This meant another lesson canceled for me and Yekaterina Alekseyevna.

Bastygy Mektepovna, Yekaterina Alekseyevna and I crossed the playground and walked towards Yavlenka's town center.

Although spring was upon us and the snow had melted, it was still cold and overcast outside. It was a dreary day.

The Esil Region's education department was not far from the school. It was in a grey two-storied brick building. We entered through a large door that creaked loudly. Inside was a small maze of hallways. Different secretaries directed us this way and that until finally we made our way upstairs to the director's office, where the three of us waited for the regional educational department's director.

The ed. department's director, Nadezhda Konstantinovna, was a middle-aged woman. Unlike most directors in Kazakhstan, she was not Kazakh. She was a *ryzhiy* (redheaded) Russian. Her office was like Bastygy Mektepovna's, austere. Her framed picture of Nursultan A. Nazarbaev was of him as generalissimo, the supreme leader of the Kazakhstani military with a large-brimmed military hat and all.

With the department's director, we went through the same motions as earlier with the school's director. However, this time Bastygy Mektepovna joined us in the head nodding.

After the formalities and business was discussed, Yekaterina Alekseyevna translated: "Tim, Nadezhda Konstantinovna has been in contact with the *akim*. You know *akim* is equivalent of mayor? The *akim* wishes to speak with you."

I was confused even more. I had met the village *akim* before at a beauty pageant, but he had not been interested in talking with me, the foreigner living in Yavlenka.

"Okay? Does Nadezhda Konstantinovna know why he wants to meet?" I asked.

"I will ask," replied Yekaterina Alekseyevna.

Yekaterina Alekseyevna spurted Russian words back and forth with Nadezhda Konstantinovna. Bastygy Mektepovna interrupted abruptly. The triad of dialogue went back and forth between the women for several minutes, with greater stress and debate on every new word spoken.

From the interaction and drama, I saw unfold in front of me, it seemed my question was not so innocuous. Maybe I should have kept my mouth closed and just gone with the flow.

When the discussion ended between the women, Yekaterina Alekseyevna turned to me and said, "Nadezhda Konstantinovna does not know, but she says it is imperative that we go to see our *akim*."

She was perturbed with what she was told to translate.

We bid farewell to Nadezhda Konstantinovna, and Bastygy Mektepovna returned to school. Yekaterina Alekseyevna and I went on to our next stop on this wild goose chase. Next up was to see the village *akim* at the *akimat* (townhall).

It was a ten-minute walk from the regional educational department's office to the village *akimat*.

The Meaning of Peace Corps

The two-story building was located on one of the only two paved roads in Yavlenka. The building was plastered with white trim and light-blue colors to cover up the austere-grey brick common to northern Kazakhstan. Elaborate emblems of Kazakhstani power were embossed on its façade, balancing the rickety tin roof of the building.

We walked into the front door of the *akimat*.

Inside the building the halls were lined with fancy, wood paneling. A pretty penny was spent to embellish this building.

Upon entering the building, we were blocked by the front secretary. We approached her desk. The secretary didn't look up, but rather she continued to scribble notes on a pad of paper. We waited. Yekaterina Alekseyevna gave a cough for attention.

"*Chto?*" asked the secretary in an indignant manner.

Yekaterina Alekseyevna returned right back at the woman with her own annoyed tone.

The secretary huffed and puffed and finally left her desk, walking down the long hallway for the office of Yavlenka's *akim*.

We continued to wait and stand at the front desk for several minutes. We waited longer for good measure.

The woman finally returned with a note in hand. She gave the piece of paper to Yekaterina Alekseyevna. She reviewed it, gave a look of disgust and handed it to me.

It read: «Я занят. Пойдите к акиму района.»

Even I understood the brief message.

The village akim wanted nothing to do with us. In fact, he hadn't even sent for us. He suggested going to the Esil Region's *akimat* and inquiring there.

As the regional center for the Esil Region, Yavlenka had two *akimat*. One ran village affairs, and the other *akimat* managed regional issues.

We left the village *akimat* and headed to the regional *akimat*. Yekaterina Alekseyevna and I did not say a word as we walked through the cold dreary temperatures.

The regional *akimat* was larger than the village one. The light-blue-and-golden-colored flag of Kazakhstan flew high over the building.

We entered the front door. We both slipped around on wet slick tiles as we walked to the front desk.

Yekaterina Alekseyevna introduced ourselves at the desk. The secretary seemed to know who we were. The wait was surprisingly and uncharacteristically short for the day's events. We were soon ushered upstairs into the *akim*'s office.

The *akim*'s office was large with a single desk sitting in the middle. Two chairs sat facing the desk. The regional *akim* sat working on the other side. To my surprise, the *akim* was not Kazakh. He was a Russian man, perhaps in his fifties, maybe sixties. A picture of the *akim* shaking hands with Nursultan A. Nazarbaev sat on his desk, strategically facing his visitors.

"*Zdravstvuyte!*" welcomed the *akim*.

"*Zdravstvuyte,*" we replied.

I sat down in one of the two chairs. Yekaterina Alekseyevna took the other one. The *akim* extended his hand, and he shook mine with unexpected force.

He began to rattle on in Russian complexities that I couldn't follow. Yekaterina Alekseyevna shook her head rapidly. I took note and shook my head with every word the *akim* said.

When the *akim*'s monologue was complete, it was explained to me by Yekaterina Alekseyevna the reasoning for our meeting. The *akim* handed me a letter with an official-looking stamp adhered to it.

I tried to read the letter, but it was in Kazakh. To me, Kazakh was more indecipherable than Russian.

"It says that you must report to the police station," interjected Yekaterina Alekseyevna.

"Police?" I exclaimed.

The Meaning of Peace Corps

First the school director, then the educational office and the akim... Now I have to deal with the police. When will this end? I asked myself.

Dealing with the police in the former Soviet Union was a tricky matter—even with my host father, Äke, having been a retired cop. The talk of the police made me worry. I thought of another volunteer, Jackson in Petropavlovsk. He had been visited twice at the college where he taught by the KNB. The secret police had grilled him and his college's director about Jackson's "true motives" in Kazakhstan, accusing him of being a spy. Apparently, for the KNB, volunteers were security threats.

"Yes, I don't know why exactly," assured Yekaterina Alekseyevna. "To my mind, it is something having to do with the inauguration of a new police chief. The letter states he is new to our Esil *raion*... region, I mean. And he has been decreed by the *oblast akim* to check all certifications of foreigners in the area, and you are our one and only foreigner in the Esil Region."

"But..." I paused in confusion. "I already showed the police my paperwork and passport in the fall when I first arrived to Yavlenka." I reminded Yekaterina Alekseyevna.

When I first arrived in Yavlenka in November, I had done all the proper checks with the police and local officials. The Peace Corps made great efforts for thorough transparency and to ensure volunteers were known by all local authorities.

"Yes, I know this," agreed Yekaterina Alekseyevna.

I glanced at the letter again. The words looked like hieroglyphics to me. At that moment, I wished I had been back in my classroom, even with my rambunctious laughing sixth graders.

Yekaterina Alekseyevna continued, "but the *akim* has been commanded by the police chief. It is our national duty to follow directions in Kazakhstan. To my mind, in English you can say there is a 'method to madness.' Kazakhstan has madness. Yes, we have much madness, but little method."

A Five Finger Feast

Yekaterina Alekseyevna chuckled. She often did when she assured me to not worry. I just needed to "go with the flow."

With her final words, we shook the *akim*'s hand, bid him *adieu* and left for Yavlenka's police station.

Well, Mrs. Braun's Fifth Grade Class, as I pack up my class-room for the summer, I hope you enjoyed learning about Kazakhstan. It sure is a learning experience for me. I hope I've been able to teach you a thing or two about this fascinating country on the opposite side of the planet.

Thank you for reading,
Your Peace Corps Volunteer

Soviet-era mural in School № 1, Timofey Pozolotin

Part III
The Tests of Service,
Year Two

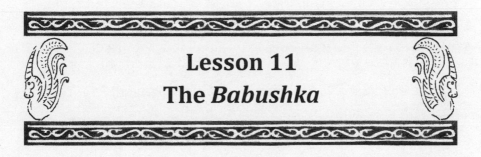

Lesson 11
The *Babushka*

«Вернешься - пути не будет.»
"Do not leave and return from a trip prematurely."

Russian Superstition

"Come back to Kazakhstan!"

"Come back to Kazakhstan!" demanded Stasia, talking very loudly over the hum of the office's swamp cooler.

I ran into Stasia, a Peace Corps staff member, at the Almaty headquarters, where I stopped on my way out of the country. She was in her late fifties or early sixties, *babushka* age, but she didn't play the part. She was as fit and spritely as a woman half her age.

"Of course, I'll come back." I assured her with a confident smile, though surprised that she doubted my commitment.

"To my mind, I see too many volunteers go home to the US on their furlough. They do not come back," affirmed Stasia. "You must return."

That evening I would be leaving for the US, where I would spend two desperately needed weeks of leave back home in Nevada. It was also my sister's wedding.

I was excited to go home and share my Kazakhstan experience with anyone who would listen. I was excited to see family and catch up with friends. I was excited to eat American food, like hamburgers and pizza. I was excited to speak "real" English to those who understood me. It would be a dose of "normalcy."

"I promise I'll come back." I told Stasia. "I've got work to do. People expect me back. Plus, my stuff is in Yavlenka."

"Ok! We like you here, Tim, and we want you to keep up the good work you've already done," continued Stasia. "Yekaterina Alekseyevna would not like it, not one bit, if you did not return. She would be heartbroken. I know because I personally talk with her on the phone. She thinks of you as a son. I am sure your host family too would not like it, not one bit. Home is tempting! Be careful! Come back to Kazakhstan! Come *home* to Kazakhstan!"

Why wouldn't I come back? I thought to myself. *Well, lots of reasons. The toilets, the drunks, the work conditions, the living conditions, the loneliness, the boredom, the winter... Lots of reasons, but I'll come back. I know I will, I think.*

As a Peace Corps employee, Stasia knew something that I didn't quite understand. She knew the numbers and stats from her fifteen years of employment. She knew that many past volunteers went home on leave, thinking the same thing that I did about returning to their site to finish the second year of service, but they never came back to Kazakhstan.

Who could blame them? I thought as I parted ways with Stasia. *America is comfortable. The language, people, environment and culture, they all make more sense than Kazakhstan.*

The *Babushka*

In the evening, I left for the Almaty airport in a taxi with two other volunteers. The airport sat on the far edge of the city from the Peace Corps office. The other volunteers were heading for Turkey, a popular vacation spot for volunteers.

At the airport, the customs agent, a woman dressed in a crisply ironed uniform and a large-brimmed military hat, scrutinized my visa and passport with a grin. I handed her a crumpled piece of paper, my migration entry card. It had been given to me when I had entered the country a year prior. She threw the insignificant scrap of paper into a large stack of disorganized papers of various colors, prints and sizes. The only acknowledgment she showed me was the sound of a stamp slapped down onto a page of my passport.

Home sweet home. I thought as I walked away from the customs window. *Free at last! Escaping Kazakhstan!*

As I boarded my flight to Frankfurt—then to San Francisco, and finally to Reno—I could hear the sweet sirens of far-away America. They sounded so lovely and sweet. I found my seat and made myself comfortable. I looked out the window towards the terminal building.

I read a large neon-lit sign that stood above the airport building: *Әуежайы.* '*Aii-ooo-yee-zhh-aaa-yyy...*' '*Ai-woo-ye-zh-a-yi...*' '*Äwejayi...*' *A weird-looking word,* '*Әуежайы...*' I thought to myself. *Whatever it means? What a weird, uncomfortable word for a weird, uncomfortable place, Kazakhstan.*

The plane took off from Almaty. I quickly fell asleep.

Night Out

"We've missed you, buddy," said Mark, speaking over the bar's music. "You've missed out on a fun year in Reno!"

Mark had led the charge, getting our group of college friends out for some fun. We had ended up at an Irish pub downtown. It didn't seem to matter to the group that we were going out on a worknight for a party on the town.

Of course, Reno didn't get too much rest, even on week-nights. It was a town fueled on twenty-four-hour bars and late-night liquor shops, decrepit casinos and midnight diners. It was filled with shady-looking alleyways, where drunks and drug addicts roamed in a haze. For better or worse, Nevada was home to me. It was where I went to college at the University of Nevada. I grew up down the road in Carson City.

"Yeah, man, you've missed all the fun," interrupted Jim. "Lots of partying, man. You're missing out!"

"No partying," corrected Nick. "We're hermits. We don't do anything but hang out with each other. Anyways, what have you done so far at home—a nice break from the K'stan?"

"Shots on me," interrupted Mark. "I'll go get them."

"I am loving being home!" I began answering Nick's question, anxiously awaiting the round of drinks Mark was ordering for the group. "It's so normal here, and I can do stuff like this, go out and be with friends. I can't do this in my village—too much gawking by the locals. I'm not anonymous there. People seem to know what I'm up to all the time. They'll bother me with annoying questions, or they'll just stare as if I'm something for their amusement."

"I guess anonymity has its benefits," commented Grant. "It's like you're either famous or a freak to the Kazakhs."

Like me, Grant was home in Nevada visiting family. He was passing time in between college and whatever would come next in his life.

In fact, most in the group of friends were having trouble finding work right out of college, even though it had been over a year since graduation. Grant had already spent the year at a mediocre internship and many "in-between" jobs, not yet applying his $100,000 degree. While Nick was figuring out ways to hustle money out of people on the internet, low hanging fruit for a few dollars here and there, Mark was preparing for a second round of law school applications. He had already been rejected by a handful. Jim was still working part-time for a former professor. Little did any of us know that the job outlook would go from bad to worse in about two months, October 2008 to be exact, when economic collapse would loom over Wall Street.

"I kinda get what it's like to be a celebrity." I continued to the group. "It's like everyone in my village knows who I am. They all have an opinion of me, whether they actually 'know' me or not."

"Tim is famous," joked Grant. "Internationally famous!"

"What do you mean famous?" asked Mark as he returned with a tray of shot glasses filled with Jägermeister and cans of Red Bull. "Time for Jägerbombs!"

"Jägerbombs?" shouted Jim, repulsively eyeing the concoction. "I've got to work tomorrow!"

"Man up, buddy!" retorted Mark. "We're drinking to our famous friend here!"

We all drank down the Jägerbombs. I gagged from the taste.

"So how's Timmy famous, Grant?" asked Mark.

"I took him to a gathering up at Tahoe the other night," replied Grant. "It was with a bunch of lifeguards I worked with this summer. When we were there, he ran into some guy from Kazakhstan! Very famous, our Tim!"

"Well, kind of"—I paused, deciding how to recount the strange encounter—"since, I guess, 'famous' is the wrong word. It was more coincidence than fame."

"What's the story?" demanded Nick. "And it better not be one of your long, boring stories!"

"No, it's kinda interesting, I guess. Well, Grant and I went to, like, this party up in Incline Village. It was mostly ski bums."

"That's Tahoe for you," interrupted Grant. "In the summer, the ski bums work as lifeguards."

"The party wasn't huge, but definitely had a crowd." I started back up with the story. "I happen to overhear this girl and guy speaking Russian, so I interrupted them with my own Russian. They were impressed. I guess, the girl was from Ukraine and the guy was Turkish, like, from Turkey."

"This story is boring," interrupted Nick. "I'm getting us another round of beers."

Despite the interruption, I continued with the story: "They were confused how this random American at a party in Tahoe could speak Russian, so I told them I lived in Kazakhstan. Well, the girl points to the Turkish guy and says that his family lives in Kazakhstan."

"Small world, huh?" stated Grant.

"It gets even smaller. His family not only lives in Kazakhstan, but they live in Petro. This is the city closest to my village, and his parents own this café, Café Döner. My Peace Corps friends and I always go there. Long story short, the Turkish guy and I exchanged info. Maybe we'll meet up when he returns to Kazakhstan in a few months."

"See, Tim's a celeb," said Grant. "What an experience!"

"Yeah, it's been an experience for sure, but I envy you guys, especially on the lonely winter nights when I'm stuck at home, trapped by the cold outside. I'm the only twenty-something who isn't married with kids in my village."

"Sounds lonely," exclaimed Jim. "Depressing, dude, don't bring down the vibe."

"I'll get another round to lift up our spirits," said Mark while he headed to the bar.

The *Babushka*

Nick just returned with his own round of beers.

"Not to sound more depressing, but I saw your ex," said Jim in a non sequitur.

"My ex?" I knew who he was talking about, but I didn't want to say her name.

"Yeah, I saw her on campus a week or two ago. Do you talk with her?"

"No, I haven't spoken with her in a while. She called me once, way back in October, but that's when my Nana passed away, so I wasn't chatty and in the mood for catching up."

"If it matters to you, she's doing well," confirmed Jim.

"You're too polite, Jim. She still talks too much," exclaimed Nick. "I ran into her a couple months back, and she wouldn't stop talking about you. 'Tim this… Yatatata… Tim that…'"

"You dodged a bullet there," smiled Grant.

"She's a clinger!" shouted Nick.

Nick liked to tease me about my ex-girlfriend.

It was partly true about my ex-girlfriend, though. I knew leaving for the Peace Corps hadn't been easy on her. I broke her heart. A year had already passed since we broke up before I left for Kazakhstan. It had been a tearful epiphany for me and, eventually, for her, when we realized that me leaving for the Peace Corps would end our relationship. We knew that the distance and the time would be too much. In Kazakhstan, I had begun to move on, but I heard through the grapevine that it had been tough on her.

"It was rough leaving, but I'm glad I did it." I assured them. "Kazakhstan is tough, but worth it."

"Hey guys!" shouted Helen as she walked into the bar entrance from outside.

"Helen!" yelled the group at our old friend.

"You've got to catch up with us on drinks," demanded Mark.

"You guys are ridiculous," laughed Helen. "It's a worknight, but sure. Get me a drink."

"What do you want to drinnnkkk..." stuttered Mark in a moment of intoxication, staring out the bar's window to the flashing neon lights across the street from the bar. "I've got an idea!"

"What is it? I'm down for whatever it is." I prematurely answered Mark's call to action since the alcohol was beginning to take its inebriating effects.

"Let's go to that strip club! Look! It's across the street. I'll close my tab now."

Groupthink took hold, and we all agreed the club was the right move to make, including the sober Helen. We stumbled through the dry desert air, crossing Virginia Street. We followed the warm neon glow of the club's entrance. We entered the club, crowding the ticket counter. The air smelled sweaty with hints of stale perfume.

"It'll be twenty dollars a person," stated the girl manning the front counter at the club.

"What about a group discount?" demanded Mark, the future lawyer. "We've got a big group and need a big discount!"

"No discount," replied the girl, looking repulsed by his demanding nature.

"No discount," repeated Mark. "New plan! To the casino!"

The girl didn't budge to the group's demand, so we headed off into the neon-lit night to find another adventure.

Russo-Georgian War

"Are you sure it's safe there?" asked Lloyd. "I mean that part of the world..."

As Lloyd's words trailed off, I looked around my current surroundings of my parents' backyard. My parents were throwing a pre-wedding barbecue at their house in Carson City. It was a perfect late-summer's evening in northern Nevada as the sun set over the Sierras. The backyard was filled with close friends and family. Lloyd was one of my parents' long-time friends.

"Perfectly safe, I think!" I spoke with some confidence.

At least, I had been one of the volunteers who had escaped major run ins with drunk Kazakhstanis, so far. Other volunteers hadn't gone without safety issues.

"Personally," I continued, "I think Kazakhstan is such a safe place: little crime, no war, no jihadists. The biggest issue is dealing with the drunks, lots of drunks."

"But"—interrupted Lloyd, still seeming unsure—"but what about that war with Russia?"

"You mean the war in Georgia?"

Lloyd referenced the war that had been taking place in the nation of Georgia with its neighbor, Russia.[26] The war shocked me when I watched the news announced during the opening ceremony of the Beijing Olympic Games. The Kremlin said they fought the five-day war in the name of the separatist regions of Abkhazia and South Ossetia.

"Yeah, Georgia!" shouted Lloyd excitedly. "You're near there. Aren't you?"

"Well, near is a relative term in that part of the world, but yes Kazakhstan and Georgia have a lot in common..." My words trailed off as I looked around the yard again.

The people who came to the barbecue cared for me. It was home. They missed me, and I missed them.

A year felt like a long time, especially a year in my early twenties. It hadn't been the easiest year. Kazakhstan tested me, my nerves, sanity, happiness, resilience and endurance.

I was relieved to be around my present company. I saw my mom. She was talking with one of her friends. Since leaving for Kazakhstan the year before, my mom had become my biggest advocate and fan. This hadn't always been the case. It had been an emotional roller-coaster for her, for me. Her little boy, after

---

[26] Georgia is a former Soviet republic in the Caucasus region. A war was fought there with Russia in 2008.

all, had been shipped off to the far reaches of the planet to live and work with people, in her mind, vastly alien and different than anything she knew. Before I left for the Peace Corps, she even tried to convince me not to go. It didn't help that her mom, my Nana, passed away a couple months after my departure. Since leaving, she became my number one cheerleader.

"This Putin guy? He's *Time's* Man of the Year!" interrupted Lloyd, perturbed.

"Umm, well, that's complicated." I replied.

"So, what's this war about anyway?" demanded Lloyd.

The war... It is difficult to explain. I thought to myself. *How do I explain the complexities of post-Soviet geopolitics?*

"The war shows the world that oil-rich resurgent Russia is back." I tried to summarize. "Vladimir Putin's Russia will play by its own rules, and the West, with its democracy, is not free to mess around in Russia's backyard, whether it is in Georgia or in Ukraine or in Kazakhstan."

"I am going to grab a burger," stated Lloyd, walking away.

Massacre

It was hot in the August sun, and the dirt road was parched and dry. Luckily, my walk from the bus station to the house at Four Sovietskaya Street was a short one. It was a beautiful late-summer evening outside. The mosquitoes which had plagued the village in June and July had mostly died off now. The people of Yavlenka were out and about tending their gardens. They were talking with each other in their yards, enjoying the last bit of summer warmth before winter's arrival.

This isn't so bad. I thought. *And to think I almost didn't get on the airplane. I came back, Stasia, and I beat your statistics!*

On my walk through Yavlenka, I felt the emotions that racked my brain and tore at my gut when my time back home ended abruptly. My parents dropped me off at the Reno airport, and I broke down in tears. To leave them again, to leave America for Kazakhstan again, to leave friends again, to leave a chance to live a "normal" life of a twenty-something again—it felt too unbearable. The fears of returning to the cold, the mosquitoes, the drunks, the weird foods, the inability to communicate like a real person—they ran through my mind in a wave of anxiety

'If you don't go back, you may regret that decision for the rest of your life,' echoed the words of my father in my mind.

These words, when my parents dropped me off at the airport, pushed me to keep going.

At the airport, I gave my parents hugs goodbye and darted to the terminal. I had to get through security quickly. I needed to get onto the airplane before I changed my mind. This was my assurance that I wouldn't go AWOL from the Peace Corps.

I had already made it 8,000 miles, and I hadn't turned back yet. It helped that I was met by Dylan and Leo at the train station in Petro when I arrived back.

While I approached Four Sovietskaya Street, I was beginning to forget the pain I left 8,000 miles behind. By now, I actually looked forward to returning to life with my host family, the Zheltoqsans. I was away for large parts of the summer, and it felt surreal to return to Yavlenka.

My life in Yavlenka had been a surreal one, for sure—very surreal. It was like a lingering 1990s sitcom, although with more alcohol consumption than would be allowed on TV by the FCC. The whole cast of characters was in place at Four Sovietskaya Street. In the family we had the goofy, yet stern father, Äke; the working mom, Anasi; the funny and silly brother, the comic relief, Ağasi; the brainy older sister, Ülkenapa; and the playful younger sister, Qoyan. I also had those characters who made appearances two or three times a season: the loud and obnoxious uncle, the loyal dog, the up-to-no-good school friend, and the friendly neighbor. My sitcom life at Four Sovietskaya Street was even complete with the moralizing commentary at the end of each episode. These remarks on how I should live my life usually came from Äke and Ağasi at evening teatime. In Kazakhstan, father and son always know best!

As I approached Four Sovietskaya Street, I noticed a small sign that read, "*Продётся Дом*." It hung from the front door.

Pro-dyo-tsya Dom? I read. *Hmmm, what does that mean?*

I heard a chopping noise. The noise echoed from the back of the house. *Thud! Clunk! Thud! Clunk!* Quacking and pitter-patter stirred into the mix of the strange ruckus.

What is going on back here? I asked myself.

I turned the corner of the house to see what was happening.

Lo and behold, Ağasi stood with a mighty axe in hand. A pool of blood soaked the ground; a pile of heads lay at his feet. He was lopping off the heads of the family's gaggle of geese.

"Timati! You home!" exclaimed Ağasi. "I happy I see you!"

Live geese cowered in a corner of the yard. They sensed their impending doom. It would only be a matter of minutes before it was all over.

"I'm happy to see you too." I replied. "You're working hard."

"My faahterrr say, 'Ağasi, keeell *gusi*.' You know, Timati, '*ga-ga-ga*' *gusi*?"

"You mean '*honk-honk*' geese?" I corrected him.

"No, Timati, no '*honk-honk*.' I keeell '*ga-ga-ga*' *gusi*! Faahterrr say, 'Ağasi, *gusi* money, money,' and we get money! We rich boyz from *gusi* money."

"Big money, of course. Where is everyone today?"

"Sister Qoyan at frrrend house. Mama at work. Sister Ülkenapa go to Karaganda. You know she leave for uoooneeeversity?"

"Oh, yeah, I remember—medical school. I didn't say 'goodbye' to her."

I knew my older host sister, Ülkenapa, was leaving for school at a university in the city of Karaganda. I didn't realize it would be so soon.

The *Babushka*

"Yes, Timati, medaseeena school! She no here. She go fife days now. You know faahterrr leave for Presnovka today? You know village Presnovka?"

I visited the village of Presnovka with Ağasi earlier in the summer to see his extended family. The Zheltoqsan family once hailed from this small place before they settled in Yavlenka. The brother of Äke was the *akim* of Presnovka village. The village hugged the Russian border, three hours by bus from Yavlenka.

"When will he return?" I asked.

"He no come back! Timati, he haff *rabotaet*... ahh... work. He director of departaahment in Presnovka *akimat* now!"

This was news to me! Äke had a new governmental job, and he would be in Presnovka indefinitely. I had realized Äke was unhappy with his life of retirement from the Yavlenka police force. Äke was a military man, a man of swift action, a man of *Blitzkrieg*-like speed, a man of impulse—and now, just like that, he was gone. I didn't know what to say or how to react.

"Zheltoqsan family all go Presnovka!" added Ağasi. "We say 'bye bye' Yavlenka."

The shock hit me again with Ağasi's words. I stared at Ağasi. The corpses of slaughtered geese laid at his feet.

Of course, Äke's family would follow him to live in Presnovka. It made sense. The sign on the door was a "for sale" sign for the house.

With Äke gone, and soon to be the rest of the Zheltoqsans—I began to think—*what will happen to me?*

"Tea, Earl Grey, hot"[27]

It was raining outside. The sound of rain patter hit the tin roof and echoed in the attic space above the small cottage. The wind occasionally lashed rain against the windows with a loud *whoosh*. The sky was dark-grey, and air temperatures were near

---

[27] *Star Trek*'s captain Picard's favorite drink.

freezing. This was just the start of fall.

Summer quickly ended in northern Kazakhstan with *babye leto* (Grandmother's Summer). *Babye leto* was an Indian Summer, a brief interlude of warm, dry weather during autumn. It was the time of the year when the birch-tree forests that dotted northern Kazakhstan turned orange and yellow and the golden fields of wheat were harvested. This made the concrete-block drabness of the towns and villages shimmer in golden glory.

Babye leto quickly ended, though, with heavy rains and the dreaded quagmire of mud that accompanied them. It reminded me that winter was coming to northern Kazakhstan, and it would be here very soon.

The *plip plops* of rain began to come down harder on the house. A roar of water now splashed down on the tin roof above. Outside, it looked wet, cold and miserable.

Inside, though, was warm and welcoming. I sat at the kitchen table with a Russian *babushka*.

Her name was Baba Toma, a nickname other villagers affectionately gave her. Baba Toma was in her late sixties, although she looked more like eighty. She wore a nightgown-looking outfit that many *babushka* wore, a dress reminiscent of a Hawaiian-style *muumuu*.

Earlier that day, Baba Toma's grandson came with his car to the Zheltoqsan's house to help me move to Baba Toma's. It was strange leaving Four Sovietskaya Street. The Zheltoqsan family had treated me well, but now my time with them was at an end.

Äke had already been gone from Four Sovietskaya Street for several weeks. The others in the family were packing for the move to Presnovka. Ağasi and Qoyan would be transferring schools. The house was sold, along with the cow, Adriana Lima. Even the Zheltoqsan's loyal dog, Rex, would be sold.

"*Timochka, chai?*" asked Baba Toma, interrupting my reverie.

'*Timochka*'... I thought. *Teem, Timati, Timka, now Timochka...*

The *Babushka*

That is a new Kazakhstani nickname for me.

Timochka was the Russian equivalent to "Timmy." I would soon learn that Baba Toma was fond of using diminutives for every other word she spoke. Baba Toma's cat was always a "kitten" (*kotyenok*), although it was an old fat cat. Her dog was always a "doggy" (*sobachka*), even when it was a nasty barking monster, chained to its doghouse. For all other nouns Baba Toma turned them into cute, playful, teeny-weeny words.

Her choices for words were fitting for her. She was a short, small woman. She was no more than five feet tall. She radiated the ease and comfort, the look that grandmothers around the world gave.

She poured me more tea and smiled. Her grin was sweet, even with its gaps and gold teeth.

Baba Toma was making things comfortable for me on my first day living at her house on Proletarskaya Street. I was also starting to get to know this fascinating woman.

From our chat, I learned much about Baba Toma's life—and, of course, family gossip. I learned that she was born in the taiga forests near the deepest lake in the world, Lake Baikal. She loved to cook and garden. She watched Russian and Turkish soap operas in her downtime. Her late husband was a school director until he died from complications with diabetes. She had two daughters. One was a biology teacher at School № 1, Timofey Pozolotin, married to a "hot-headed" husband, a truck driver. They lived in Yavlenka with their twenty-three-year-old son and his pregnant girlfriend. She was half Armenian, a source of controversy in the family. Baba Toma's other daughter was the more rambunctious sibling of the family. She lived in Petro with her teenage daughter. She was twice married, twice divorced.

"*Pelmeni*?" asked Baba Toma.

I love pelmeni. I nodded in agreement. *At the Zheltoqsan's, they never fed me homemade pelmeni.*

"*Tarelkochka i vilkochka.*"

Baba Toma scooped homemade dumplings onto my "teeny weeny" plate (*tarelkochka*). She gave me a "cute little" fork (*vilkochka*) to accompany my *tarelkochka*.

Although my Russian skills were getting better, I could tell that living with Baba Toma would improve them greatly. I would be forced to speak and listen to Russian to communicate with Baba Toma since she didn't speak a lick of English. I also knew I'd be well fed.

I was hungry, so I scarfed down my *pelmeni*. In the process, my nostalgia for the Zheltoqsan's quickly disappeared. In fact, my homesickness for Reno, and my friends and family there, slowly subsided since returning to Kazakhstan. Baba Toma's gracious welcome to her home helped speed the process.

Is it safe? While I ate my *pelmeni* and drank my *chai*, I thought back to my conversation with Lloyd back in my parents' yard. *Is it safe? Is Kazakhstan safe? Well, Baba Toma certainly makes it feel safe. For now, I think I'll stay here.*

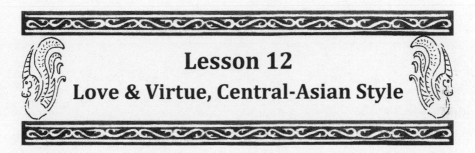

Lesson 12
Love & Virtue, Central-Asian Style

"Capital punishment and life-imprisonment are equally immoral; but if I were offered the choice between them, I would certainly choose the second. It's better to live somehow than not to live at all."

From "The Bet"
by Anton Chekhov

Lubov

Lubov! I thought, caught in a daydream, a fantasy... *I'm in love!* It had already been a few weeks since I met Aizere at the volunteers' party for the *Krishenia* holiday. In the weeks that followed, I often found myself in reverie about her. This fantasy for my newfound love was all I could think about. I found myself frequenting Petropavlovsk much more than usual, just to see her. These visits to Petro were more than what the Peace Corps allowed, and I was spending a lot of money to make these extra trips into the city. But I didn't care what the rules said or at what cost. I needed to see her, desperately. I thought I was in love. I was a foolish boy.

I was heading into the city on a small Chinese-made bus. In recent years, Kazakhstan had imported used busses from its neighbor to the east. Chinese characters were posted above the emergency exit:

紧急出口[28]

It means 'love.' I thought to myself. *Chinese for 'I'm in love!'*

Aizere was beautiful, intelligent, gregarious and ambitious. Since she was Kazakh, and also Muslim by cultural default, she had a sort of exoticism about her. She was twenty-three, and she had just graduated from the local university in Petro. Her English was near-perfect, perfected by time working in America for a summer. She worked in Petro as a translator for an adoption agency. She understood American culture and American people. Unlike most of the local girls, she had plans that went beyond getting married and having lots of Kazakh babies. She wanted to get her master's degree in London. She was exciting and different.

Gulag

Life in Kazakhstan had been exciting during my first year of service. Everything I did was filled with enchantment and novelty. Everything—even banal, ordinary and even crude things like toothpaste and toilet paper—was enchanting, different, strange, wondrous and fascinating. Kazakhstan, during that first year, had truly been a new world to explore.

When I returned to Kazakhstan from my two-week interlude in America in the summer, things seemed to change. Something

---

[28] 紧急出口 means "emergency exit" in Mandarin Chinese.

shifted in my second year of service. The dark and cold winter, and the dreaded *moroz*, began to set in. I was also beginning to feel the drag, the banality, the routine of village life even more than the first year. Boredom was the norm, but this wasn't just a normal type of boredom that one might experience from the mundane of our daily lives, and it wasn't ennui. It felt insidious. The boredom felt lonelier. Life in Kazakhstan during my second year began to feel very lonely. It felt like a trap, a prison, that I couldn't get out of. The more I struggled to free myself from loneliness' grasp, the tighter it gripped—and believe me, I tried all sorts of ways to escape the isolation.

"Cultural integration" had been one of Peace Corps' convictions, so I told myself that I should push myself to achieve more "cultural integration" into village society. The year before I had easily integrated into my host family, the Zheltoqsans. I truly felt a part of their family during the first year. When the Zheltoqsans moved away from Yavlenka shortly after I had returned from America, I moved in with my new host *babushka,* Baba Toma. During that fall we took to each other nicely, although the language barrier proved to be an obstacle. I felt that if I could integrate into these two families so easily, then why not "integrate" into Yavlenkan society as a whole? "Cultural integration" would surely save me from banality and loneliness.

I tried to delve deeper into my job as an English teacher at School № 1, Timofey Pozolotin. I thought I could escape boredom and loneliness by working harder. I would not only work harder in the classroom, but I would start community projects to make myself more visible around town. Peace Corps HQ loved that sort of stuff.

During my second year, Yekaterina Alekseyevna and I started an English class for adults. We thought, if we held classes at night for local villagers in Yavlenka, we could generate momentum. Perhaps the parents of our students would want to help their kids with their own English studies, or maybe students from the local agriculture college would attend. Afterall, I was a local celebrity in town. Who wouldn't want lessons from me, a real, live American? On the first night of the class, we had a dozen, maybe even thirteen or fourteen, fresh and energetic students ready to learn English. The next week's lesson, we had five. The week after we had three. The last week of lessons we had one student. It seemed hard to get anyone to show interest past the initial novelty.

After the adult English class failed, I thought maybe I could delve into my work in other ways. I double downed on other community projects. I ran an English club after school for my students. The students showed up for a couple club meetings, but after a while, the enthusiasm fizzled out. I tried to start a book club at the village library. We read *Treasure Island*. I had received a boxful of *Treasure Island* copies donated by an American patron, so the book was a convenient choice. Only three people came to the meetings—one being my Russian tutor and best English student, Ksenia. She went to everything I organized.

Whatever I tried, whatever activity I planned, I felt like nothing captured the attention of the locals. My work felt like it was stalled. My projects brought me no closer to the Holy Grail, the Peace Corps Nirvana of "cultural integration." I felt defeated.

I changed directions. I decided to learn more Russian. That would surely help me in my quest for "cultural integration." I needed to speak to the locals in their language to become part of their society. I studied a lot of Russian in the fall months. I met with Ksenia often to read stories and practice my speaking. Over time, though, I could tell that I wasn't making much headway. I stagnated, maybe even regressed in my Russian. Simple Russian words and phrases seemed harder for me to remember and retain, much less to spit out coherently to others.

If I couldn't make progress on my Russian, then I would improve on my own native language. I began spending more and more time reading, alone. I went home every cold afternoon from work and read for an hour or two, sometimes three. I read all sorts of books, books I had picked up at the Peace Corps' office. Most were history books about Central Asia and the former Soviet Union: *Lenin's Tomb* and *Resurrection* by David Remnick; *The Great Game* and *Setting the East Ablaze* by Peter Hopkirk.[29] I tried to read Aleksandr Solzhenitsyn: *The Gulag Archipelago* and *One Day in the Life of Ivan Denisovich*.[30] Those two books didn't help to improve my plight on the dark afternoons. Reading about oppression in the Soviet Union's prison camps was depressing.

Personally, though, I found that I could only read so much before I began falling asleep. I came home after work, wrapped myself up in my bed's warm blankets and started reading a few pages. I found myself waking up an hour or two later. Ultimately, I started to take a lot of naps, especially as the temperatures outside dropped.

At night, after watching an episode of Russian soap operas with Baba Toma, I retreated to my bedroom to continue watching shows and movies. I brought a laptop computer to Kazakhstan, so I watched the same DVDs over and over. I can't tell you how many times I watched seasons one and two of *The Office*.

I was very lucky, as far as volunteers' internet access went, because I had the internet directly hooked up to the classroom that I shared with Yekaterina Alekseyevna. It was the *one* place in Yavlenka with *consistent* and *unlimited* internet.

As the afternoons began getting colder and darker in Yavlenka, I found myself spending more time hanging out in my classroom long after school had finished. I checked Facebook all

---

[29] David Remnick (b. 1958) is an American journalist and editor of *The New Yorker*. Peter Hopkirk (1930-2014) was a British journalist.
[30] Alexander Solzhenitsyn (1918-2008) was a Soviet author and dissident.

the time. Through Facebook, I felt like I could somehow live my "American" life vicariously through my online social network. I spent countless hours on Facebook searching profiles and feeds of friends back home. I saw my friends living their exciting lives. They were doing the exciting things that twenty-somethings were supposed to do: going out with friends, dating, advancing their budding careers, etc.

Seeing Facebook only made my loneliness grow. I became envious, jealous even, of my American friends back home. My stay in Kazakhstan prevented me from living the young "American" lifestyle they were living. I felt like I was missing important milestones of a young man's life. At the same time, Facebook was interfering with my ability to fully live my Peace Corps life.

Other volunteers in Kazakhstan helped get me through the long, cold winter nights. Like Facebook, volunteers possessed a complex and extensive social network of our own, a closed and exclusive network of 140+ users. We texted each other often. These brief, often-humorous messages helped fill the void of loneliness. Most volunteers were also alone in small villages in the middle of nowhere. They were lonely, cold and bored just as much as I was.

I hadn't quite reached the tipping point by New Year's Eve of my second winter. It was a social and exciting time. The excitement and fervor of New Year's Eve celebrations brought parties and delicious foods. New Year's celebrations brought a week of parties in Yavlenka and Petro. But the festivities ended in a vodka-induced hangover. I was like a manic depressive—fervor and blithe one moment, depression and sickness the next.

Around the middle of January, I felt like I had punished myself with a self-imposed prison sentence. I understood when I shipped out with the Peace Corps that I would encounter difficulties. I knew I would be cut off from the American way of being, but little did I understand or appreciate what this would mean. I didn't understand how the scourge of monotony and the distress of loneliness would punish me. This was the loneliest time in my life, only to get lonelier.

"To love..."

" *M* *akhabbat ishu!*" shouted Aizere.

"*Za lubov!*" repeated Dylan with a giant smile.

To love! The third toast of the evening was always "to love."

The large group of twenty volunteers and our Kazakhstani groupies gathered in Leo's small apartment. Everyone in the party took down their shot of vodka. We had all come to Petro to celebrate *Krishenia*.

Krishenia (January 19) was the "Christening" (the Epiphany). This was the revelation of Jesus Christ as the Messiah, the moment when the Holy Trinity of God the Father, God the Son and God the Holy Spirit is said to have manifested on Earth.

We gathered in Petro for *Krishenia*'s main event: three icy baptismal dips into the Ishim River to cleanse body, mind and soul of sin and evil. Not only did the polar bear swim give us bragging rights to friends and family back home, but the event was also a special time for volunteers to meet up after not seeing each other for a long time. It helped us take a needed break from the realities of Kazakhstan and hang out in the city.

Most volunteers stuck around Petro the day after the holiday to watch the inauguration of Barack Obama as the forty-fourth president of the USA.

Leo's connection could barely stream the live feed from Washington. Leo's small laptop hummed loudly as it loaded the inauguration taking place on the other side of the planet.

It should have been a sleepy winter evening, but the crowd in the apartment was loud. The neighbors in his apartment block must have wondered what the hell was happening in their typically quiet neck of the woods. It must have seemed like a den of foreign agents, an American nest of spies, had gathered in their building. It was an invasion, the fifth column gathered on the fifth floor of the apartment.

I saw Aizere across the small living room. She was still talking with Dylan. I made my way nervously over to her.

"Bros! You hear about the Kaz Eighteen out in Ust?" I overheard the boisterous Simon talking with some volunteers.

"I've heard," replied Leo. "He got arrested by the KNB, right?"

"Yeah, that's what I heard," whispered Ben as he stared nervously around the room with his balding forehead, making sure no one could overhear their secret talk. "The Almaty office doesn't want it to get out, but we all know what's going down."

I minded little concern to this "secret" conversation. I had another mission to fulfill. I kept moving forward.

"Uhh... Hi!" I anxiously said to Aizere.

She smiled and replied, "Tim, how you doing?"

"I'm getting another beer," stated Dylan, understanding my intentions to talk with Aizere.

"This place is packed!" I was nervous and lost for words.

"Very busy," replied Aizere. "Americans are crazy! You are all so excited about this Obama man."

"I suppose most volunteers voted for him. He's young, hip and will be our first black president, but maybe some voted for McCain—probably not many, though."

Aizere looked at me confused. I think the subtleties of American politics were lost for her.

Am I boring her? I questioned myself. *Don't talk politics or anything that's boring. Talk about something interesting!*

"So what a day, yesterday, huh?" I asked a dumb question.

"*Krishenia* was so fun," replied Aizere as if she was interested in my question. "Americans are so funny and so crazy!"

"All so crazy, I guess." I parroted her nervously.

"It is loud and crazy in here," stated Aizere. "Maybe you and me, we can go to a café to talk."

"Just the two of us?"

"*Da*! I want to talk with you, *and just you*. Let's go!"

Aizere and I took our Irish exit just as Leo's laptop computer finished loading. Obama took the stage on Capitol Hill.

The noise and cheering from the crowd of Americans could be heard down the stairwell of Leo's apartment building. Even outside on the snowy street, the sound of muffled shouts drifted down from five stories up.

None of the fervor and fun upstairs mattered to me, though, not in that brief moment. I was infatuated by this Kazakh girl. I was still nervous, but nothing else seemed to matter to me as Aizere and I snuck off to a café near Leo's apartment. In that moment, life felt perfect...

A Conspiracy

*B*ut life isn't perfect.

Word went fast through the network of volunteers, spreading like wildfire. No, it was not word of my tryst, not my new relationship with Aizere. No, this news was graver.

One of our own had been arrested, a Kaz 18. The word was that he had been arrested at his own going-away party. He had been set up by his counterpart—the person that, as a volunteer, you work with the closest and trust most in two years of service. It was a Soviet-style trap with trumped-up charges and false accusations by the secret police, the KNB. He was accused of "international terrorism!"

How? Why? Many of the details remained nebulous to volunteers in the country. Nevertheless, as much as the Peace Corps wanted to keep the incident under wraps, we all talked.

It was as early as December when volunteers began to figure out that something was wrong. The Kaz 19 volunteers had been in Almaty for our Mid-Service Training (MST), marking the beginning of our second year of service. About sixty of the Kaz 19s still remained from the original seventy-five who came to the country a year prior. MST would be our chance to reconnect and refresh after not seeing each other for months. While volunteers and Peace Corps staff gathered at the conference, our safety and security officer, the fiery Küzetşi, and our new country director, John Sasser, were mysteriously absent. Peace Corps staff answered questions with vague and ambiguous messages that led to more questions. Some left MST disappointed that our director wasn't there. All left MST with more questions than answers.

Soon the volunteers of eastern Kazakhstan, where the incident occurred, began to leak information out. The story began to piece together something like this: The Kaz 18's town had some sort of mine located there. While at his going away party in late November, his counterpart introduced him to a man who claimed to be the manager of the mine. Like many parties in Kazakhstan, alcohol was present, so when offered to tour the mine the volunteer enthusiastically agreed. It didn't matter that it was midnight. It was the last chance to see this local attraction before going home. The three went to the mine, where they had to climb over a security fence. The volunteer was given a tour, but on the way out of the facility things didn't go the way he expected. He was asked to hold a backpack while the counterpart and the other man climbed over the fence. Just as they did this, a group of police with video cameras busted into the facility. They grabbed the volunteer, asking him what was in the bag. He opened it. It contained old dynamite sticks. The volunteer was promptly arrested. The Peace Corps was involved. The American ambassador was involved. The higher ups in the Kazakhstani government were involved. They were negotiating his release, trying to keep things under wraps and out of the media, but an element of the Kazakhstani government was stalling the process.

From what we heard by mid-February, Küzetşi had helped negotiate house arrest rather than jail time. This volunteer was waiting, wasting time, instead of being home after two years of Peace Corps service.

Wasted Weekends

*B*zzzzzz!!!! I rang the aging buzzer. I was impressed that it even worked for this Soviet-era apartment. In Petro, most apartment complexes had little security and fewer had a call box. *Bzzzzzz!!!!* I rang the buzzer again.

"You have arrived, already?" answered a muffled voice on the other side of the call box.

The door lock buzzed open, and I walked into the building. Aizere walked down the stairs to get me. She greeted me with a peck on the lips. We walked up to her apartment on the fourth floor of the building.

"You have a good bus ride?" asked Aizere.

"Yes. It wasn't bad; it's cold outside." I replied.

We didn't say much as we walked through her hallway. Our conversations had, over the past couple weeks, grown stale, but I wouldn't let that get in the way of "*lubov.*"

We had a date planned for tonight. I had been looking forward to this date all week, waiting for five days in my cold lonely village. For our date, she was taking me to a nightclub, what Kazakhstanis called a "disco." I hadn't been to a disco in Kazakhstan before.

"This is the apartment," explained Aizere, matter-of-factly.

The moment we walked through the apartment's door her cell phone rang.

"I need to answer this."

She answered her phone in Russian. She ran into another room of the apartment.

I guess I will make myself comfortable. I thought.

I sat on the couch in the main room of the apartment. The TV was on with Kremlin-propaganda news playing. Aizere still lived with her mom, although her mom was not at the apartment

217

at that time. Her dad was largely absent from her life, so it was an apartment for two. The decor was plain with hints of modern Scandinavian-chic.

She spoke on the phone in another room, sometimes pacing back and forth. I could hear bits and parts of her conversation.

At first, I assumed the phone call was work-related since she was on call for her adoption agency. She had American and European clients, couples who flew to Petro with the sole purpose of adopting a child from Kazakhstan. She seemed to make herself available at all hours, which sometimes interrupted our time together.

From what I could hear, though, this conversation sounded more personal than professional, almost flirtatious. I waited patiently for her for what seemed like a half hour. This turned into forty-five minutes, and then an hour. I was beginning to feel antsy. Aizere finally emerged from the room.

"Tim," started Aizere, "I am not done with my phone call, but I will be done soon."

"Take your time?" I said un-assuredly.

"Of course, I will."

She returned to the other room.

I shouldn't have said 'take your time.' I thought, annoyed at myself. *It has already been plenty of time.*

I continued to wait. It seemed like hours, but it was probably only a few minutes, ten, maybe fifteen. She finally emerged from the room.

"I need to change; get ready," stated Aizere. "I will be back soon, okay?"

I continued to wait.

Play it cool, Tim. Play it cool. I said to myself. *Don't want her to think you're a clinger or too pushy. We will go soon.*

After waiting for twenty minutes, Aizere returned to the waiting room. She was dolled up in a tight dress. She wore makeup that lightened her dark face. She looked thoroughly rusified, a Russian in a Kazakh's body. We got on our winter coats and left for the disco.

L eo met us at the entrance of the disco. He had started to date Aizere's friend, Sveta. Tonight, we were going on a double date. He was outside the disco, smoking a cigarette.

"Howdy folks," greeted Leo with his smoke-exhaling breath muffling his voice. "Took you guys long enough."

"Leo, give me a cigarette," demanded Aizere.

"Cigarette?" I asked, not realizing Aizere was a smoker.

"Of course, Tim! I like to smoke."

"Where is Sveta?" asked Leo.

"She joins us inside," replied Aizere. "Let's go. I know the bouncer. We need not pay the door fee."

The large Kazakh man who guarded the front door of the discotheque greeted Aizere with a kiss on her cheek. She whispered into his ear. He nodded and motioned us inside.

"Welcome to the disco," laughed Aizere.

After checking our jackets at the coat check, we entered a large dimly lit room, mostly empty. Couples danced on the dance floor. Some gangster-looking characters sat in a dark corner. Eurotrash beats vibrated through the room. Seizure-inducing lights flashed from the disco ball. The air was heavy with cigarette smoke.

Sveta sat at a table near the dance floor. The Russian woman was smoking a cigarette.

"Hello all," greeted Sveta with a puff of smoke and a mixed drink in hand.

In Kazakhstan, mixed drinks or "cocktails" were limited to vodka and soda. They were uninspiring and non-imaginative— no frills, no thrills.

We all sat with Sveta. A waitress arrived to take our orders. Leo and I ordered beers, Baltika 7.[31] Aizere ordered vodka.

"Oh my god, this is my friend here," stated Aizere when she glanced across the room. "I will go talk with her. She probably has a cigarette I can have."

Aizere disappeared just as our waitress brought several shots of vodka and the Baltika 7.

"Where's your lady going?" asked Leo. His voice could barely be heard over the blaring Russian pop music.

"Don't know." I told him. "It's been happening all night."

"Maybe she has another man," stated Leo, jokingly.

"I've been wondering the same." My tone was beginning to sound more perturbed as I lost my patience with Aizere.

Leo and I had another round of Baltika 7. Sveta sat at the table, smoking cigarette after cigarette. She didn't talk much. Music blasted. It was Dima Bilan.[32]

"My ride's here," said Aizere when she finally came back from the void of the disco.

"What? Ride?" I was confused. "I didn't realize you were leaving us."

"Yes! I must leave now," stated Aizere.

"Really? I didn't, uhh... You never said you had to leave us so early tonight."

"Yes, I am meeting my friend Mustafa. You know Mustafa? The Turkish guy."

"Of course, I know Mustafa"—the Turkish guy I had met at Lake Tahoe the summer before had returned to see his family in Petro, and I had introduced him to Aizere and to all the volunteers—"but why are you going to meet him now?

"He invited me to a birthday party! Don't look so worried," exclaimed Aizere.

---

[31] Baltika 7 is a lager beer brewed by the Russian brewery Baltika.
[32] Dima Bilan (b. 1981) is a popular musician from Russia.

"You are going off to another party." I told her anxiously.

"I think he is gay, he won't admit it, but I think he is, so you no need to worry about him."

"Still, you're leaving all of us in the middle of our date."

"This is a date? It will be fine. You will have a good time with Sveta and Leo. I must go now. My ride is outside."

"Can I at least walk you to your car?" I asked her.

"*Da*, I guess."

We walked out of the disco into the freezing winter temperatures. I had left my jacket at the coat check. I quickly gave her a kiss goodbye. She got into the car, seeming familiar with the driver. He was a young Kazakh man. I felt sick to my stomach sending her off. I stood there in the cold. The car drove off.

Did I just hand her off to another 'boyfriend'? I asked myself. *Was her conversation on the phone another lover? Maybe it's just a friend or a cousin...*

I was paranoid.

Paranoia

It was said that the mental health among volunteers in Central Asia was the worst in the service. Blame the cold. Blame the food. Blame the culture. Blame the isolation. Blame the alcohol. I think all seventy-five Kaz 19s who had arrived in the country in August 2007 felt the pangs of Kazakhstan. We felt the highs and the lows—the deep, deep lows—of Peace Corps service. Some felt it more than others. Some left Kazakhstan, the infamous ET or Early Termination. A select few were sent to hospitals in Washington or the Peace Corps' hospital in Thailand. They were Medically Separated (MedSep), or they were somehow patched back together and sent back to Kazakhstan.

The Kazakhstani nationals we were supposed to serve and support didn't always appreciate our presence. They didn't always make it easy for the volunteers. For example, one volunteer had been walking down the street in his city when he was assaulted by a local drunk. He had just left the public *banya* with volunteers and local friends when a drunk man approached him. Without warning, the drunk punched him in the face. His skull was fractured, and he was evacuated from the country. He served two weeks in Thailand at the Peace Corps hospital there.

The very government which had invited the Peace Corps to Kazakhstan didn't always make it easy on us either. The KNB, it was said, was filled with "old guard" hawks. In the post-Soviet world, the KNB aligned themselves with Russia and Putin, another former KGB member. The Peace Corps, NGOs and other international aid organizations, which were initially invited to Kazakhstan with open arms in the 1990s, were beginning to find it more difficult to operate in Kazakhstan. It was said that the KNB bugged our incoming phone calls from the US. One volunteer swore that each time his parents called his cell phone he would hear strange clicks on the line. It was as if someone was listening in on the call.

The Peace Corps told us to be careful with whom we befriended and trusted. A couple years after leaving Kazakhstan, I heard a story about a Kaz 20. At his going away party, his two best local friends disclosed a secret to him. Unbeknownst to him, the KNB had paid them to befriend the volunteer and spy on him during his two years in Kazakhstan. They spied on the volunteer, reporting back to the KNB on his whereabouts, visitors, activities, etc. However, these two guys took a liking to their target over the course of their two years of spying. When their target was about to take off from twenty-seven months of service, the two disclosed that they had been spies. Of course, they realized that the volunteer wasn't up to anything nefarious. According to them, the Kaz 20 was an outstanding guy. They told him they were going to miss him, and they even asked if they could visit him in America someday.

Like the Kaz 18 who was being held under house arrest on

"international terrorism" charges, Kazakhstan became our prison. The local drunks. The KNB spies. The deathly cold climate. The impossible language. The food. The loneliness. At times in Kazakhstan, it felt like a million mosquitoes were biting and feasting on the soul. It could drive a person mad.

Feast of a Million Mosquitoes

"Aizere has soooooo many boyfriends," laughed the red-headed, freckled Kentuckian. "She's got her boyfriend over yonder in Almaty. She's got one in Astana. She's got that one in Petro who drives her around town everywhere."

Even though I already suspected that I wasn't the only guy in Aizere's life, my stomach sank. The Kentuckian didn't know that, in his audience, another one of Aizere's boyfriends sat.

"Let us not talk about this," grinned Aizere nervously.

The rest of the dinner party of volunteers looked over at me while this man brought the obvious out into the open. Aizere had invited the Petro volunteers to dinner to meet her newest American couple.

The Kentuckian and his wife were in Petro to adopt a child. Aizere was their translator and fixer while they navigated the complexities of adopting in Kazakhstan.

Kazakhstan was a big exporter—if "exporter" is an appropriate word for international adoption—of orphans. For local orphanages, there was big money to be made from Americans and Europeans. The process was relatively cheap and easy for them compared to adopting a child back home. In Kazakhstan, it took about seven weeks and $15,000.

"Oh, yeah," continued the man, laughing, "she's got boyfriends at her beck and call!"

Aizere's phone rang. She took the call away from our table.

"One of her boyfriends," shouted Dylan, smiling at me.

Well, this is what I suspected... I thought to myself. *I guess I am not as crazy as I thought.*

A Five Finger Feast

For several weeks, I had felt sick to my stomach. I suspected that something was off in our relationship, but I couldn't quite figure it out. At first, I thought maybe it was the distance—me living in the village, her living in Petro. During the week it wasn't easy being in the village, usually bored, and her being busy with work and friends in the city. I grew jealous.

A big issue that interfered in our relationship was how busy she was. She said that her job forced her to work seven days a week. She had to cater to the needs of her adopting couples. Then on top of this she had friends and family too, so when I came in on the weekends to see her, I was competing for her attention. I grew more jealous.

At first, I thought my jealousy was a language or a cultural-barrier type of thing, some sort of miscommunication or mis-understanding between me and Aizere. It turned out there was a communication issue, indeed. It wasn't necessarily a cultural issue. It was that I was too afraid to bring up my frustrations with her, and she told me nothing about her life happenings.

I felt like it was eating me up inside. It was as if the millions of mosquitoes that festered in the swamps of Petro during the summer months had returned to attack me in the cold winter.

There had been passion and excitement in the very begin-ning of our relationship. Now, it was pain, angst. I felt unsettled and unsatisfied. I felt like I was going mad. I was a young man in love, after all. I was jealous. I had become very, very jealous.

Aizere returned from her phone call. The gregarious Ken-tuckian continued talking to the table. The volunteers were mostly silent afterwards. It was as if we were giving Aizere the cold shoulder when she returned.

At the end of the dinner, Aizere sent her adopters back to their hotel in a taxi. The volunteers and Aizere stood outside of the café. It was snowing out, although it wasn't particularly cold.

"What are we all doing?" asked Aizere.

"I think we are just going to walk home," answered Dylan.

"Yeah, I think we are going to go home," affirmed Rebecca.

I stood in silence.

"I'll go home too," replied Aizere with a tone of uncertainty.

The group of volunteers moved as a pack down the snowy sidewalk. We left Aizere standing there alone as she called up for a ride from one of her boyfriends to drive her home.

"Tim, you've got to figure that situation out," stated Dylan.

"Dump her!" exclaimed Rebecca. "I've never really liked Aizere that much anyways."

"Yeah, you've got to break up with her," stated Leo. "She has been playing you. Anyways, I just broke up with Sveta. We can be single bachelors together!"

"It's just a fling," laughed Dylan. "You will get over it. You will be way happier without her. You haven't been yourself lately, and I blame Aizere."

I mulled over what happened tonight. I ruminated on the volunteer's advice in silence as we walked.

We eventually made our way back to Leo's apartment. I would be spending the night here before leaving for Yavlenka the next day.

As we entered his warm entryway, I checked my phone. I had received several text messages from Aizere.

"Well, looks like Aizere was busy messaging me." I announced to the group.

"What did she say?" inquired Leo. "Let me see!"

I dodged his question as I read through Aizere's texts:

Why did u leave me @ cafe? :(You've turned the other Americans against me! I don't want 2 be left out :(

Her second message read:

It's not true @ cafe. I only have u 4 boyfriend :) Miss you!

And a third text:

What are u doing? XOXO Let's meet tomorrow, before u go 2 Yavlenka. It's Women's Day, after all. U must get me a gift ;)

"Well, what did she write?" demanded Dylan.

I handed him the phone.

"Hmm... It's your call on this one, buddy," stated Dylan as he passed my phone to Leo.

"She seems to still like you enough to text you," stated Leo. "But dump her!"

"If it were me, I would get rid of her," interrupted Rebecca. "I never really liked Aizere. I know she is Sveta's friend, and I work with Sveta, but she sucks! Plus, she stood you up so many times."

"I am not sure what to do." I told the group. "I like her, but I don't like how she treats me. I feel way too stressed waiting on her. I spend so much money coming into the city and going out with her."

"Women are expensive," stated Leo.

"I just don't know. I like her, and she does make me feel good, sometimes. It's nice to have a girlfriend." I sighed.

"If it was that nice, we wouldn't be having this conversation," replied Dylan. "You're a prisoner of your own doing."

Exiles/Prisoners

Aleksandr Solzhenitsyn, the Soviet dissident and former *gulag* prisoner, published his extensive narrative history, *The Gulag Archipelago*, in 1973. In his work, he wrote about a web of *gulag* camps that imprisoned millions of Soviet citizens. Yet, this "archipelago" lay hidden just under the surface of Soviet society, with the Soviet State acting as if its massive network of prisons and concentration camps was invisible.

During the Stalin years, Solzhenitsyn had endured forced labor camps, known as a *gulag*. At one point, he was even internally exiled to a village near Almaty. After he was released from prison and exile, he wrote a short fictional story, *One Day in the Life of Ivan Denisovich*. This story detailed the horrors of the *gulag*. Amazingly, the Soviet censors allowed him to publish his work in the early 1960s.

He continued his momentum by gathering interviews and accounts from the *gulag*. *The Gulag Archipelago* went too far for the censors, though. He landed himself into exile again in 1974, Vermont of all places. He would only return to his motherland when the Soviet Union collapsed in the 1990s. In a bit of ironic vengeance, it had been the spark started by *One Day in the Life of Ivan Denisovich* that helped usher in the Soviet Union's collapse thirty years later.

In a strange way, the modern nation of Kazakhstan was a direct product of this archipelago of prisons and *gulag*. The Russian Empire and the Soviet Union manifested the idea of the modern-day Kazakhstan when they forcibly settled mass numbers of people in the mostly empty lands between the Volga River in the west and the deserts and mountains of Xinjiang in the east.[33]

For millennia, outside of the Almaty region and the far south of the country near Tashkent, Uzbekistan, the area of Kazakhstan was a place where people mostly passed by, but rarely settled. People moved goods up and down the Silk Road. Mongol conquerors sacked settlements in southern Kazakhstan on their way to richer lands in the Middle East and west in Europe.

Some nomads herded livestock around the steppe of modern-day Kazakhstan. However, the land could only sustain so many people and so many sheep, because it was a land of ex-

---

[33] Xinjiang is the westernmost province of China. Its biggest city is Ürumqi. It is home to the Uyghurs, a predominately Muslim ethnicity related to Kazakhs.

tremes—extreme winters, mosquito-infested summers, and a million square miles of arid steppe.

The extremes of Kazakhstan—and, subsequently, its larger, colder neighbor to the north, Siberia—were the reason why people were forced into exile here by the Tsars and later the Communists. It was extremely cold and extremely far from Moscow and St. Petersburg. Tsar Nicholas I exiled the writer Fyodor Dostoyevsky first to Omsk in Siberia—a city just over the border from where I was stationed in Yavlenka—and then to Semipalatinsk, Kazakhstan, the area where the Soviets would eventually test their nuclear bombs. Stalin made Kazakhstan his dumping ground for his unwanted minorities: Volga Germans, Vladivostok Koreans, Armenians, etc. These groups were accused of "collaborating" with the Nazis and Japanese during the WWII. They were deemed "untrustworthy" by Stalin, which was a good enough reason to deport them to Kazakhstan.

If you look at a map of Kazakhstan, the center of Kazakhstan is pretty much a large desert. There is, however, one lonely city right smack in the middle. This is the city of Karaganda—the capital of the Karaganda Oblast, a province larger than Sweden. Five hundred thousand called this lonesome city home. The city was largely built up during the 1930s and 1940s by forced labor. Stalin built a large *gulag* around Karaganda, where he sent all sorts of notorious criminals: writers, composers, professors, painters, journalists, Jews and *kulak* (wealthy peasants). The Soviets packed these people into cramped cattle cars and then shipped them off to *gulag* barracks around Karaganda.

Psychotherapist and Auschwitz survivor Viktor Frankl published his book, *Man's Search for Meaning*, in 1946. In his book, Frankl wrote that suffering and death are interconnected to every human life. Without suffering, we cannot be human. To understand how to live a better and more fulfilled life, a person must also examine the suffering that comes with living.

Love & Virtue, Central-Asian Style

The masses of people who were exiled to Kazakhstan and sent to the *gulag* experienced the extremes of this suffering that Frankl wrote about. The Kaz 18 who was under house arrest also experienced this suffering. In fact, most, if not all, of the volunteers serving in the Peace Corps in Kazakhstan experienced this suffering during our time in the country.

Our service in Kazakhstan was tough, but as Nietzsche said, "what doesn't kill me makes me stronger."[34] Kazakhstan, Aizere and all the unpleasantries in between were making me a person, a better one, even if it hurt along the way.

Frankl also said man must make choices. Choose to perish or choose to survive. Those who were imprisoned in Kazakhstan had a choice. Die in the labor camps or live in the camps. Survive! Many of the prisoners found meaning in this suffering. They chose to build new lives. From prisoners and exiles, a nation would be born. Today, many of the descendants of those who were sent to the *gulag* have made Karaganda and Kazakhstan their homes.

Like those in the *gulag*, I came to realize, with Aizere, I had to make a choice. My time with Aizere slowly became torture. I can reflect clearly on it now, many years later, after finding true love and experiencing the happiness that comes with it. I had a choice to make.

International Women's Day

"Why are you doing this to me, Tim?" asked Aizere rather miffed. "Are you breaking up..." She paused. "Are you breaking up with me?"

Aizere and I stood on the front steps of the orphanage where she worked. The air was biting cold for March.

"Yes, I guess so." I stated, fighting back the tears. "I think we are doing different things. We are going in different directions."

---

[34] Friedrich Nietzsche (1844-1900) was a German philosopher.

"But we have fun together," said Aizere.

Aizere and I had made plans to hang out today. We were supposed to have the day to ourselves to get food and simply hang out for March 8, International Women's Day.

In Kazakhstan, this holiday had lost the political and socialist undertones of the original holiday. It became a mixture of Valentine's Day and Mother's Day. Men were expected to treat and give gifts to mothers, wives, girlfriends and daughters. People went out to cafes on dates, or they went to parties to celebrate the women in their lives.

When I woke up in the morning, Aizere had been quiet in answering my text messages, until she finally texted me in the late morning to cancel our plans. I had already bought her flowers by the time I heard from her. Nevertheless, she let me know that I could drop the flowers off with her at the orphanage. I left Leo's apartment, flowers in hand, frustrated by Aizere.

"Yeah, we do have fun together, I guess." I answered Aizere. "But you are so busy with work, and I don't think you realize that you are overlooking our relationship."

On the way from Leo's apartment to Aizere's orphanage, I kept thinking of a problem my *babushka*, Baba Toma, experienced recently. She had been complaining to me for weeks about a toothache she had. I told her over and over to go to the dentist. Of course, in Kazakhstan, the solution for toothaches sometimes meant more gold teeth. Dentistry was not a popular profession in Kazakhstan. She acquiesced. She finally went to the dentist. Her toothache magically went away. On my walk to meet Aizere, I realized I had my own toothache.

"You are right," answered Aizere. "I do sometimes overlook our relationship. It's because I'm so busy, and I don't want to change that, because it's my work. If I don't respond to your text message, it's not because I don't like you. I'm busy."

"Well, like, it feels like you don't respond to my texts more often than not." I told her. "I want to have someone to be with. It feels like you just like the idea of dating an American."

"*Da*, I like being with your friends too," responded Aizere. "But I like you. You know, like... I 'like' you?"

"I like you too"—answering as I continued—"but we're from completely different worlds. We're going in different directions. You want to get out of Petro. I just need to get out of my village. I need someone to help with the loneliness. I'm not sure what you want."

"I want to have fun together. Just think this over again," stated Aizere matter-of-factly.

On my walk before arriving at the orphanage, I had come to terms with what I needed to do. Inspired by Baba Toma? Maybe. Influenced by Leo, Rebecca and Dylan's opinions from the night before? Perhaps. But this was my decision. I needed to do it to continue in Kazakhstan and to get through the nine months I had left of Peace Corps service. I was nervous as hell. I knew I wasn't good at confrontations like this. I had little experience breaking off relationships.

"I think..." I choked up. "I think I have made my decision. We should not be together. I have these flowers for you. I bought them for Women's Day."

"Tim, why are you doing this?" asked Aizere as she took the flowers in hand. "Just think this over," stated Aizere.

Don't cave! I told myself. *Don't back down!*

"I've got to go. I've got a bus to catch." I was fighting off tears. "Happy Women's Day."

I left Aizere on the steps of the orphanage, holding the bouquet flowers for Women's Day. I walked quickly as I could to the bus station to return to Yavlenka.

A Five Finger Feast

I had a broken heart. That day, I thought the agony would go on forever, but the pain subsided, eventually. By the time I returned home to Nevada, months after the relationship ended, the pain would be gone, almost. I realized that the relationship was flawed. It was lust. Looking back on the relationship years later, it is easy to see why it was a doomed affair. Yes, it was a distraction from the pain and the loneliness of Kazakhstan—my personal *gulag*.

Perhaps, though, Kazakhstan hadn't really been a *gulag*. The second winter was tougher than the first. The experience of the Peace Corps was difficult at times. There were moments I questioned my ability to survive, let alone thrive, in Kazakhstan. I often questioned my ability to continue on with my service, but it is natural for anyone to question the difficult parts of life.

Years later, as I write about Aizere and Kazakhstan and that second winter, I cannot say if there are any true regrets from my time back then. *"It's better to live somehow than not to live at all."* I came to realize that even struggling over the heartbreak or dealing with the loneliness and the boredom of Kazakhstan—surviving my *gulag*—can make you truly live a life worth living.

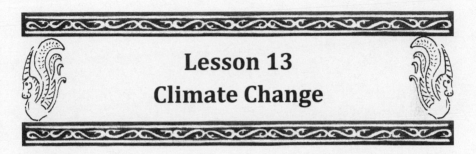

Lesson 13
Climate Change

"The Aral Sea was the fourth largest lake in the world. The former seabed is now a salt desert... The dying Aral Sea is one of the world environmental disasters."

From English - Английский Язык: Учебник для 11 Классов *by T. Ayapova*

A Cemetery

As our Soviet-made jeep sped along the crumbling road to the Aral Sea, we passed desolate villages—long ago sustained by the once-fruitful bounty of the Sea. Now these meek settlements stood in states of decay, some totally abandoned, and others still inhabited by the meager and desperate. These small villages had been forever stranded in an ocean of sand and desert, a brown and grey waste that stretched out as far as the eye could see.

Our driver flew through one such village like a madman, a silent madman. He never said a word to his four American passengers—instead, he feverishly put his foot down on the gas pedal. The jeep zipped through this dilapidated settlement. The driver seemed to have no concern

for the safety of a group of children playing soccer in the middle of the dirt road.

These children, and a lonely camel tied up to a mud wall, were the only signs of life in the village.

The jeep continued along the road. It drove over small hills, bumping and thumping and then sliding through patches of mud and sand.

We raced by small mausoleums and tombstones built long ago by the ancestors of the Kazakh people of the region. These cities of the dead seemed to outnumber the villages of the living; those in the ground were more plentiful than those above.

We eventually arrived at the former seashore, but our car didn't stop here. Like an intrepid ship facing down a storm, we drove over what was once a beach and continued onto the Martian-looking seafloor. Dry, brown tufts of grass grew on the mounds of sand and the seashells that once formed below the water's surface.

The engine of the jeep revved with fury over every sandbank we traversed. The loud clatter from the pistons blasting and gears shifting was muffled by bizarre Arabic-inspired music roaring from our driver's stereo.

Ahead in the distance, we happened across a lone figure. It was a grimy old man watching over a herd of camels and sheep. He sat on his dirty grey horse, wrapped in a torn jacket and topped by a grungy fur hat. He was like a specter from a time long forgotten by the receding waters of the Sea. The car slowed as we passed the old man.

Our driver rolled down his window to shout a simple, yet, courteous show of respect to this gentleman: "*As-salam aleykum!*"

"*Wuleykum as-salam*," replied the congenial man.

The engine revved. We continued our way along the seabed.

Across the wasteland of what had once been a large harbor rested the ship cemetery. The rusted bones of three boats remained of the dozens of ships that were abandoned by their crews over two decades before. Like vultures, people had come and picked apart the hulls and inner mechanics of the ships, selling what scrap metal they could in distant places—Almaty, Ürumqi, Chelyabinsk, Tashkent.

Our car drove up to the boats. It came to a sudden stop at the biggest of the ships, berthed forever in the shifting sands. Our driver said not a word as the four Americans jumped out of the crowded vehicle to look around the graveyard.

The wind howled, blowing through what was once the stern of a large vessel. What was left of the hull had turned a rusty red. Whatever trace of majesty and dignity this boat once possessed was stolen twenty years ago when the Sea retreated away from this sad place. It was sinking into the sands of the apocalypse.

We continued on our way. Our chauffeur rolled down his window and lit a cigarette, flooding the cabin of our vehicle with fumes of smoke and particles of dirt from outside. Our driver continued to drive furiously over every hill like a madman.

Was it twenty minutes? Thirty minutes? I couldn't tell. The waving and bouncing and bumping of the car obscured my sense of time. We bounced up and down violently. I was slightly amused, but mostly frightened for my life.

It was while our vessel was recklessly airborne over one large hill when I first caught a glimpse of the retreating waters of the Sea. There it was, stretching out along the horizon in front of me—enchanting, yet unsettling. It stretched before me like a faceless ghost, still and silent in a world of waste that surrounded it.

Our driver landed the jeep back down into the sand with a thump. With a crash, my view of the Sea became obscured. The Sea was gone.

Carson City

"Alright, class." Mr. Clemens raised his voice, trying to get his student's attention.

Mr. Clemens, a stout man with grey receding hair, was in his late fifties. Only a few more years of teaching and he would be living the sweet life of retirement, but first, get through one more day of teaching middle school social studies.

"I have a treat today," said the aging teacher sarcastically.

The word *treat* quieted up the seventh-grade class.

Mr. Clemens, a cantankerous and crabby man, usually didn't give out treats to his classes. The treat, we soon learned, wasn't really a treat. It was a lesson on the former Soviet Union—a seventh grader's delight.

"So, we've been learning about the Soviet Union and its geography for a couple days," Mr. Clemens continued, "and I want you all to be aware that we have a quiz coming up next class. It will be based on what we have learned so far. The test will be difficult, and I am sure many will not pass it." He smirked. "If you have been paying attention in class and doing your homework you might have a chance."

When I was in the seventh grade, the collapse of the Soviet Union was barely history at the time. Back then the largest nation on Earth had only passed away five years prior. To many Americans its demise was a sudden shock and relief. With the collapse, the world had changed dramatically.

However, to children of the 1990s, the end of the Cold War and the news events that followed were barely blips on TV for us. *Ducktales*, *Saved by the Bell* and *TGIF* kept our attention and perverted our memories. Anyways, how could an American six-year-old comprehend the events that unfolded in 1991?

In 1997, I was twelve going on thirteen. In Nevada, it must have been a seventh-grade standard to be educated on the geography of the world, including the former Soviet Union.

"As for my treat," Mr. Clemens resumed, "I have a video."

The ears of the students in the class perked. We almost never got to watch videos in his class.

"This isn't a cartoon or any tween TV show," exclaimed Mr. Clemens. "Oh, it's a real gem! It's on the Aral Sea. A real gem! It is one of the ecological disasters of our time. Does anyone remember this term, *ecology*, from your vocab sheet?"

Mr. Clemens scanned the room. No one dared flinch.

"Well, I see you all have some studying to do for the test. Okay, let's do this."

Mr. Clemens hit the lights in the classroom and turned on the TV. He hit play on the VCR. The video started, flickering a few times with static across the screen. The video played as a desert scene panned on the screen.

A strange song began playing. It was a woman's voice in a strange tongue, and she sang a ghastly tune. The rhythm and beat were unfamiliar and exotic. The music was oriental and unfamiliar to the ear, especially to a seventh grader in Carson City. It was a distant song from a distant land.

The narrator's deep masculine voice bellowed: "The Aral Sea is the greatest manmade environmental disaster of our time. The remnants of the Sea border the newly independent nations of Kazakhstan and Uzbekistan..."

The Aral Sea

What remains of the Sea straddles a border in southwest Kazakhstan and northwest Uzbekistan. It clings to an imaginary manmade line in the middle of a lonely wasteland.

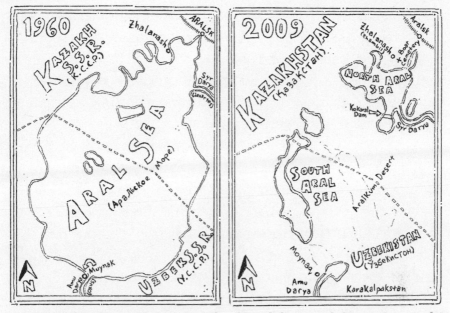

In 1960, the Aral Sea was the fourth largest lake in the world after the Caspian Sea, Lake Superior and Lake Victoria. However, from 1960 to 2009, it shrank to twenty percent of what it once was.

The Sea's fast disappearance is due largely to over irrigation and water usage from its main tributaries, the Amu-Darya (Oxus River) and the Syr-Darya (Jaxartes River). These two rivers—known best in the Western world for their role in Alexander the Great's conquests—pass through several politically antagonistic countries: Afghanistan, Tajikistan, Kyrgyzstan, Turkmenistan, Uzbekistan and Kazakhstan.

The death of the Sea began in the 1950s with Soviet leader Nikita Khrushchev and communist planners. Their vision was to transform Central Asia into a socialist utopia where cotton would be king. Planners knew the Sea would shrink, but the profits from cotton were too alluring.

The Soviet's slogan went: "The Aral Sea must die, just as a soldier in battle!"

Just as God had condemned Sodom and Gomorrah, the communist leaders, acting as their own gods on Earth, condemned the Sea to a similar fate.

The Sea shrank quicker and more drastically than planners expected. The rivers were diverted into poorly designed canals and irrigation ditches. Central-Asian sunshine and water-intensive cotton sucked the region dry.

In 1989, the northern and southern halves of the Sea split, creating the North Aral Sea and the Greater (South) Aral Sea. As the Sea divided and shrank, desertification intensified, especially in the fertile Amu-Darya delta in Uzbekistan. Farming in the delta diminished. The salinity of the Sea increased, and fish began dying. The fishing industry collapsed. Once-popular seaside resorts were abandoned. The already extreme winter and summer temperatures of the region intensified. Dust storms carried salts and pollutants into the air for hundreds of miles.

In 1991, the Soviet Union collapsed, and the Kazakh and Karakalpak peoples of the Sea's region were abandoned to suffer. People in southern Kazakhstan and in Karakalpakstan, a region in Uzbekistan with a population of over a million people, began suffering from new cancers and strains of tuberculosis.

The newly formed Central-Asian nations competed against each other for political and economic dominance in the region. The regional rivalries, added by rampant government corruption, have taken their toll on the Sea.

There has been little success and cooperation to solve the Sea's problems. The Sea continues to disappear. It is a place forgotten—discarded, swallowed by an ocean of desert sand.

A Textbook

Over the years, that video from Mr. Clemens' class faded into my own distant memories, just as the Soviet Union had drifted into the annals of history. I forgot the Sea existed. Even when I arrived in Kazakhstan for Peace Corps service, the Sea was a thousand miles away from where I was stationed. I didn't think much of it, until I came across a passage in the eleventh-grade English textbook I used for lessons.

Like most educational materials used in the classroom in Kazakhstan, the Ministry of Education issued the book. The textbook was cheaply printed. It was barely one hundred pages thick, filled with many typos. The contents contained disconnected, complicated passages on "relevant" topics like Queen Elizabeth II's Diamond Jubilee. It used antiquated or rarely used words like "furlough." The books were more hindrance than tool for English-language learners. These issues probably didn't concern the textbook's author, a person named T. Ayapova. Nevertheless, I tried my hardest to make do with the textbook.

As I flipped through the textbook, trying to lesson plan and adapt its contents for practicality, I came to the unit after the Diamond Jubilee, a lesson on the Aral Sea. It appeared that Ayapova was an environmentalist, in addition to being an expert on Her Majesty.

I began reading: "The Aral Sea was the fourth largest lake in the world. The former seabed is now a salt desert... The dying Aral Sea is one of the world environmental disasters."

The Aral Sea piqued my interest during lesson planning. It was a topic more relevant to my students than anything else contained in the textbook. The topic actually had to do with Kazakhstan! I began doing more research on the topic, and I tried to figure out how to adapt the materials to my students' limited English comprehension.

I began delving deeper and deeper into the topic. I started to possess a strange, obsessive fascination with the Sea. I read more about it, beyond the brief chapter in Ayapova's textbook. I talked about it to locals and other volunteers. I needed to learn more. I even dreamt about it...

One day a visceral voice deep down inside of me echoed: *Go to the Sea while you are in Kazakhstan! While you can! While it still exists!*

The Sea was a phantasm that I needed to put to form, so I began planning. Visiting the Sea would not be an easy task. Even in Kazakhstan the Sea was a distant apparition. Most Kazakhstanis only knew a little about it, and even fewer ever visited. None of the locals in my village could direct me along the right path to get there. An expedition to the Sea required time and patience, as well as a bit of mental and physical endurance. After all, the journey from Yavlenka in northern Kazakhstan to the Sea in the far southwest was a fifteen-hundred-mile forty-five-hour trip by train. The epic journey would take me through never-ending steppe and inhospitable desert.

During *Nauryz*, the Kazakh new year celebration in March, the time had finally come to go to the Sea. I needed to get out of my village. The second winter of service had been particularly rough on my spirits. The winter had been bitterly cold and lonely. I had also just ended my brief affair with Aizere. The Sea offered me a way to escape the cold north. The Sea offered me a chance to forget Aizere. Most importantly, it offered me an adventure to explore the unknown.

I collected my team of three other volunteers. Our small crew would soon be some of the very few Peace Corps volunteers to ever venture to the remote region of the Sea. Since we served in different parts of Kazakhstan, we met in the southern city of Shymkent, a junction on the train line between Bishkek and Moscow.[35]

The Evil Eye

It was a dark, rainy night at the station in Shymkent. Jose, Jonathan, Carolina and I waited for our train to arrive from Bishkek. We sat talking in the cavernous lobby of the station, giddy with the notion we were venturing into the unknown.

---

[35] Bishkek is the capital of Kyrgyzstan.

Climate Change

The other passengers waiting in the lobby heard the echo of our talk and laughter. They stared and looked at the strange foreigners with curiosity.

Our American guises and bizarre jibber jabber ultimately attracted the scorn of a wrinkly down-and-out beggar wandering through the station. This old woman approached us with her leathery hands held out.

"*Dengi!*" she demanded with great vehemence. "*Dengi!*"

"Money? *Nyet,*" replied Jose tersely. "*Nyet dengi.*"

Of course, this was a lie. We all had money in our pockets, but we needed to save it for our journey into the wilderness, where ATMs would be far and few between.

"*Hiiiisssss!*" hissed the woman. "*Hiiiisssss!*"

She stepped backwards away from us hissing, casting the evil eye upon us.

She chanted a mysterious, unintelligible curse to our faces: "You will find nothing but desolation at the dying Sea. *Hiiiisssss! Hiiiisssss!* You will only find your own graves..."

We laughed to ourselves as the woman wandered off to go bother other passengers in the lobby. Every so often her evil eye wandered towards us with disdain.

"Will is gettin' kicked out of the Peace Corps," started up Carolina in her southern drawl.

Will was a volunteer stationed near Almaty. He had planned to be on the trip to the Sea with us, but he mysteriously canceled on us at the last minute.

"Is that why he bailed on the trip?" I asked. "He was quiet when I tried to confirm if he was joining. He was secretive."

"He's always secretive," stated Carolina. "That's why I took his place and joined y'all! Anyways, he wouldn't have even been able to come. Sasser is makin' an example of him, Will that is. He's gettin' kicked out of Peace Corps as we speak!"

Gossip! I thought. *There's nothing better than Peace Corps intrigue, and Carolina will be able to give the inside scoop.*

"Aren't you and Will dating?" asked Jonathan.

"Were." She replied tersely.

"What?" I asked.

"We *were* datin' until this Sasser th'ang came up."

"Tell us the story." I demanded.

"Do tell!" interrupted Jonathan.

"First of all, he was never in his village," laughed Carolina. "Always at my place, and when he wasn't in the city with me, who knows where he was. I guess he stopped showin' up to work, and his host family never knew where he went off."

"He went AWOL." I stated.

"He certainly did. I think Peace Corps had their suspicions, but Sasser caught him at the wedding," explained Carolina, referencing another volunteer's recent marriage to a local girl. "All the volunteers in the area were at the wedding, and so was all the Peace Corps staff. We all put in leave log, especially knowin' staff would be there, well, except Will didn't. He saw Sasser at the wedding and didn't even leave log, the easiest th'ang to do!"

She was right. Leave log was one of the easiest of the Peace Corps' protocols to follow. Leave log was the way the Peace Corps tracked where volunteers went around Kazakhstan—a simple rule to keep volunteers safe and accounted for. We were required to leave log if we spent the night anywhere outside our assigned sites. We simply texted the Peace Corps security office each time we left site. Simple as that, but some volunteers chafed under the requirement. They felt that it was too much "Big Brother." As adults, they felt they shouldn't have to report their where-abouts. Nevertheless, we signed up for the service. We had to follow their regulations. The Peace Corps' intentions were good, after all. Safety and security of their volunteers—especially in a country as vast, and sometimes dangerous, as Kazakhstan—was of the utmost importance.

Climate Change

"Sounds like Will was pulling stunts volunteers used to do in the nineteen seventies," stated Jose.

"What do you mean?" I asked.

"In the seventies, volunteers were infamous for leaving their sites for weeks at a time," explained Jose. "They would drive Peace-Corps-issued motorcycles to parties in the middle-of-nowhere and drink and do drugs. Some crashed and died."

"*BLYAAAAAT!*" screamed the woman from across the train station, glancing at our group with her glaring evil gaze.

"I think that means it's time to catch the train." I said.

We escaped the woman's malice and her evil eye when we boarded the Bishkek-Moscow express.

Our destination: Middle-of-Nowhere, Kazakhstan—a town called Aralsk, fifteen hours from Shymkent.

While we prepared our bunks for bed, our train sped out of the city limits. We were chasing the Sea...

Fish without a Sea

We woke several hours later as the sun began to rise over the flat landscape. Our train slowly chugged through the desolate Kyzylkum Desert. Every so often we passed a lonely homestead. I measured the distance not in miles, but by how many times the immigration police came by our bunks to check our passports and visas. Luckily, they didn't try to shake us down for a bribe as was a popular pastime for the police. Our train slowed as it approached a lonely city with dusty collapsing factories—crumbling monuments of the not-so-distant Soviet past. They looked dystopian and derelict, bleak and dreary.

A rotund elderly woman wearing some traditional Kazakh garb—a velvety night-gown-looking dress and a loose shawl covering her devout Muslim head—passed through our wagon to sell stinky dried fish. Where she got these fish in a parched land with no water was a mystery to us. As she cradled the dried fish over her arms, she grinned with a smile of gaps and missing teeth. One gold tooth shone brightly.

"*Riba, riba!*" She quacked in her high-pitched Russian.

She stopped at our bunks. She expected us to buy her pungent cargo, though we showed her no interest.

"*Riba, riba!*" repeated the woman, holding her suffocating goods towards our faces. "Feeesh!" She attempted English.

"*Nyet, spasibo.* No, no fish, please," replied Jose. His face was closest to the mass of fish shoved towards our direction.

"*Riba!* Feeesh goood!" exclaimed the woman, smiling at us with her gold tooth.

"*Nyet, spasibo,*" replied Jose again.

As a group, we politely smiled at the woman, rejecting her offer. A smiling rejection was an unfamiliar American mannerism in Kazakhstan, but she understood. She continued down the long train...

"*Riba, riba! Riba, riba! Riba, riba...*"

Hours continued to roll by while we glided down the tracks through the desert. There was nothing but sand and desolation for miles to see until we finally steamed into lonely Aralsk. The sun was beginning to set.

At the station, we were met by our fixer in Aralsk. Our contact worked for a local organization that took scientists and journalists to the Sea. He arranged our home stay for the next two nights, and he set up our driver and vehicle to get out to the Sea the following day.

Climate Change

Ghost Town

While we walked through Aralsk's train station, I admired a beautiful large mosaic hanging on the wall. This piece of Soviet art glorified the state and attested to the splendor of Aralsk. The mosaic depicted fishermen standing on docks overlooking a vast sea. Red banners flew in the breeze. Lenin's head surreally floated over the scene, watching over the proletariat like God. It was a socialist paradise, a utopia conjured by the leaders of the October Revolution.[36] It depicted Aralsk's heyday when it was the largest port on the north shore of the Sea.

The moment we stepped onto the street outside of the station, we saw the true Aralsk, a skeleton of a city. It was neither prosperous nor glorious, neither paradise nor utopia. Lenin and the Soviet Union had left the town to die a long time ago. Aralsk was a dirty, trashy town of 30,000 people. The main drag was muddy and potholed. Every other building was boarded-up and looked abandoned. A once-elegant four-story hotel overlooked the harbor. The hotel was rundown and falling apart. Swamp coolers hung perilously from the hotel's windows as if they were just about to fall and smash onto the street below. Next to the hotel was the former

---

[36] During the October Revolution (November 7, 1917), the communist Bolsheviks led an armed *coup* in Petrograd (St. Petersburg). They overthrew the provisional government of Russia, which had overthrown the Russian tsar eight months prior.

harbor extending along a dry seabed. Plastic bags blew in the wind across the waterless harbor like tumbleweeds. Old canneries were crumbling and collapsing. Rusty docking cranes were turned with their backs to what was once water. Three corroded ships with graffiti all over their hulls had been pulled up onto the embankment. They were all but empty shells, standing motionless in the wind.

Posters of President Nursultan A. Nazarbaev dotted the main road in Aralsk. The posters depicted the president as a provider and giver to his people. One poster showed the leader turning on a water faucet, allegorically bringing water back to the Sea. These posters seemed unreal and inappropriate. They were lies broadcast from the state put into ostentatious propaganda. It was obvious that the town was dying slowly of a horrible, terminal cancer, but no one from the government wanted to admit the truth to this poor patient.

While we walked through Aralsk, a surreal feeling overcame me. Surreal? Yes. It was one of the weirdest places I have ever visited. Sad? Yes. The town was largely a dump. That was for sure, but there was still a glimmer of life in the town. At first it felt as though we existed separately from Aralsk. It was like we were walking amongst ghosts. It was a place that the greater world outside of Aralsk tried to "un-see," pretend it didn't exist. Yet, we began to see it. We began to see them.

As we continued to explore Aralsk, the people became less like apparitions to us. They manifested themselves through their humanity. They became real and alive, flesh and blood.

Climate Change

Elderly Kazakh men wearing old suits and Muslim skullcaps gathered in front of cafés chatting about their daily happenings. A middle-aged woman herded sheep down the street. A teenage boy whipped his cow home from the pasture. A young man was washing his new BMW from a water pump on the street.

During our walk through Aralsk, we gradually became a part of their world. To put this surreal experience best, we crossed over and entered Aralsk's reality. Crossing over wasn't difficult. After all, four Americans walking around Aralsk, a city seldom visited by Westerners, caused a commotion among the locals. We were alien, exotic and bizarre—anything but quotidian.

Small children followed us around town. They asked us questions and shook our hands. Two young teenage girls giggled at us as we passed by them. A caravan of young tuxedoed men driving polished cars slammed on their brakes when they saw our group walking down the road. They were heading to a wedding. They wanted us to give them an American blessing for a prosperous marriage. We obliged.

Though the Sea was gone from Aralsk, people somehow continued on with their lives. They hung on to whatever dignity they could still muster, and they lived life with the rights entitled to every human being on this planet.

Hospitality

We checked into our homestay that evening. A Kazakh family rented out rooms and provided food to foreigners visiting the Sea. Our house was clean. Kazakhstanis were meticulous in keeping their homes clean. There was little furniture in the house. Couches were used as beds for visitors while the family slept on thin mats on the floor.

The family was a young one. The father was a husky man in his early thirties. He was a watchman at Aralsk's train station. The mother was in her late twenties. She was traditional in her dress and manner, yet, curious to learn more about her foreign visitors. The parents had a daughter. She was a shy six-year-old. She took to Carolina as the two began to play with each other.

"*Krasivye volocy*," repeated the daughter while she played with Carolina's blonde hair. "*Krasivye volocy*."

Her curiosity with Carolina's hair made it obvious to us how the girl didn't see many blonde women in Aralsk.

The family showed us all the hospitality dictated by Kazakh culture. The first night we ate dinner with the family. We sat on the floor with pillows cushioning us, and we ate at a *dastarkhan*. The mother laid out before us Uzbek *plov* (rice and lamb pilaf with raisins and carrots). We shared the *plov* from the same bowl in the center of the table. The American guests ate with forks while our hosts ate with their hands.

"*Tost!*" bellowed the father. "*Druzya pyut vmeste*." *Friends drink together.*

To friendship! He was insistent that we drink quickly to our new friendship. Glasses clinked and drinks went down. The father poured each of us another shot.

"*Za zdravie!*" slurred the father. *To health!*

The cultural barriers between the family and their American guests were torn down with each successive and customary toast. And with each successive shot of alcohol, the conversation loosened up and the words began to flow. We talked about families and friends, dreams and aspirations. Russian. English. Kazakh. It didn't matter what language we used. We understood each other.

An inebriated father began doing much of the talking. He explained to us that most people in Aralsk were too poor to move away. He explained the soil of the area was too salty and dry to grow most crops. There were some shepherds and camel herdsmen left in the area, but small-scale husbandry didn't bring in much profit. Since the fishing industry collapsed in the late 1980s, schools, hospitals and other governmental services were the only things keeping the town afloat. He alluded that Aralsk had a problem with mafia-like gangs, only compounding the town's predicament.

Towards the end of the night, he mentioned the Aral Sea dam. This highly controversial dam was recently built at the confluence of the Syr-Darya and the North Aral Sea to save what was left of the Sea in Kazakhstan. It kept the North Aral Sea from completely evaporating into oblivion. The water had returned within thirteen miles of Aralsk. The dam was a catch twenty-two. While there was a glimmer of hope for the north, the dam condemned the Greater Aral Sea in Uzbekistan to evaporate into a desert oblivion.

Even with the best scenarios provided by the dam, the father seemed to lament that the Sea was gone forever.

"*Za moré!*" cried our host. *To the Aral Sea!*

We took one last drink in honor of the dying Sea.

"The Sea is dying..."

Our group was ready to venture onward to the Sea. We bought groceries from a shop for a seaside picnic. We met our driver, loaded up the car and headed out of town in our jeep.

The old asphalt road quickly dissolved away once we passed under the rusty metal arch welcoming tired travelers to Aralsk. The road was in horrible condition, and we violently bounced about the vehicle. We passed by abandoned apartments a mile outside of Aralsk. Like ghastly phantoms, they stood haunting the lonely steppe. In the distance past the apartment blocks, we saw the desolation that once formed the seashore.

Our drive from Aralsk to the Sea lasted about two hours. We passed the village with the burly camel and the children playing in the streets. We passed the Kazakh cemeteries. We passed the old shepherd guarding over his flock. We passed the skeletons of ships in the desert. They were strewn across the desert like an archipelago.

We sped at ever greater speeds along the flat seafloor, driving for miles and miles. We drove over scraggly bushes, and we traversed over sand dunes.

We pushed on until suddenly our driver slammed on the brakes. Our driver did not say a word, but we knew we had arrived at the Sea.

It was disorienting being at the bottom of a once-expansive body of water. Except for small cliffs a couple miles behind us, everything was flat. We could not immediately see the water from where we were parked.

A cold strong breeze blew.

We grabbed the picnic food and walked into the wind. We clambered over small dunes and bushes. We cautiously approached the strange void ahead of us—a chasm to the center of the world, a black-hole of inescapable power.

We walked for several hundred feet until we saw a mirage-like image of water. The water appeared like a mirror reflecting the inclement clouds hovering above. We walked further along, losing sight of the car behind us before we confirmed that the mirage was no mirage. It was indeed the object of our desires.

At that moment of realization, we began running towards the water with fervor and excitement. After such a long and tiring journey, we had finally arrived at the water's edge. What had begun so many years ago with the planting of a seed in Mr. Clemens' class had finally come to fruition. Here it was before us, the Aral Sea.

We came to the muddy shore. One hundred feet from the spot where we stood extended a line where the surf broke. Beyond the break was an immense body of water. From where we stood the Sea stretched on forever, but it did not. Beyond our view were newly formed deserts encroaching on the Sea.

While the Sea was still remarkable in size, its former self must have been a goliath. The Sea had once stretched for hundreds of miles, from Aralsk in the north to Karakalpakstan in the south. It was truly amazing to witness firsthand the power by which man can play God and alter his environment, manipulate the physics of the world. The Sea was a testament to the power by which humans could turn something that provides sustenance and life into a barren waste.

The wind picked up as we stood in awe at the water's edge. Seagulls flew overhead. They were attempting to escape a fast-approaching storm coming over the water.

We sat down and quickly ate a modest picnic of cheese and bread. Cold wind blew dirt into the food, filling every bite with grit and sand.

After finishing our meal, we stood in a circle, uneasily looking at each other. We had a five-liter bottle of water with us, so we ceremoniously poured the water from the plastic bottle onto the dry ground. We silently stood looking down at the small mucky puddle of water which now formed at our feet. We glanced at the landscape around.

The wind howled. A storm approached. Birds flew, escaping the storm's path.

"Ayapova was right," exclaimed Jose, nervously breaking our group's silence. His voice was muffled by the howling wind. "The Sea is dying."

No one responded. Instead, we all turned and walked back to the car, occasionally peeking back at the Sea we left behind.

We left what remained of the Aral Sea, and the ships lying in their sandy tombs, and the old shepherd tending his herd, and the lonely cemeteries honoring the dead, and the neglected village with children playing in dusty streets, and Aralsk with our gracious Kazakh hosts. We departed that distant, lonely, forgotten corner of the planet, and we went back to the world from which we came.

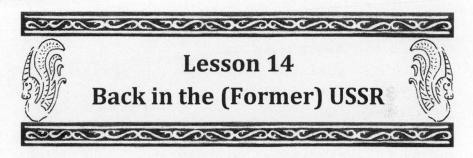

Lesson 14
Back in the (Former) USSR

Vladimir Vysotsky

Sam and I cautiously approached the bus station in his village. We learned in our time in Kazakhstan that you had to sneak into train and bus stations. Otherwise, you'd be attacked by a line of men loitering outside the station's doors. Gypsy taxis were what we called them—entrepreneurial-minded, and often cash-strapped, men who charged outrageous prices for rides in beat-up vehicles.

Sam's village had been one of many stops on my summer tour around Kazakhstan and beyond. By mid-summer, I had already spent much of it away from Yavlenka. I traveled from one volunteer-led camp, like the one Sam, a Kaz 20, organized, to another. The work helped fill the downtime of summer after school closed down on May 25. I spent much of my summer also using some of the forty-eight vacation days Peace Corps allowed during service by traveling out of the country—three weeks in Ukraine and Kyrgyzstan.

A Five Finger Feast

Sam and I were on to our next job via Petro, an outdoor-adventure and English-language camp somewhere in Middle-of-Nowhere, Kazakhstan. Our friend Simon organized it.

"Success!" spouted Sam. "Too easy sneaking by the drivers. There's a bus at four o'clock, so let's get tickets for that one."

We approached the kiosk to purchase our fare. It would be ₸350 (about four dollars) for the two-hour bus ride to Petro.

"*Dva*," said Sam as he held out two fingers and handed the attendant a wad of cash for two tickets. "Petropavlovsk."

"*Nyet, avtobusa nyet*," replied the worker, a middle-aged woman with a perm and maroon-colored hair. *No bus.*

"*Nyet*?" asked Sam, trying to understand why there wasn't a bus at the usual departure time. "No bus?" questioned Sam as he turned to me.

"*Nyet!*" confirmed the woman. "*Avtobusa nyet.*"

The attendant turned away, disinterested in the conversation. She began filing papers in a cabinet behind the kiosk.

"*Pochemu*?" I asked why, trying to get her attention back.

The woman glanced scornfully back at us with a disdainful, un-answering look.

We walked away.

"I don't know what her problem is," stated Sam.

"There's no problem." I replied. "That's the Soviet way."

"It's that mentality that I hate," laughed Sam. "Waste time and money. No customer service, and there's no efficiency, because that's just how it's done."

"So, no bus." I stated.

"*Avtobusa nyet*," mimicked Sam. "And the train to Petro won't be here for several hours. Let's go to plan B, gypsy cab."

We wandered back outside from the bus station. The drivers moved in like wolves feasting on a fawn. While the woman in the station reflected the Soviet mentality of Kazakhstani economics, these men demonstrated what truly ruled: money. There was an art to negotiating with gypsy cabs that Sam and I hadn't quite perfected. Drivers shouted at us and tried to pull us to their cars. They argued amongst themselves to undercut or inflate prices.

One Kazakh man stood to the side, though, leaning against his car, smoking a cigarette coolly. He nodded at me with his wrinkly face and greying hairs, motioning me to come over to him. I stumbled to the driver and his slightly beat-up BMW sedan. Sam remained behind trying to negotiate with three screaming taxi drivers.

"Petro?" I asked the man.

"I go Petropavlovsk."

He spoke English to my surprise. It was rare to find an English speaker in the village.

"You really speak English?"

"*Da*," replied the man as he took one last drag on his cigarette and flicked it to the ground. "I *really* speak English. Live in Seee-ttaaal, Vaaashington—ninety-nine to two thousand six. You know Seeettaaal, Kurt Cobain, Nirvanaaah?"

"Never been." I replied.

"Amerikaaan?" He asked. "I can see it. Your friend too."

He pointed to Sam, who was still haggling with the other cab drivers. The man chuckled and shook his head.

"*O bozhe moy*," laughed the man. *Oh my god.* "We do not see foreigners here. I mean we have people from Russiaaah, but not true foreigners. They think they trick your friend into paying big money for drive."

"I give you both ride for cheap, ₸500 each. I already go to Petro anyways. Deal?"

The driver put out his hand. I reached back and shook it.

"Deal. Sam!" I shouted at my friend who was still being swarmed by cabbies. "I got us a cheap ride to Petro!"

"Why are you here?" asked the man as we waited for Sam to break free of the pack.

"Here? In the village?" I asked.

"*Da*, *nu*, Kazakhstaaan?"

"Peace Corps, *Korpusa Mira*. Have you heard of it?"

"*O bozhe moy*! My friend in Seeettaaal left for Peace Corps in two thousand one. He go to Afrikaaah. I not know Peace Corps, I mean *Korpusa Mira*, in Kazakhstaaan. We poor, I guess, third world. Don't believe what President Nazarbaev says, we third world." The man chuckled while Sam stumbled up to us.

"This is..." I trailed off since I hadn't caught the man's name.

"Call me Charlie. My Kazakh name sound like Charlie, so that is what my friends in Seeettaaal call me. Give me your bags."

Charlie packed our bags into the trunk. Sam and I sat in the back seats. The seatbelts had been tucked deep into the crack of the cushions with no way to secure them to our laps. Charlie got into the driver's seat and started the car.

The Russian singer Vladimir Vysotsky's deep smoker's voice and acoustic guitar blasted from the car speakers.[37]

"Sorry," apologized Charlie. "I love Vysotsky," said our driver as he turned down the music's volume. "You know Vysotsky? He Soviet Bob Dylan. More populaaar than Secretary Brezhnev in nineteen seventies.[38] Amerikaaan not know Vysotsky, but we love Vysotsky. Rest in peace..."

"I've listened to him before!" I told Charlie.

"*O bozhe moy*! You know him? I love Vysotsky. Vysotsky got me through war. You know war in Afghanistaaan?"

"Yes, we know," replied Sam.

"Not war with Taliban and America. I talk about Soviet war—the first war in Afghanistaaan."

"Yes, we know." I affirmed.

"Smart Amerikaaan! I was there, eighty-seven to eighty-nine. Two year."

---

[37] Vladimir Vysotsky (1938-80) was a Soviet-era musician and dissident.
[38] Leonid Brezhnev (1906-82) was leader of the Soviet Union from 1964-82.

"My host father was there too." I interjected. "Don't know what years, though."

"Host father?" chuckled Charlie. "He good man to host an Americaaan in his house. He is Kazakh? Soviet army like using us Muslimaaans from Kazakhstaaan and Kyrgyzstaaan. We fight Afghaaan, although we Muslimaaan brothers. Koraaan forbid, but Lenin permit!"

The car left the station parking lot.

"Tim was just in Kyrgyzstan," explained Sam.

"*O bozhe moy*! I had many friend from Kyrgyzstaaan. I know them in Afghanistaaan, but..."

"But?" empathized Sam naively.

"They stay in Afghanistaaan," trailed off Charlie.

He turned up the volume on the car stereo. Vysotsky sang louder and louder—something about alcoholism, a common theme for the dissident singer. With the volume of the music increased, the car became silent. It seemed as if our talk about Afghanistan had touched a note with our chauffeur.

Our car turned onto the main highway that ran from the Russian border, through the village, and onto Petro. We sped faster and faster, with the village's famed pride, a ten-story grain silo, getting smaller and smaller in the rearview mirror.

The lack of conversation reminded me to pull out my journal. I kept good notes on my recent trip to Kyrgyzstan and Ukraine. I had been meaning to write home about the journey before we headed off to Middle-of-Nowhere, Kazakhstan. Maybe in Petro we'd be able to get to a computer and email. I opened my journal. I had filled up half the small book with travel notes. I began to read through it.

Bicycles

June 29, 2009 – An apartment in Almaty, Kazakhstan – Waiting for our Kyrgyzstani visas

"We were supposed to go to China," I said, "but the Chinese

rejected our visa app. Swine Flu scare, Uyghur unrest in Ürumqi or something.[39] We never got the story. Jonathan and I went to Ukraine instead. It was the cheapest place to fly, last minute, without visas."

"Ukre'en, we'll be 'en Ukre'en 'en two m'enths," said the Kiwi. "Don't w'erry about Ch'ena! You don't want to go there," affirmed the New Zealander. "Their feed 'es *sheeet*! K'ez'ekhst'en has betta feed."

"Arrgreed," replied the Irishman.

He had been quiet for most of the conversation, but food seemed to strike the gaunt Irishman's fancy.

"Haaar yee haff milk and cheese," continued the Irishman.

"Right, 'en Asiya they j'est have rice," interrupted the Kiwi. "I mean in Ch'ena they j'est have b'ewl after b'ewl 'ef rice. You've also ge' meat here—very l'ecky!"

"Do we have meat!" laughed Jonathan with a delightful smirk on his face. "Have you guys tried *our* national dish of Kazakhstan, *Beshbarmak*? If you like meat, you'll love *beshbarmak*."

"C'en you ge' it 'et the Green B'ezaar?" asked the Kiwi.[40]

"Maybe, probably you can," replied Dylan. "The bazaar is like the Walmart of Central Asia."

"We don't have W'elm'ert where 'em fr'em," laughed the Kiwi, "but I assume you ge' pretty m'ech 'ell you'd need there. I'll look f'er this *pisssh-ba-mark* or wheteva' 'et's called 'et the b'ezaar. 'Ef 'et is meaty, I'll take 'et."

All this talk of the national dish of Kazakhstan prompted me to go to the stove top and get a second helping of noodles. Ironically, we had made *lagman*—the national dish of the Muslims of Western China, the Uyghurs. It was a spicy, noodly, oily,

---

[39] The H1N1 (Swine Flu) pandemic occurred from Jan. 2009 to August 2010. Uyghurs are a predominately Muslim ethnicity in western China. Uyghur protests against the Chinese government took place in the summer 2009.
[40] The Green Bazar (*Zelenyy Bazar*) is a large market in central Almaty.

meaty stir fry. Our guests loved it.

We met the Kiwi, the Irishman and an American girl earlier that day while waiting in line at the Kyrgyzstan embassy. We had arrived at noon to get visas to Kazakhstan's southern neighbor, but the guard on duty said it was the lunch break and to return in an hour. When we came back from lunch, we were turned away from the embassy again. They processed new visas only in the mornings starting at eight in the morning.

As we walked away from the embassy, we ran into the trio. They too were trying to enter Kyrgyzstan on a biking trip across Eurasia. They too were frustrated by the inefficient process of receiving visas in Central Asia.

"It's *besh-bar-mak*. Not *pisssh-ba-mark*," clarified Jonathan to the Kiwi. "It's an acquired taste but has lots of meat."

"I'll take 'et," said the Kiwi. "We've been protein deprived f'er two m'enths. That's h'ew l'eng 'et took to bike through Ch'ena."

"I've been hardest hit," chimed in the American girl. "I lost so much weight there. This beer is going to my head, by the way."

The girl took a sip from a bottle of Baltika 7.

Jonathan, Dylan and I had invited the trio to our rented Almaty apartment to help school these cyclists on Central-Asian culture and etiquette.

"You g'eys are Peace Corps, *eeeh*?" asked the Kiwi. "You're roughing 'et here. Respect to you! Nothing like h'ew we lived 'en Korea, where we had cars and l'exuries."

"We had all been English teachers near Seoul for about four or five years each," explained the American.

"Well, it sounds like you guys are the ones really roughing it now," said Dylan. "Tell us about your trip."

"Where to st'ert?" exclaimed the Kiwi. "We've been 'en K'ez'ekhst'en f'er five days—cr'essed the border somewhere near T'eldeee Koorg'en. That was a big hassle. The Ch'enese and K'ez'ekhst'eni border guards hate each 'ether. And before we spent two m'enths riding through Ch'ena."

"Where are you headed?" I asked.

"To 'Ereland," responded the Kiwi. "We're t'eking our friend here back to 'Ereland. Send him home 'en style."

The redheaded Irishman nodded in agreement.

"If we hadn't found you Peace Corps," continued the Kiwi, "we'd be 'en a real bind. There were no English speakers 'et the K'ergeez consulate. We need to get 'ento K'ergeez so we can ge' to the Azerb'ejani emb'essy 'en B'eshkek f'er Azerb'ejani visas. We need to do this 'en five days, and then to the Ferg'ena Valley and T'eshkent. Then we cross a couple deserts to catch a ferry on the C'espian Sea back 'en K'ez'ekhs'ten. We need to do this before our K'ez'ekhst'en visas run out 'ef time."

"Less t'an t'irty days," chimed in the Irishman.

"Why not just get the visa to Azerbaijan in Kazakhstan?"[41]

"Ha!" laughed the trio in unison.

"The Azerb'ejani emb'essy 'en K'ez'ekhst'en 'es over one thous'end kilometers north 'en 'Est'ena. Try biking that, so 'et is K'ergeez 'en five days!"

"Sounds like an adventure," said Jonathan.

"Would've been crazier 'ef we could get 'ento 'Eran." The Kiwi maintained most of the conversation as the American girl and Irishman continued to drink and eat. "We had a C'en'edian member, but the b'est'erd went 'ehead 'ef us. He wanted to go 'ento 'Eran, but we can't ge' 'en with our 'Emeric'en—and we can't leave her behind."

The American girl smiled and took another sip of beer. It was now quite noticeable that she was a lightweight.

The morning would be filled with a slog of headaches for her and her biking friends in order to get visas into Kyrgyzstan. Hungover or not, we had all discovered the bureaucratic mess

---

[41] Azerbaijan is a former Soviet republic on the Caspian Sea.

of travel through Central Asia.

Alcoholic

"Much of Kyrgyzstaaan friend, they drink," shouted Charlie over the Vysotsky song. "Help get through war in Afghanistaaan. All Soviet men drink, much alcohol. Help get through life."

We moved steadily down the north Kazakhstan highway at a fast clip. Birch-tree and pine forests blurred, only to come into focus as we slowed down to roll through potholes.

"Vysotsky, he alcoholic. Sad end for him. I no drink," clarified Charlie as he flicked his neck. "I no true Muslimaaan, but I no drink—only tea and, of course, coffee! Thank you to Seeettaaal!"

Charlie pulled a cigarette from his shirt pocket and lit it. Sam coughed in passive-aggressive disapproval.

"Soviet men drink too much! It no good," continued our driver. "Death come early for men here, maybe sixty. Across border in Russiaaah it worse. Maybe it fiffy-eight or fiffy-nine. Alcohol do it. You live in villages. They're worse than cities. Afghanistaaan so bad too."

It was true. The life expectancy of men in the former Soviet Union was low, and it dipped to record lows in the late nineties when the economic situation was dismal. While the cities were bad for encountering drunks—in the cities they were often present in café life—villages had a different insidiousness to alcoholism. There were the men who drank themselves to death in their decrepit, dirty hovels, or the men who fell over drunk and passed out outside in the freezing winter temps. It was all too real in the villages.

"In the war, didn't they stop soldiers from drinking?" asked Sam naively.

"*O bozhe moy*! Soviets try, but no luck. Soviets were useless, but Putin change attitude now. He like me and no drink. Role model for man—tough, sportsman, clever. Soviet men idolize."

"Putin, *Time Magazine*'s 'Person of the Year'." I stated.

"I see this. He strong man, this true, and this why 'Man of the Year.' Maybe good for Russiaah, maybe good for Kazakhstaaan."

"He's also a dictator," said Sam.

"You smart, Amerikaaan! He true rule Russiaah, not this new man, President Medvedev, and he own all news in Russiaah."[42]

"Over a year ago," I started, "I was watching TV with my host father, the one who fought in Afghanistan. Putin held a press conference at the Kremlin, and he had Medvedev there next to him. I asked my host father what was happening, and he explained that this was the 'new president' of Russia."

"Continue," interrupted Charlie, staring at me in the rearview mirror with a smile.

"I asked him if there had been an election. I hadn't read anything about an election in the news. He said no, it will come soon, but 'what Putin *says*, *is*' in Russia."

"He smart man and he know politico!" laughed Charlie. "You Amerikaaan have it good in Amerikaaah! I know because I live there. Here we only have strong men. All them no good. Islam Karimov, Turkmenbashi, Nazarbaev, they bad, but Putin he smarter.[43] He know he must do some good to stay in power."

"What good has he done?" asked Sam. "Russia is still crap! Plus, he meddles in Kazakhstan's economy and politics, and he meddled in Georgia last year. What's next Ukraine?"

"*O bozhe moy*! My friend, you speak true! Lenin declare Soviet Union. He bad. Stalin build Soviets, but he evil. Khrushchev less bad, but alcoholic.[44] Brezhnev was stupid and alcoholic. Gorbachev, he smart and see problems. Amerikaaan love him. I

---

[42] Dmitry Medvedev was the president of Russia from 2008-2012.

[43] Islam Karimov (1938-2016) and Saparmurat Niyazov, aka Turkmenbashi (1940-2006) were the leaders of Uzbekistan and Turkmenistan.

[44] Nikita Khrushchev (1894-1971) was the leader of the Soviet Union from 1953-64.

know, because I live in Seeettall, but Soviets hate. Yeltsin alcoholic too.[45] Yeltsin destroy Soviet Union with others, like Nazarbaev and Karimov. Putin may be bad, but he make Russiaah powerful again."

"Powerful?" spouted off Sam. "What good does that bring?"

"He bring Russiaah back to world power. Sochi Olympics. It put Russiaah back on world map. It help economy. You know Sochi? It on Black Sea. I go to Black Sea, one time. I go to Ukraine in Soviet time. I love Odessa and Black Sea."

"Tim just went to Ukraine too," explained Sam. "Didn't you go to Kiev, Lviv and Odessa?"

"Yep!" I replied. "I was in Ukraine right before Kyrgyzstan."

"*O bozhe moy*! You world traveler! I fall in love with Ukrainian girl. Blonde and beautiful. She from Lvov, I mean Lviv. Now Ukraine say Lviv, don't they? We go to Odessa and Crimea, and even Sochi for 'world travel'! We made much love!"

"What happened to her?" I asked.

"We marry in nineteen-ninety! She was visiting family in Petropavlovsk. We marry. My family no like, because she no Kazakh. We move to Lvov from Kazakhstaaan, because it easier to live there than here. We travel all over Ukraine and make much love."

"Where is she today?" asked Sam.

"*O bozhe moy*... In the ground..." Charlie began to choke up. He wiped away a tear. "*SPID*... You Amerikaaan call it AIDS. She get from surgery, blood transfer from infected druggie."

HIV/AIDS was officially recognized by the Soviet Union in the late eighties, after much denial. Since then, Russia and Ukraine have been hit hard. Today Russia and Ukraine have some of the highest rates of HIV/AIDS in Europe.

"When did she die?" asked Sam tactlessly.

---

[45] Boris Yeltsin (1931-2007) was president of the Russian Federation.

"This in ninety-nine," replied Charlie. "This why I move to Seeettaall. I leave her in Lvov. She in the cemetery there and I move far, far away. I never go back..."

Roads Paved with Tears

June 23, 2009 - Wandering the city and the Lychakiv Cemetery in Lviv, Ukraine

"I still can't believe the woman at McDonald's refused to speak Russian to me," laughed Jonathan. "Come on! It's not like she could speak English to me. She had to know how to speak Russian. Every-one speaks Russian in Ukraine."

Jonathan and I had found that the farther west we went in Ukraine the trickier it became to use our Russian skills. While we were in Kiev, a huge city of two and a half million people, we could easily get by with our Russian. In Lviv, formerly called by its Russian name of Lvov, we had hit the hotbed of Ukrainian nationalism. At our hostel, bars, and even at McDonald's—a place Jonathan and I frequented on our vacation to Ukraine— people refused to communicate in Russian.

Lviv was a beautiful city. We had been wandering around the city that day, waiting to leave in the evening on the train for our next stop, Odessa.

We happened upon a cemetery while wandering. A recent rainstorm was clearing out, as late afternoon shadows were beginning to creep in on the necropolis. A cemetery sounds morbid, but the Ukrainians, as we found with much of the former Soviet Union, had a different relationship with their dead than Americans. The entrance to the cemetery was crowded with passersby and picnickers.

"I still can't believe that lady at McDonald's," continued Jonathan. "Ukraine is so funny! Such a surprise!"

Like the cemetery that we stumbled into, we were surprised by Lviv. Lviv had been an afterthought for our Ukraine trip. We landed in Kiev with ten days until departure and almost no plans in between.

In fact, Ukraine was an afterthought of a journey to a much larger planned one. Conjured by images of Marco Polo and the Great Game, we had made plans to venture into Western China, also known as Xinjiang. We would travel from Ürumqi to the fabled city of Kashgar and then into Kyrgyzstan along the old Silk Road. We had planned far ahead of our proposed departure, but the Chinese government put a stop to our plans. The reasons were unknown and unexplained to us when our travel agent returned empty passports to us. The agent still took her commission, even though her services were not rendered. A year's worth of planning had been flushed down the metaphorical Turkish toilet. With only three weeks before our planned departure, Jonathan and I decided to find the cheapest and easiest—meaning no visas needed—place to fly out of Almaty. We found Ukraine. Dylan decided he would join us for the Kyrgyzstan portion of the trip.

"Well, I'm surprised by Lviv. Who'd have known we'd be in this random, beautiful place!" I said.

"The cemetery is like a park," stated Jonathan.

It was true. The cemetery was almost like a small forest of large trees and greenery everywhere. In the cemetery, we continued to walk along the cobblestone path. We passed large, ivy-covered crypts and mossy tombstones.

While we stumbled through Ukraine, we found many surprises. This journey to Ukraine had been so random. It was truly an adventure, albeit a meandering one. Sometimes those types of journeys are the best. Journeys both near and far, allow one to begin to learn about a place and its history. One begins to discover truths, sometimes just hidden under the surface about a place's past and its people. Ukraine offered us just this. Every day, we learned more about its secrets. We began peeling away at the hidden histories of the former Soviet Union. Lviv had layers and layers of history, hidden within its people, its buildings, its roads, its graves.

Most of the tombstones and crypts in the cemetery were old, very old, at least from the nineteenth century. We noticed that the older ones had German and Polish inscriptions on them. The ones dated after World War II had Russian with black and white photographs stuck to them. The photos of very sternly looking Soviets stared at us from their places in purgatory. The newest graves had far less ivy and moss growing on them. Ukrainian inscriptions were carved on these ones.

One of the Ukrainian tombstones read: *Ще не вмерли Україна ні слава ні воля!*

"Shhh...che neee veee...merly Ooo...kraina ni sla...va ni vol...ya." I read out loud.

"Tim, that was the secret password," replied Jonathan. "the password from last night."

"What?" I was confused. "What do you mean?"

"From last night, the nationalist bar we found."

"The speakeasy!" I answered. "It was a nationalist bar?"

"Yeah, we had to say the secret password in Ukrainian to get in," continued Jonathan. "'*Shche ne vemerly Ukraina ni slava ni volya.*' 'The glory and freedom of Ukraine has not perished,' that's what it means."

It was ironic that Lviv was now the heart of Ukrainian nationalism. Ukraine, at the time of our trip in 2009, was a country that was not even twenty years old. Lviv, like much of Eastern Europe, had a changing and shifting history.

It had not always been Lviv (Львів). The city was founded by a distant Rus king, naming the town after his son, Lev. Later, the Tatars sacked the city (İlbav) in the Middle Ages, and the Lithuanians came next (Lvovas). The Polish conquered the town (Lwow) and kept it for centuries. The Ottoman Turks attempted to take it (Aslanlar), but never could. It passed to the Austrian

Habsburgs, calling it Lemberg in German. Ukrainian and Polish nationalists fought a civil war to lay claim to the city after World War I. Would the city be called Lwow or Lviv? The city went back to Lwow until the Germans returned as the Nazis (back to Lemberg). The Soviets took control after World War II. They called it Lvov (Львов). After independence in 1991, the town became Lviv. It became the seat of Ukrainian nationalism, power and contention with the eastern and ethnic Russian part of the country. A civil war in the east in 2014 and later invasion of Ukraine in 2022 was instigated by Putin, destabilizing Ukraine.

We eventually left the cemetery, and we began walking back towards our hostel to grab our bags. We had to catch our overnight train to Odessa.

"Tim, look down!" interrupted Jonathan.

"What?" I answered.

"Just look at the sidewalk!"

I slowed down. I looked down.

"What am I looking for? Did you drop something?"

"The sidewalk! Look what it is made of!"

After a second, I gasped.

To our astonishment, we were walking on headstones. They were worn down and cracked from years of people tromping and trodding down the sidewalk. Puddles of water remained from the rainstorm, pooling where the tombstone path was most worn down. Etched on them was the Star of David and Hebrew letters.

The Jews had a long history in Lviv too. (They called it Lemberik, לעמבעריק.) In Lviv, they prospered; for centuries they prospered, and their community thrived. They grew to become one third of the city's population. But Ukraine has a complicated relationship with its Jewish people and history. *Pogroms* and mass emigrations happened in the late-nineteenth and early-twentieth centuries. The Nazi's Final Solution was the culmination of their history in Lviv.

And here we were, Jonathan and me. We had found this history, and we were walking right over it. Jonathan took a particular interest in the Jewish history of Ukraine. Jonathan was Jewish. Like millions of Americans, his family emigrated from Eastern Europe a hundred years before, escaping a *pogrom*.

"The sidewalk must be from the Holocaust," claimed Jonathan. "It must be!"

"Why would they still leave them like this, sixty-five years later?" I asked. "It just seems so wrong. I mean people just walking on the tombstones as if it was a sidewalk."

"Well, it is a sidewalk," replied Jonathan.

"Just seems like they would've put them back after World War II."

"The Soviets probably didn't want to do the work," stated Jonathan. "I read somewhere that the Ukrainian nationalists at the time of the War were collaborators with the Nazis. Plus, there are probably no Jews left in Lviv to complain."

"Sad to see this part of history. Isn't it?" I asked.

"At least their history hasn't been totally wiped away," answered Jonathan. "We have something from their past."

We continued back to our hostel, where our bags and belongings were. We'd soon be on our overnight train to Odessa.

Potty Talk

"Say me, how long in Ukraine? How you find Odessa? It beautiful, no?" asked Charlie. "My wife, she love this place, the beach."

"Almost two weeks in Ukraine, but I didn't like Odessa." I replied matter-of-factly.

"*O bozhe moy*! Say me, why no like?" asked Charlie in a concerned tone.

"It was dirty. I thought it was supposed to be a nice beach town, but it was dirty."

"What? But you have Potemkin Steps, and many lovely buildings and avenues, and palm trees, and the Black Sea, and many beaches! When Soviet Union, it beautiful," affirmed Charlie. "My wife love it. I know why you do not like Odessa!"

"Why?" I asked.

"Yes, because it have much garbage! To my mind, I hear in news—Amerikaaan news. I sometimes listen still, because they do not say true in Russiaah and Kazakhstaaan news."

"It was dirty." I told Charlie. "The beaches were crowded with trash and Russian tourists."

Charlie began to chuckle.

"What is so funny?" asked Sam.

"Russian tourists! In former Soviet Union, we no take care of nature," began Charlie, "and our tourists are worst."

Even Charlie saw how his fellow citizens didn't treat their natural wonders and resources with care.

A year earlier, I discovered Kazakhstani environmental stewardship hiking to the top of Kazakhstan's most prized natural wonders, a unique rock formation at the national park at Borovoe Lake. As I climbed the steep thirty-foot formation, I stepped into a pile of human feces. Apparently, the whole rock formation was a convenient squat toilet for day hikers.

"Well, we also had just come from Lviv to Odessa." I stated. "It was a stark contrast between the two cities."

"Lviv is beautiful, no?" asked Charlie. "No garbage there, but also no Russian tourists!"

"It was an amazing city, and true, it is not very Russian-friendly." I replied.

"You take train from Lviv to Odessa?" asked Charlie.

"Yes, yes we did. Why do you ask?"

"Just curious. Soviets make very good trains. Very good system, and it put Amerikaaah system to shame."

"True," chimed in Sam. "Most don't use trains in the US."

"Yes," answered Charlie, "because Amerikaaah love cars. Soviets make good trains from Leningrad to Pacific. It reach even wilds of the Turkmen and Tajik. But Soviets and Russians and Kazakhs and Ukraine people they know how to trash a place, even trash their trains."

"Explain," asked Sam.

"You see in train, toilet have no plumbing. Toilet go straight down to ground, to train track," laughed Charlie. "We poop on our most prized possessions, our trains!"

432nd Hour

June 13, 2009 – On a train to Almaty somewhere on the steppe between Petro and Karaganda

"Where you from?" asked Oksana, a young suntanned woman from Sochi.

"*Ssss.Shuh.Ahhh.*!" I replied with "USA" in Russian.

"*Amerika*!" gasped the girl. "I no meet *Amerikanets*."

The mullet-sporting teenage Tatar boy sitting next to Oksana whispered something into the girl's ear.

"Ilsat, he say how many cars you have in *Ssss.Shuh.Ahhh.*?"

"*Pyat*! Five, at least!" I replied as I held out five fingers, smirking from my inside joke.

Ilsat gasped in amazement. The Russian girl laughed.

I was heading to Almaty from Petro to meet Jonathan at the airport. We were heading to Ukraine.

Over my two years in Kazakhstan, I had already spent days, weeks on the train. On this trip, I began totaling up the hours. I was approaching my 432nd hour of train travel in two years in Kazakhstan. The train time added up, and the trains had become an integral part of my experience in the Peace Corps. The train had been the place where I experienced Kazakhstan from all facets of its society. Every-one, rich and poor, needed to take the aging Soviet-built train system to get around the country.

To many, the trains reeked of a fading, imagined golden age

of the Soviet Union. They were the mighty diesel engines that helped industrialize and unify the Soviet man, expanding his communist utopian dream. That dream ended in 1991, but the trains did not. The trains kept running, because they were the webs that connected the remotely populated and vast nations of the former Soviet Union.

Because the train held an utmost importance in Kazakhstani society, it was a place where I learned about Kazakhstan as much as Kazakhstan learned about me. I met all types of travelers—most wanting to get to know the strange foreigner sitting in the bunk next to theirs.

In the beginning of my service, the Peace Corps paid for volunteers to travel by second class, *kupey*. These were cramped stuffy four-bed compartments that could be closed off from the main hall outside by a sliding door. They were reminiscent of 1960s James Bond movies. Midway through my service the Peace Corps changed their policies for the trains. They would only pay for *platzkart*, the equivalent of third class. *Platzkart* was not only cheaper than *kupey*, but ironically more comfortable. The open floor plan of *platzkart* wagons allowed more airflow than stuffy *kupey*. It allowed travelers to stretch out their legs and meet fellow travelers in the bunks nearby.

This is how I met my current travel company: Oksana, Ilsat and Vanya.

"*Amerikanets*," interjected Vanya, "*vy zhenati*?"

Vanya was the archetypal villager. Rough with dark, tan skin from working outside. Piercing blue eyes. Chiseled high cheekbones. Bad teeth caused by smoking and poor dental hygiene.

"You... ahhh... marry wife?" Oksana translated Vanya's culturally ubiquitous question.

This curious group asked all the questions typically asked to volunteers. Are you married? If not, then why aren't you going to bring one of *our* beautiful girls back to the States to marry her? Why are you in Kazakhstan if you are not looking for a wife to take home? Are you a spy then? What's your spy salary? Do you have any American money you can show us? How much does a car cost in America? How many cars do you own? How many cars do Hollywood actors typically own? Speaking of Hollywood stars, do you know any movie stars? Did you know actors can become politicians in America? Have you ever seen the governor of California, Arnold Schwarzenegger? Did you know the Governator is not a "true" American, because he is a foreigner? Did you know Obama is a "foreigner" too? You do realize your president is a black man, yes? The group asked me the all questions expected to be asked to an American riding *platzkart* in Kazakhstan.

As the funny and absurd questioning subsided, we shared food, drink and conversation into *our* night on the train *together*. For these few hours, my three train companions adopted me into their world—expanding their cultural horizons, and vice versa, mine.

The next morning, the train chugged into the city of Karaganda, and my new *platzkart* friends disembarked. They headed back into their own worlds outside the one we had shared on our train ride.

In Karaganda, I knew I only had a few minutes to make the meeting before the train would continue on. I got off the train and pushed my way through the busy crowd of porters and passengers to meet my host sister, Ülkenapa.

Ülkenapa had left Yavlenka the previous summer to attend college in Karaganda.

I texted her the night before, letting her know I'd be passing through the next morning.

"Helloo Timati!" waved Ülkenapa through the hectic crowd.

"Me so happy see you," smiled Ülkenapa with glee. "Me pleez to see you!"

"I am so happy to see you too!" I exclaimed. "Thanks for meeting me on short notice, I just wanted to say 'hello.'"

"My... my aunt make food at home. Come, pleez," commanded Ülkenapa with a smile.

"I can't." I tried to explain, pointing to the train.

"Timati, where you *bagazh*?" interrupted Ülkenapa.

"Baggage? It is on the train." I replied.

"*Pochemu*? Why? You no stay in Karaganda?"

I realized at that moment we were lost in translation. Ülkenapa thought I was going to stay the night and visit her and her family.

"No, I am going to Almaty. I am flying out of the country for vacation. I texted you because I wanted to see you and say 'hello.' Also, I leave Kazakhstan in a couple months, and I want to say 'goodbye' before I leave."

Ülkenapa mulled over my words for a second. Her English was elementary and basic.

"Ahh... Okay!" smiled Ülkenapa. "Wait here, pleez."

Ülkenapa wandered off into the crowd and disappeared.

Hweeeeee! Hweeeeee! Hwoooooo! Hwoooooo!

The train whistled. People began boarding back onto their prospective wagons.

Where did Ülkenapa go? I asked myself. I *need to board, but I can't just leave without saying goodbye.*

I waited for a few more seconds, but realized I needed to get to my *platzkart*. I began to walk back to the wagon. As I reached for the handrail, I heard my name being called.

"Timati," yelled Ülkenapa. "I have you gift, food."

I turned to face Ülkenapa, and she handed me a bag of freshly made *piroshki*.

"*Spasibo!*" I said in thanks for the fried pastries.

A Five Finger Feast

"Pleez, eat! Pleez, go!" commanded Ülkenapa with a smile.

A conductor blew a final whistle to usher passengers onto the train. The wagon's door closed behind. I went back to my bunk. I tried to open the window to wave goodbye to Ülkenapa, but it had been welded shut. I stared out through the scuffed-up window at Ülkenapa as the train chugged out of Karaganda station and back onto the tracks for the lonely steppe.

As the 432nd hour turned into the 433rd, the 434th and so on, my travel companions changed at each train station.

Unlike the faces of my fellow passengers, the steppe's landscape didn't change much. Outside was a flat landscape of brown and golden hue, offset by a clear blue sky. This lasted into the 435th hour, 436th hour and so on.

Engine Problems

I woke suddenly. The car jerked and a loud noise came from the engine. I had nodded off into a light slumber.

When there weren't potholes, roads in Kazakhstan tended to undulate. They rolled up and down and swayed back and forth, easily putting passengers to sleep.

"Wha... what's happening?" I jumped up in my seat as the car slid to stop on the grass shoulder of the road.

"No worry!" declared Charlie. "I pull to side of road."

"Is everything okay?" asked Sam.

"*Alles gut*!" replied Charlie. "We stop here for a minute."

The car jerked again. Something was clearly wrong with the engine. It began to smoke.

Where Charlie pulled the car over, there was no one in sight along the stretch of lonely road. We pulled over to a spot with a field to one side of the road and another large field to the right. Birch trees lay in the far-off distance.

"*O bozhe moy*... Okay, this will only be a few minutes," explained Charlie while he jumped out of the car.

He opened the hood of the vehicle. A puff of smoke blew up into the air.

"*Blyaaaaaaaaaaaaaah*," shouted Charlie in this nondescript Russian epithet.

"Sam, I think we are going to be here a while." I was concerned about the recent developments of our trip.

"Yeah," agreed Sam. "I think we are going to be late to Simon's camp. We are already pushing it to catch the train in Petro, anyways."

"Well, maybe we can stay at Dylan's place. I'm going to see what's the problem." I told Sam and I got out of the car.

Charlie was leaning headfirst into the smoking engine.

"What's the problem?" I asked.

"*O bozhe moy*! I do not know, Amerikaaan. I know cars, but this bigger problem for me."

"What are we going to do?"

"I call friend in Petro, but it will be long before he here."

Sam stepped out of the vehicle.

"We will be here for a while." I told my friend.

"I guessed so," replied Sam.

Charlie sat on his car's trunk. He was talking on his cellphone. He was calling for help.

"There's not a whole lot out here," explained Sam as he panned around to the surrounding fields. "Wheat fields to the left. Wheat fields to the right. Not much here."

"There's a road"—stating the obvious—"and a rather nice one for that matter." I smiled.

"My Amerikaaans," shouted Charlie. "We have help in two hours or maybe three or four. My friend, he mechanic, say he come with truck to help us, but he is at celebration—cousin's wedding, I think. He need to be less drunk to drive here," smiled Charlie as he flicked his neck. "But he come soon enough. Come sit with me. We wait."

Sam and I jumped on the back bumper and sat down on the car's trunk. Although it was the middle of summer, this was Siberia. Cool grey clouds floated from the arctic north. Rain was coming down in a field in the distance.

My journal was in hand. To kill the downtime, I perused my journal again.

The Tent Mountain
July 6, 2009 – The mountain chalet and a yurt at the Altyn Arashan, Kyrgyzstan

"She haff two song," introduced the proud Valentin. "One Kyrgyz, other *ruski*. First song she sang when she varrry young *devochka*... ahh... varrry young girl."

Valentin's voice had an air of urgency as it flowed through his bushy mustache. The Russian wanted to make sure his many guests were taken care of in his mountain hut.

The Kyrgyz woman, who would be our entertainer for the night, bashfully began plucking at her guitar strings. The petite woman sat in front of the crowded dining room on a stool.

Plick! Pluck! Ding! Dong!

"Now she haff three *deti*... ahh... three children," stated Valentin matter-of-factly.

The Polish guests in the room gasped from hearing the news.

"*Da, da,*" smiled Valentin proudly. "Three *deti!*"

The American guests whispered in the back of the room, anticipating the woman's song.

We had all come to drink and eat in the main cabin of the valley, a sort of "chalet" in the alpine wilderness of the Altyn Arashan. To our surprise, we had entertainment that came in the form of the woman who also cooked our dinner.

Plick! Pluck! Ding! Dong!

"*Spokoi, spokoi*... ahh... *shhhhh!* Quiet, pleez," whispered the gruff voice of Valentin.

Plick! Pluck! Ding! Dong!

The shy woman continued plucking her guitar strings, warming up to the tune. Valentin grabbed her by the shoulders to rotate her to face the guests. She bashfully smiled.

"*Lalalalalaaalalaaalalaaa,*" started the woman in song.

Her guitar twang was plucked with the rhythm, tune and tradition of the Eastern world. Her music was the bearer of a heritage going far past the Soviets and the tsars, and Tamerlane and the khans, and even Alexander the Great. The music resonated like classical flamenco, but it wasn't Iberian in origin. The music was plucked like a banjo, but this music wasn't *Americana*. The tune was of Central Asia, distinctly Central-Asian through and through—haunting and melancholy, epic and heroic, communal and hospitable.

"*Lalalalalaaalalaaalalaaa...*"

The Kyrgyz words that followed were indistinguishable to my American ears. Yet, I felt that I knew them well. They were as beautiful as the mountains and forests and the meadows and the streams and the alpine valley that surrounded us. They were as beautiful as the people who sat and listened, this international gathering of newfound friends. The music that came from the woman's guitar-plucking fingers and her soft Central-Asian voice reflected the beauty of the moment, a fleeting moment that I would never have again.

This is what travel is all about. It is not always about seeing great cities and monuments dedicated to great and tragic events or great and terrible men who came and passed years ago. Travel is a meditation on life. Travel is about experiencing these fleeting moments of beauty. Travel not only allows us to view other cultures and learn their histories, our histories, but travel goes even deeper. It is a reflection on the soul of humanity. We connect with others and learn to open our hearts. Travel puts us in uncomfortable and comfortable situations, sometimes simultaneously, so that we can grow and become better people.

With the song's end, my mind came back from its wanderings. My mind drifted back down to the valley floor of the Altyn Arashan. I came back to the room in the rickety chalet.

"*Izviniti, slova zabila,*" stated the petite woman with rosy, blushed cheeks.

"Ahh… she say, 'excuse me, forget some words.' Pleez, forgive," clarified Valentin.

"It so good!" shouted the Japanese man.

The guests in the small room clapped fervently.

The concert at the chalet had been an unexpected surprise, a reward, after the nine-mile four-thousand-foot climb that Jonathan, Dylan and I took earlier that day.

We began our hike in a drier arid climate lower down the mountains near the town of Karakol. The temperatures that day were perfect for a hike, and the skies were clear. As we began hiking, the landscape immediately turned into an alpine wonderland with pines and green pastures filled with sheep and yurts. On our walk to the valley of the Altyn Arashan we only spotted the occasional foreigner mountaineer and a few local Kyrgyz shepherds. Otherwise, we had the mountains to ourselves. Five or so hours after we began our journey, we entered the magnificent valley of the Altyn Arashan, meaning in the Kyrgyz language, the "golden spa."

Steep, grassy and pine-tree covered slopes walled in the narrow valley. A small river ran along the right side. Hot springs flowed into the river from its banks. A few yurts and houses sat on a small plateau above the river in the middle of the valley.

At the far end of the valley was the snow-capped sixteen-thousand-foot Palatka—the tent mountain. The "Tent" towered above the valley like a khan sitting on his golden throne.

We had booked our night to stay in the Altyn Arashan at a guesthouse down in Karakol. The guesthouse in town and its chalet in the mountains were owned by a Russian man named Valentin. He was a lively character, around sixty years old.

To our surprise, we ran into four other volunteers from Kazakhstan at the chalet. They too were vacationing in Kyrgyzstan. We were also joined by a group of five mountaineering Polish men and women. There was a Russian couple too and two Australian women traveling from Tashkent to Moscow. A Japanese man rounded out the international guest list at our retreat.

"*Amerykański!*" shouted two of the Polish men when the music was on pause. "*Amerykański!*" shouted the two men again from across the room, pointing to me.

"What? Me?" Confused, I pointed to myself.

"*Tak*, yes," replied the man with glasses and a bookish look.

"*Komm zu mir*," commanded the other Polish man in German. "Come here!"

He was bald and had a giant's stature.

I followed their command and approached the two at their table. They had been drinking vodka, which Valentin served voluminously to the Poles. The bald man's face had become bright red. The bookish man rose to his feet from the bench that the two were sharing.

"Sit!" commanded the man.

I sat down next to the bald giant on the bench. The man with glasses sat back down. I was trapped between the two. Hijacked!

"Veee drink vodka," explained the man with glasses. "It is deee best course of action for us tonight."

"It is," agreed the giant.

"You seee," continued the man with glasses, "veee climb deee Palatka. Soon veee be at deee top, so veee must celebrate veeeth our *amerykański*. It veeell bring us good luck."

"*Glück*! *Tak*, yes, luck," spurted the loquacious giant.

"My friend here," continued the man with glasses, pointing to the giant. "He is doctor. I am engineer. Veee are from Katowice in Poland, and veee climb mountains."

The giant began filling vodka into three glasses set in front of us on the table.

"Veee veeell drink to you, *amerykański*!" commanded the man with glasses.

When in Rome (or the Altyn Arashan)!

Together, in unison, we downed the vodka. The giant then grabbed our glasses from our hands, and he poured another drink for the group.

"Second one," explained the man with glasses, "it is a toast to deee great Palatka!"

We drank our shot in respect to the goliath mountain that sat on the far end of the valley of the Altyn Arashan.

"Tim!" shouted Dylan as he ran up to the table I was sharing with the Polish men. He was holding the guitar. "I've secured us a yurt!"

"A yurt?" I asked for clarification.

"Yeah, a yurt! One of the Polish guys was going to sleep in it but he gave it to us!"

Dylan had a huge smile on his face.

"How'd you get him to give up his yurt?"

"Well, one, he is drunk, but two, I told him it was my granddad's dream for me to sleep in a yurt while in Kazakhstan. Well, I guess, technically we are in Kyrgyzstan."

"I've always wanted to sleep in a real yurt too!" I laughed.

"My granddad has been emailing everyone back home that I was running off to Central Asia to live in a yurt."

Jonathan overheard our conversation, and he joined our triad at the table with the Poles. He had broken rank and conversation from the Aussies across the room.

"I heard 'yurt' and I just knew!" stated Jonathan with a smile. "You got the yurt! You know this is my dream?"

It was clear to me that Jonathan was drunk too. Everyone in the chalet, especially Valentin, for that matter, was drunk. Why else would three Americans care so much about sleeping in a yurt, after all?

"I actually have this childhood dream where I watched this Discovery Channel show," started Jonathan. "It was on the Kyrgyz cowboys, and it was about these cowboys who went into the mountains and did all this cowboy stuff, but, like, it was in the absolute middle-of-nowhere. Getting this yurt is my dream come true, Dylan! We are in the middle of, god, who knows what mountain range we are in…"

"The Tien Shan," answered Dylan.

"Yeah, whatever, some extension of the Himalayas. We're going to be living in a yurt, next to some Kazakh, I mean, Kyrgyz named river. This is pretty cool. I have reached the highpoint of my life tonight."

"Final drink," interrupted the Polish man with glasses, "is to deee yurt, your yurt!"

Three shots of vodka had already been poured for me, Dylan and Jonathan. We toasted with our two Polish friends.

Eventually we slipped away from the festivities to our awaiting yurt. The lights and the noise from the chalet reflected down our path to the yurt. It was a short walk.

We entered the round wool tent with one flashlight in hand to illuminate the round room. The inside space was larger than expected and we could stand straight up. The ground was laid with wool tarps and blankets. We unrolled our sleeping bags with enough room to spread out from each other.

Although it was July, it was a cold night in the mountains, so we slipped into the warmth of our bags. The party in the chalet could faintly be heard in the distance. To the soft, rhythmic gurgling of the river running through the Altyn Arashan—and with the strange, yet comforting smell of damp wool that floated in the air—we fell asleep in our small yurt. We were khans of the Altyn Arashan.

Fellowship

"This time remind me of when I leave Afghanistaaan. *Da, da,* it does," affirmed Charlie.

I lifted my head from my journal. We continued to sit on Charlie's trunk. The rain in the distance encroached closer on our position.

"Tell us the story," requested Sam.

"My battalion get command," started Charlie, "Gorbachev to leave Afghanistaaan. This was in eighty-nine, January. It was cold, some rain, some snow. Soviets leave Afghanistaaan in caravan of armored cars. I was driver. Can you picture me in uniform and helmet?"

"I can see that," replied Sam.

"My friends, my brothers, so happy to survive war and finally leave, but we were so tense that day. We still scared. It was like bad hangover. We happy not dead, but we still had much fear. Mujahideen, you know? They jihad soldier. They attack Soviets as we leave Afghanistaaan. Our vehicle breakdown, like my car today, and we stuck. Fields and farmland on both side of road, but big hills in distance. That's where Mujahideen watch us. We know it."

"What happened next?" I asked.

"*O bozhe moy,*" laughed Charlie. "I still live today!"

Suddenly, we heard a vehicle zooming towards us from down the highway. We all turned and looked. In the distance, a small bus was barreling towards us.

"Bus!" stated Charlie. "*Tovarishchi,* you go with bus."

"But, but... umm... what about you?" asked Sam.

"We can't leave you." I told Charlie.

Sam and I had grown fond of our gypsy taxi.

"You will go with them!" demanded Charlie. "I good. Soon my friend come help. You know *Lord of the Rings*?"

"Ahhh... yeah?" answered Sam, seeming confused at the randomness of the question.

"*O bozhe moy*! You confused, Amirikaaans. I love *Lord of Rings*, movie! I watch in Seeettaaal. Tolkien's books greater!"

"What are you getting at?" asked Sam.

"My car, it is like Ring. It bring Kazakhstaaan man and two Amerikaaan together. It unite us, but it also break us. Our fellowship is over. You Amerikaaan, you are like my Hobbit friends. I will be fine here with my car."

Charlie laughed at his strange analogy.

The bus got closer to us. Charlie stepped out in the road, raising his right arm to hail down the driver.

"I have much Vysotsky song to listen," explained Charlie. "Your time in Kazakhstaaan, in my country, it is precious. It is limited. You can't waste it. I know! *O bozhe moy*! I waste much time in Seeettaaal! I waste much time with my wife. You will go with bus."

The bus began to slow down. It approached us at a bumpy but slow speed. The brakes jolted and jostled the bus to a complete and uncomfortable stop. The bus doors opened with a rusty squeak. Charlie jumped onto the bus to talk with the bus driver. After a moment with the bus driver, he stepped back down to the road.

"My Amerikaaan, I get good price for you to Petro. I give you discount for broken car," explained Charlie as he held out ₸500 to me.

"No, Charlie, keep it. It'll help with your car." I told him.

"*O bozhe moy*! You rich Amerikaaan," chuckled Charlie. "I keep the money. Let us grab your bags from my car."

"Charlie, what happened, I mean, what happened next in Afghanistan?" I wanted Charlie to finish his story before we departed. "What happened out there?"

Charlie turned and smiled at me revealing gold crowns.

"Of course, I finish, but you not too excited," stated Charlie.

"Nothing happen on the side of the road, nothing but brothers together one last time. We sit there on the side of the road. The battalion keep moving, vehicle after vehicle. We tense and scared, but we also happy—happy to leave Afghanistaaan. Finally, our mechanic fix engine. It only took an hour or maybe two, and we go, back to Uzbekistaaan, back to Soviet Union. We all think we home after long journey, but home disappear in just a year or two after Afghanistaaan. Soviet Union vanish. Now, go!"

Charlie shooed us to the bus door.

"Goodbye!" shouted Sam and I in unison.

"*Poka*, my Amerikaaan, Hobbit friends," smiled Charlie.

We boarded the bus. It began to drive off before we took seats. We tossed our bags on empty seats in front of us, and we sat down.

All the time in the taxi and sitting on Charlie's trunk, I still had my journal in hand. I opened it back to read and jot down new notes.

The Border Crossing

July 9, 2009 - Kyrgyzstan-Kazakhstan Border, the Chu or Shu River

The fellowship was broken... Over three weeks of travel in Ukraine, Kazakhstan and Kyrgyzstan with Jonathan and Dylan finally came to an end. We would each go back to our Peace Corps sites. For us, there was only four months left of service in Kazakhstan. We would all be setting out on our own separate paths home. Dylan and I said farewell to Jonathan at the Bishkek bus station. He was heading back to his site in Balkhash on a bus that left directly from Bishkek. Dylan and I were heading for Shu, a town on the Kazakhstan side of the border. There we would catch a train back to Petropavlovsk, and off we would go to Sam's village for his camp.

From a busy tree-lined avenue in Bishkek, Dylan and I hailed a taxi driver, an elderly man. We threw our bags into the Russian's trunk, and his old sedan sped out of Bishkek. We sped out of the city limits through farmland.

We were leaving Kyrgyzstan behind. The border was on the outskirts of Bishkek.

For reasons unknown to us, the taxi was avoiding the main highway and border crossing that most travelers took when entering and leaving the country. Instead, as the driver explained, we would be taking an "alternative" route. Dylan and I could care less which route we took back into Kazakhstan as long as we made it to Shu on time to catch the train.

Across a field, I could see the border post. It sat at the edge of a bridge. Kazakhstan lay on the other side of the Chu River. On the Kazakhstan side of the murky river, the Chu was called the Shu.

The taxi slowed as we approached the post.

The border post was tiny compared to the one we had taken to enter Kyrgyzstan a week prior. It was no more than a glorified metal awning.

As we stopped under the awning, a half-dozen men with large-brimmed hats filed out of a small office. They were caught off guard by the taxi's approach. One guard approached the car. The driver rolled down his window.

"Passport," commanded the guard, leaning into the window.

The taxi driver passed his passport to the guard. He turned to Dylan and me in the back seat of his car. He extended his hand out to us. We passed him our American passports. He gave the documents to the guard.

"*Amerikantsy?*" asked the man.

"*Da,*" answered our Taxi driver.

The guard left our car while he flipped through our passports. He entered the office door. There was a lot of commotion that we could hear coming from the open door. There was movement and commotion in the office between the guards. The guards at this post weren't prepared for "foreigners" to cross at their outpost.

While we waited, another car approached the post. The car was quickly searched by guards. The guards confiscated a small package of water bottles from the trunk. As soon as the driver drove off through the post's gate and across the border, the guards opened up the bottles and started drinking down the water—a cool treat on a hot afternoon.

Our guard returned to our car with his box of stamps and our passports in hand. We received the correct stamp in our passport, and he passed our passports back to our driver.

Our taxi driver was ready for us to take off for the Kazakhstani side. The car slowly began to pull forward.

"*Stop!*" shouted another guard with a large-brimmed hat and aviator sunglasses.

The taxi driver hit the brakes, and the car came to an abrupt stop. Dylan and I were confused. The man approached the driver's window.

"*Bagazh,*" demanded the guard.

He wanted to search our bags. The guard had our taxi driver

open the trunk of his car. Dylan and I were pulled from the car as well. The guard then had me pull out my large backpack.

With Dylan, our taxi driver and four guards standing around, I began pulling out my things from my backpack. I pulled out dirty underwear, clothes and my journal. I placed them on the dusty asphalt.

"What this? What that?" asked the guard in broken English while he pointed at my things with a military-grade baton.

"This is the t-shirt I wore yesterday." I answered to the point of his baton. "Those things are souvenirs." Etc., etc., etc...

Am I a suspicious-looking person? I asked myself. *What's with the interrogation?*

Chuckling from Dylan didn't seem to help the situation.

The deeper the guard dug into my bag with his baton, the more invaded I felt.

The guard pulled out my bag of toiletries as if he was a surgeon removing a tumor from his patient's brain. He riffled through my toiletries grilling me on the details of each item

"What this?" asked the guard.

"Toothpaste." I answered.

"What that?" He shook a bottle of aspirin.

"Aspirin."

"What this?"

"Sunscreen."

"What that?"

"Floss."

"What this?"

"Bug spray..."

When he pulled out charcoal tablets and Pepto-Bismol used for stomach bugs and diarrhea—stomach bugs and diarrhea being endemic in Central Asia—he stepped up the interrogation.

"When you ate?" asked the inquisitor with all of my medicines in his hand.

"At noon." I replied. "I had a Snickers bar."

"Sure?"

He looked at me with even more suspicion.

The other guards continued to stare.

"I am one-hundred percent positive."

"I no believe," replied the officer.

His reasoning behind his questions confused me.

"Are you 'transporting' drugs," suggested Dylan with a laugh.

"What? Me? How? Why?" I was astonished. "In my stomach?"

"Or worse, your butt!" laughed my travel partner.

Every day, heroin crossed the border into Kyrgyzstan from Tajikistan, originating from Taliban-held areas of Afghanistan. From Kyrgyzstan, drugs passed through Kazakhstan, to Russia and then to Europe.

Because of the problems with drug trafficking, the officer had some legitimacy in his interrogation.

I was beginning to get nervous. I had heard of horror stories where unsuspecting foreigners had drugs planted on them by corrupt police officers. Sometimes they did this to shake money and a bribe out of them. Other times they did it for politically expedient purposes.

"Passport!" The interrogator demanded our passports to be returned to him.

We reluctantly handed them over. He took them from us with a quick jerk of his hand. He turned and walked away from the car to the office. He also carried the stomach meds away.

"Damn, what the hell is going on?" nervously laughed Dylan. "This guy is on, like, a mission."

"I don't know but if this keeps up, we are definitely going to miss the train in Shu." I replied.

"Prevent the Americans from crossing at all costs," stated Dylan. "Just our day to get on his bad side."

"Well, at least, he isn't demanding a bribe from us, yet." I rebuked, jokingly.

We waited patiently, leaning against the car.

Our taxi driver walked off to the border gate. As he leaned against the gate, he lit a cigarette and took a long drag.

After ten more minutes of waiting anxiously, another guard returned to us. The new man had our passports and my meds in hand. With a toothless smile, he passed them back to us.

"*Korpusa Mira*? Peeez Korrr?" asked the guard.

"*Da*," we replied in unison. "Peace Corps!"

"Ok! Goodbye, Amereekah," bowed the smiling guard. "I love you Peeez Korrr!"

Another guard proceeded to open the gate to cross the dusty bridge into Kazakhstan.

Dylan and I quickly gathered up my bag and belongings from the asphalt. I tossed the bag into the open trunk of our taxi. We jumped into the back seat of the car.

"Let's go!" shouted Dylan to the taxi driver.

The driver put out his cigarette and jumped into the driver's seat. We slowly passed through the gate and onto the bridge that ran across the River Chu.

As we approached the Kazakhstani gate on the Shu side of the river, a Kazakhstani border guard with a large-brimmed military hat opened it for us. We slowly drove through.

"Welcome to Kazakhstan," said the border guard. "Passport."

We handed over our passports through the car's window to the guard. He walked away into a small office.

"Here goes another round of interrogation." I joked.

A couple minutes later, the man re-emerged from the office. He had our passports in hand. Another guard followed. He had a gleeful smile on his face. It was as if he wanted to catch a glimpse of the Americans traveling through his sleepy post.

"You good!" exclaimed the guard.

"*Korpusa Mira*?" asked the other guard to find out if we were really with the Peace Corps.

"*Da*," answered Dylan suspiciously.

"*Korpusa Mira*, good!" smiled the guard as he gave us a thumbs up.

"Welcome to Kazakhstan, again," stated the other guard. "Happy time here!"

With those words, our taxi driver sped off from the border.

My journey across the former Soviet Union would be coming to an end—and with only a few months scheduled in Kazakhstan, my long two-year journey in the Peace Corps would end very soon.

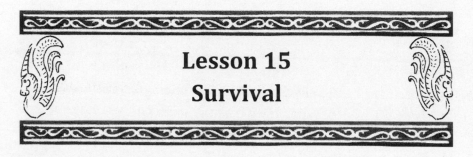

Lesson 15
Survival

"Trust in Allah, but tie your camel."

Arabic Proverb

Hospital № 1

Hospital № 1 lies on the western outskirts of Almaty. It's not to be confused with Hospital № 4, which is located a block or two away. The hospital sits immediately off a dusty, tree-lined road behind a large white wall. Young guards watch the front gate of the complex. It takes some finagling, even in cases of medical emergency, before they allow passage into the hospital's grounds.

Once inside, overgrown gardens of poplars, pines, rose bushes and weeds surround a large complex of buildings. Mosquitoes and flies buzz around the trees. Young students from a nearby college dormitory congregate and walk along the garden's beaten tree-lined paths—a courting ritual among the teenagers. Girls walk in groups and boys in packs, eyeing and flirting with each other, hoping to sneak away together to more private parts of the grounds.

The main building of Hospital № 1 is like so many other Soviet-built structures found in Almaty—several stories high, made of concrete, prefabricated slabs. Some areas of the outside façade are adorned with white marble. The entrance hardly prevents outside smoke from cigarettes and burning trash from wafting into the "sterile" hospital environment inside.

The lobby is large and cavernous with worn cracked tiles covering the walls and floor. A small kiosk sells magazines, tabloids and newspapers. Across from the kiosk hang portraits of the staff doctors and, of course, the auspicious president Nursultan A. Nazarbaev. Countenances range from Mother-Teresa-like sainthood to grouchy Mafioso. A giant poster with big English and Kazakh letters hangs near the staircase in the lobby. In English, it spells: "Sertificate." The rest of the sign, spelled out in Kazakh script, "sertifies" the hospital's credentials.

Different corridors branch off in various directions from the main lobby. They lead to the different departments in connected buildings. One passage leads to cardiology, another to maternity, and so forth. The stench of bleach resonates from every hallway, keeping the scalpels and test tubes pristine and clean. A mysterious gasoline-smelling cleaning agent also reeks here, keeping the tile floors free from dirt, blood and disease.

Up a rickety elevator to the fifth and final floor going up, where old rugs lead through the hallway, a glass door opens to an "upscale" wing of the hospital. Nurses run up and down the hall. They are dressed in white gowns. Others are capped with tall hats that would be a better fit for a chef than a hospital nurse. The nurses here run a tight ship. It is a strict policy for visitors to sign in and out at the floor's front desk. The nurses are also quite strict with visitor dress code. Visitors are required to don lab coats while visiting—just another quirk of Kazakhstan.

Before reaching the patient rooms, a small cafeteria opens four times a day: breakfast, lunch, dinner and tea. With only six small tables in the cafeteria, there isn't much sitting room for all the wing's patients. The menu ranges from exotic *beshbarmak* to mundane oatmeal. The menu suggests that mutton is a cure-all for what ails you.

The rooms in this wing of the hospital are quite nice—at least, nicer than one would expect for Kazakhstan. Depending on how much a patient wishes to pay for their healthcare will factor into the amenities a patient will get at the hospital. Pay a little bit of money and share a room with a grumpy old man or a nagging *babushka*. Pay a little more and have your own room, free from distractions and allowing you to make a restful recovery, in peace. All the rooms come with a television, a desk and cabinet, a small shower and a decent toilet. The rooms are carpeted and the windows open, perfect for microbes and pollutants to float in from outside and imbed in the room.

Survival

Despite this small oversight, each room has a balcony, and the views are magnificent. The views alone are worth the stay at Hospital № 1. From the top floor of the hospital, you can see the snow-capped Tien Shan as they rise from the city to several thousand feet above. The city's Soviet monuments and other concrete relics dot the landscape with new skyscrapers emerging from the rubble of construction and urban sprawl.

Standing on one of these balconies on a warm evening in August and gazing at the Kazakhstani sunset through the city's thick smog is, strangely, one of the most beautiful sights in the world. And for me—being one of the few Americans to ever gaze from this view as the sun sets on the western horizon of Almaty's sprawl, where the Tien Shan meets the seemingly infinite and wild Kazakh steppe—this is something awe-inspiring.

Gazing at this view was like so many other events and things, and places and people, and experiences that I encountered in Kazakhstan that took me by surprise. I would have never been able to dream up or fathom the many stories without the helping hand of Kazakhstan. The country took me on an unexpected rollercoaster of ups and downs, confusion and intrigue, ecstasy and agony. I never would have thought that Kazakhstan would become this odd and peculiar muse for me. Two years had passed since my arrival in Kazakhstan, and I knew that this was the end as I stared through the pollution into that sunset. I had finally reached the end of my journey in

my adopted home.

I knew this was the end, because it was at Hospital № 1 where my time in Kazakhstan met a surreal and unforeseen turn. It was at Hospital № 1, in August of 2009, where I had the privilege of being the American guest. While this was the end of my story here in Kazakhstan, the beginning of the end began far, far away from Hospital №1.

A Camel Past Karaganda

Three hours past the city of Karaganda, the beat-up, overcrowded bus slowed as it passed the first interesting sight since leaving the city limits. It was a camel—an unsightly and gangly beast. It stood there in the middle-of-nowhere on the blank steppe as if the rest of the world hardly mattered. The

owner of the camel sat on a crate nearby his massive wooly Bactrian, selling *shubat*[46] to truck drivers and busloads driving by.

I was never keen on *shubat*, nor the many other funky fermented milk products of the nation. Kazakhs swore by the health benefits of these yogurty alcoholic concoctions.

Our crowded bus drove over the bumpy, gravel shoulder of the road to the only pitstop along this stretch of road. It was a

---

[46] *Shubat* is an alcoholic drink made from camel's milk.

café called *Salam*. The bus stopped. The driver stepped down from the vehicle. He pulled out a pack of Camel cigarettes from his shirt's left breast pocket.

"*Rauchen kann tödlich sein!*" read German letters on the package. *Smoking will kill you!*

The driver lit up and took a long drag of the death stick.

About fifty passengers anxiously emptied the bus. We had been driving for several hours in the sweltering heat. There was nothing between Karaganda and Café Salam. The passengers ran around the café looking for a toilet, a drink, a bite to eat.

I had traveled to the middle-of-nowhere with a fellow volunteer, Rebecca. She had been stationed close to Yavlenka—only an hour and a half away, a close distance by Kazakhstan standards. Yet, over the course of two years, our relationship was anything but close. Rebecca and I did not always see eye to eye on things. Our attitudes and outlooks on Kazakhstan diverged greatly. It wasn't that we disliked each other. We tended to tolerate each other, but we had our moments that made it a rocky friendship.

Despite our many differences, so far on our trip to the middle-of-nowhere we seemed to be getting along with each other. At the rest stop we began playing a game, Six Degrees of Separation. The goal of the game was to connect Actor A to Actor B through various movies the actors had been in together.

"Ok, Rebecca." I began. "Let's see if you can get this one: singer, actress, humanitarian Hilary Duff to George Clooney?"

"Oh, God! Why Hillary Duff?" huffed Rebecca in frustration. "I hate her! She stands for the complete opposite of everything I stand for! She disgusts me!"

"Come on! That's not what the game is about. This one will be fun. Just think about it for a second. I'll give you a clue. Hillary was in *War, Inc.* with John Cusack."

She begrudgingly played. It was either play the nonsensical

game or be bored as we stood in the parking lot of Café Salam.

"Well, that makes it easier," replied Rebecca. "John Cusack was in *High Fidelity* with Jack Black. Jack Black was in *The Holiday* with Jude Law. Umm, now I'm stuck."

"He was in the comedy *I Heart Huckabees* with Marky Mark."

"Mark Wahlberg!" exclaimed Rebecca. "He was in *Three Kings* with George Clooney! I've only seen the previews."

"We have closed the loop on Hilary and George. Who's next?" I asked.

We continued to play the game as we walked into Café Salam to buy snacks. The café didn't offer much, and the lack of choices made it difficult for Rebecca, a zealous and devout vegetarian. Rebecca stood at the café counter looking at the selection of food in disgust. She walked away from the café empty handed. I bought a package of candies.

After thirty minutes passed, our bus driver honked the horn to gather up the flock of passengers. The bus loaded up, and we took off for Balkhash—another two or three hours of driving ahead of us.

Rebecca and I were headed to Balkhash to work at an English camp organized by our friend Jonathan. We had been out to Balkhash the summer before to help work on another project of Jonathan's, so we were familiar with the town.

"It's my birthday Monday!" cried Rebecca with enthusiasm.

The year before we had also celebrated her birthday in Balkhash. All the volunteers visiting Balkhash at the time had crammed into a small apartment Jonathan had rented for the group of volunteers working on his project. The apartment heated up like an oven in the July heat, and at night we couldn't air the place out because the mosquitos outside swarmed in by the millions.

"Your party was a blast last year." I exclaimed. "But that was such a miserably cramped apartment. We were so hot at night.

Survival

Remember how we couldn't open the windows, because of all the mosquitoes?"

"But it was great when all the guys got shirtless to cool off," laughed Rebecca. "I have pictures of you guys. That was a hot mess. Oh, and the apartment didn't have dishes or glasses."

"We made glasses out of bottle tops." I remembered.

"By the way, I don't work or go to school on my birthday," demanded Rebecca. "My birthday is *my day*. You guys will have to cover me at the camp that day this week."

"Well, you'll have to talk to Jonathan about that." I replied, slightly perturbed by her demand. "It will be the first day of the camp and he may need all hands on deck."

"He'll have to do without me!" demanded Rebecca.

"Well, anyways..." I scanned my brain to change the topic. "Three more months in Kazakhstan..."

The two years of service for me and my fellow Kaz 19s would be ending in the fall. We would all gather for our last meeting (COS or Close of Service) as a group in September in Almaty. Then each individual volunteer in Kaz 19—there were about fifty remaining out of an original seventy-five—would leave the country, one by one, starting in November.

"I can't believe it too," stated Rebecca, already forgetting the talk about her birthday.

"What will you do when you go home?" I asked her.

"I am never going home!" exclaimed Rebecca. "I hate the Midwest, and I hate my mom who lives there."

"You're not going home for even a little bit?"

"Well," huffed Rebecca. "Yes, I will go home at some point, but not for long. I am going to go to school in Europe. I am going to get my PhD in philosophy."

"A very practical degree." I teased her.

"Tim! Stop it!" huffed Rebecca.

"I just can't believe that two years is almost over. I don't have a clear idea of what I will do when I go home, but I might take some grad classes in Reno."

"Aren't you and Dylan going to Russia after the Peace Corps ends?" asked Rebecca.

"Yeah! We will leave in November. We'll take the train from Almaty to St. Petersburg. It'll be a once-in-a-lifetime trip."

As we drove away from the camel and Café Salam, our conversation puttered out. I opened the plastic wrapping of the candy I had bought at Café Salam. I easily went through the whole package before falling asleep.

Riviera on the Steppe

I woke up two hours later. It was dusk when our bus entered the city limits of Balkhash. A MiG jet greeted us at the city limits. It was frozen in place on top of a large pedestal that made the airplane look as if it was zooming off into flight.

Balkhash was remote, even by Kazakhstan standards—five hours from Karaganda and nine hours from Almaty, with almost nothing in between. It was a city that stood on the edge of a vast desert and Lake Balkhash, one of the largest lakes in the world.

A factory town of eighty thousand people, the city was founded in the 1930s, according to a Soviet model of industry. A metallurgical plant dominated the cityscape and the lake.

Rebecca and I were greeted at the town's bus station by Jonathan and two other volunteers, Jose and Sam. Jose and Sam arrived in Balkhash earlier that day.

"Good to see you guys!" greeted Jonathan. "I hope you are ready for a fun-filled week! The plan is to start on Monday morning with the camp. It will be at my school, and we have about fifty kids signed up."

"Well, we better get a chance to go to the beach," demanded Rebecca. "I came here for the lake and the sun."

"Don't worry about that," said Jonathan. "We will get a chance to go tomorrow. And sun! It's always sunny in Balkhash!"

Survival

"Liam is back at the apartment," chimed in Sam. "He's not looking too good. Moment we got to Balkhash he started feeling nauseous and throwing up. He thinks it's food poisoning."

"Poor guy." I responded. "One man down for the count."

We walked towards Jonathan's apartment. Above us floated white smoke emitted from the metallurgical plant on the edge of town. It eerily glowed in the night sky, wafting and settling over the city.

When we arrived at the apartment, I took no time unpacking my towel and shampoo from my backpack. After a long journey, I was in need of a shower. I hadn't bathed in several days, and I stunk badly. I went to the bathroom and turned on the hot water in the shower. The city volunteers were lucky to have showers, a luxury item the Western world takes for granted. I stepped into the lukewarm water, and I began to soap up.

I subconsciously scratched my leg.

Instantaneously, small fleshy bumps appeared where I had scratched. Quicker than I could react, they flared up on my butt and the inside of my arms as well. These hives quickly spread to my lower back. I was having some sort of allergic reaction. The red hives itched like crazy. They looked disgusting.

I quickly stopped the shower and tried drying off without further aggravating the rash.

Annoyed and uncomfortably itchy, I got dressed and went out to the living room. Jonathan and Rebecca were making dinner. Sam was talking to them. Liam, a Kaz 20, was lying on the couch, looking pale and rather dead in appearance.

"Umm, does anyone have Benadryl?" I asked the group.

I hated Benadryl because it made me feel groggy, but it was the only antihistamine that the Peace Corps prescribed in our medical kits. It would help with the rash.

"Yeah, I've got some," replied Sam. "I take that stuff like Vitamin C. It helps me fall asleep. Why do you need it?"

I showed him the hives on the backs of my arms. I lifted my shirt to show him my lower back.

"Oh my god!" gasped Sam. "What happened?"

"I don't know. They just suddenly appeared when I was in the shower. They itch bad. Well, maybe if I get some rest they'll go away. It's been a long day."

I etched out a section of Jonathan's living room floor to lay down my sleeping bag. I went to bed, hoping the hives would go away by the time I woke up.

The Zone

In Andrei Tarkovsky's 1979 film *Stalker*, the protagonist, an un-named man known only as the "Stalker," leads two clients into a contaminated and off-limits area called the "Zone."[47] Something or someone has changed the landscape of the Zone. Reality does not seem to operate on the same principles as the outside world. The area seems to have a certain presence or sentience to it.

The three characters venture into the Zone, avoiding a military blockade and the strange, unseen dangers and phenomena inhabiting the area. They navigate their way through overgrown fields and decrepit, concrete buildings to find a special room. It is in this room where wishes are granted to those who enter.

It is at the room where it is revealed one of the Stalker's clients has come to destroy the room with a bomb, so that the room's power doesn't fall into evil hands. However, after arguing with the others, this man decides to not use the bomb. The three men realize in their argument that entering the room may cause unforeseen and unknown ramifications for themselves and others.

Ultimately, the three decide to not enter the room. The infinite possibilities of creation and destruction that come with

---

[47] Andrei Tarkovsky (1932-86) was a Soviet movie director. He filmed the science fiction films *Solaris* (1972) and *Stalker* (1979).

their desires remain within themselves. They eventually return to the world outside the Zone.

In the film, the Zone provides a metaphor for the unknown. It is mankind's desire to harness the unknown—to understand, shed light onto it and to manipulate it. The effects of that manipulation, as the film suggests, can change reality in profound and often irreversible ways. The strange phenomena of the Zone and the room of wishes represent the irreversible changes we can unleash onto ourselves and the world around us. The three men's decision to turn back, instead of entering the room elicits a sense of self-healing and acknowledgment that some fruits shall not be eaten—at least, not yet.

Parallels were made with the film and the Chernobyl disaster that occurred six years later.[48] After the nuclear meltdown at Chernobyl in 1986, the Soviet government cordoned off the most radioactive area of Ukraine and Belarus, calling it the "Zone of Exclusion." Mankind unleashed the power of the atom, and we couldn't contain the consequences of discovery. Chernobyl and its surrounding area will be contaminated with deadly levels of radiation for hundreds, if not thousands of years.

Even the film's set acted as a sort of "Zone" for the filming crew. There were unknown consequences that would unfold from Tarkovsky's ignorance. The set was located at an abandoned, hydro-electric plant outside of Tallinn, Estonia. A chemical plant sat upstream. Many of the crew of the film complained of strange rashes while shooting the movie. Some, including Tarkovsky himself in 1986, died of strange cancers years later.

"Trust in *Allah*..."

When I woke up the following morning, the hives were still there. I could barely sleep that night. The sweat and heat trapped in my sleeping bag seemed to aggravate the allergic re-

---

[48] Chernobyl is a nuclear power plant in Ukraine. On April 26, 1986, Reactor 4 had a meltdown. The disaster released radioactive fallout across Europe.

action even more.

That day the allergic reaction ebbed and flowed on my skin, coming and going. My body felt incredibly uncomfortable. Over-all, it continued to worsen over the course of the day.

That afternoon, as promised by Jonathan and demanded by Rebecca, we went to the lake. Liam, still reeling from food poisoning, remained behind. He was barely functioning. I thought the beach would lift my spirits, so I went along.

The sun was hot and bright in the afternoon. It beat down on the city streets and baked the area's parched dry red earth.

The city of Balkhash was situated on an inlet of the larger lake, and the beach sat opposite of the city. The metallurgical plant loomed large over the town. The smokestacks emitted plumes of smoke that settled onto the apartments below.

The water of the bay was calm and tranquil, but the color was off from what was the natural color for water. The color was cloudy and turquoise—like the oxidized color of copper, the Statue of Liberty.

I sat with Sam in the shade on the shore while the others played in the water. Sam didn't care much for the sun, and my hives looked so unattractive that I didn't dare take off my shirt.

"Last year we came out to swim here." I started to tell Sam. "We were having a blast goofing around in the water. Two boys on a jet ski were zipping around the bay. We didn't think much of it at first, but every time they passed by us, they came by just a little closer."

"I don't like where this story is going," replied Sam.

"Well, the jet ski came around and started to come towards us. At first it was like, 'no way, they're not going to hit us'."

"And did they?" asked Sam.

"Yep, they hit the group dead on." I said matter-of-factly. "We all tried to scatter out of the way, but they hit one of the girls, this volunteer in Kostanai."

"Was she okay?" asked Sam.

"She was more shocked than hurt"—I paused for a second and continued—"but the jet ski did bruise her back, and it cut her skin up a little."

"Dang," laughed Sam.

"That's not the end. Jonathan's sitemate, this Kaz 18, was livid. I mean we were all angry, but he was more of a hothead. He started marching down the beach towards the jet skiers who had by now come ashore. The girls stayed behind, but the guys in our group, we all followed. We stormed up to the jet skiers. They were hanging out at some sort of cabana beach club over there where the fence is."

I pointed towards a fenced off area of the beach. Umbrellas stood in the sand, and loud music blasted from a beach club.

"Then what?" asked Sam.

"Well, our fearless leader marched right up to them screaming and puffing himself up like he was going to fight them. The rest of us just stood behind him. Within seconds we were surrounded by a group of Russian teenagers. A short guy with a long mullet stepped up. He pointed a gun at us!"

"What? Really? A gun?" asked Sam.

"Well, it was a flare gun." I clarified. "Mullet man pointed it right at Jose's stomach."

"You guys must have been flipping!"

"Oh yeah! My stomach dropped, and I was pretty nervous. There was a lot of shouting. Jonathan pulled out his phone and said he was calling the police."

"Did that scare them?"

"It did." I laughed. "Jonathan actually just called Küzetşi, the Peace Corps safety officer, but they didn't know the difference. They begged for us not to call the cops. Jonathan handed the Russians the phone. You could hear Küzetşi yelling at them over the phone. They even tried to bribe us with money after."

"You should have taken it."

"I wish we had. When we refused to take the money, the mullet man and the jet ski boys insisted that they apologize to the girls. We refused to let them."

"Rightfully so."

"But they still walked down the beach to apologize to them. Of course, the girl who got hurt refused their apology."

"It's like these teenagers were introduced to new technology," started Sam, "that they just couldn't understand the power behind it."

"Yeah." I replied. "They really didn't understand the consequences that crash could have had for them or us if someone really got hurt. I'm thankful that no one got too messed up." I paused. "There's something about this lake. First the jet skis, now my rash. It's cursed."

We both stared out towards the glistening water. The sun's blinding light beat down on the turquoise water as our friends played in the lake. The factory smokestacks bellowed plumes of white gasses. A group of boys sat on a platform sticking out of the water fifty feet offshore. They were fishing.

"But tie your camel..."

"It's my birthday," screamed Rebecca.

She woke the entire apartment from sleep.

"Happy birthday!" replied Jonathan from his bed across the small apartment.

"By the way," Rebecca to Jonathan, "I don't work on my birthday! Never have. Don't intend to, ever. I don't go to school or work. It's my personal rule for life. I'm looking forward to relaxing and reading today."

"Rebecca, you know it's the first day of the camp," interrupted Sam as he lay on the living room floor in his sleeping bag.

"Who are you to tell me if I work or not?" huffed Rebecca. "It's not up to you! Right, Jonathan?"

"Sure," answered Jonathan. "You can stay at the apartment."

Sam looked at me from across the living room in disbelief and annoyance at Rebecca. His expression changed immediately, though, when he looked at me.

"Uhh... Tim, you should look in a mirror," said Sam. "Something's wrong with your face."

I sprung from my bag and ran into the bathroom. Something did feel off with my eye. I gasped as I stared at myself in the mirror. My right eye had begun to swell shut. It was a freakish sight. I panicked.

My body continued to react to the mystery allergen. The hives, the itching and the discomfort persisted throughout the morning. Nothing seemed to curb its growth or stop its "infection." I took Benadryl. I avoided the sun. I stopped showering. I watched what I ate. All these measures and no results.

Finally, I called the Peace Corps medical staff. Dr. Bluma was assigned to my case. She directed me to go to the hospital and to call her when I arrived.

Jonathan was down to three people for his camp. Liam was still sick from his mystery ailment. Rebecca had taken a personal day. I was heading to the hospital. Jonathan insisted that he could manage the campers with the small group of volunteers he had left. The camp was going to begin soon, and fifty eager kids waited. I didn't quite believe that he'd be okay, but there were no other alternatives.

Jonathan sent his local counterpart to the hospital with me for any needed translations. Jonathan mustered Liam from his deathbed to be my American advisor. Basically, he sent Liam to ensure nothing weird or out of the ordinary happened to me at the hospital. In his current shape, Liam should've already visited the hospital himself anyways.

We hailed a taxi outside Jonathan's apartment. The hospital was located on the other side of town, too far to walk.

As we approached the hospital from the road, the building looked abandoned. The dirt road leading to the entrance was drenched with rainwater. Giant puddles strewn the road. The night before there had been a brief and sudden thunderstorm. The water quenched the parched red sands of Balkhash.

Jonathan's words from two night before reverberated in my head: *It's always sunny in Balkhash!*

We were let off at the front entrance. A beat-up ambulance sat empty, running idle. We entered the main doors. The aroma of bleach instantly struck my nostrils. There was no front desk nor any attendant waiting to greet visitors. Jonathan's counterpart left us by the door to find a doctor.

"Tim"—blurted Liam, breaking the silence he had maintained much of the weekend, still looking sick and pale from days of puking up his insides—"you ever hear the horror stories of hospitals right after the collapse of the Soviet Union."

310

Survival

"I know some of them." I uneasily answered while I sniffed the peroxide-laced air. "Why are you telling this to me now?"

He laughed in a maladroit manner.

"Up into the early 2000s the economic situation was so dire in parts of Russia and Kazakhstan," he continued, "that hospitals recycled used needles by boiling them."

"Well, let's hope they don't give me any shots here."

"Let's hope you don't contract HIV!" laughed Liam devilishly.

A bald goateed man in a white lab coat, blue scrubs and alligator shoes approached us. Jonathan's counterpart walked behind. He looked like the type of doctor who bribed his way through medical school.

"Teem?" spouted off the man.

"*Da?*" I replied.

"*Moi pervi amerikanets!*" boasted the enormous doctor. *My first American!*

He put out his hand to shake mine.

"*Kto on?*" asked the doctor who Liam was, nodding to my pale-faced friend.

Jonathan's counterpart intercepted this question and explained that Liam was an American friend. She explained that we were with the Peace Corps.

He seemed to recognize the organization's name. He nodded at us, and he led us all to a small office nearby.

The furnishings in the office were ancient, and a computer from the 1980s sat in the corner. There was a stiff-looking exam table in another corner.

I sat down on the table.

Jonathan's counterpart pulled out a cell phone from her purse. She dialed a number and handed the phone to the Kazakh doctor. She had called Dr. Bluma.

For several minutes, the two doctors talked on the phone. At moments, there seemed to be tension, at other moments, laughter. It almost seemed like the doctor was flirting with Dr. Bluma.

"*Ladno! Davay, moi nomer*..." He was giving her his telephone number. *When you're in Balkhash next, give me a call. I'll take you out for dinner and a movie... Ciao!*

He hung up the phone.

A nurse entered the room with some plastic bags. Syringes were sealed within.

My heart began to race. I hated needles. Liam's comment about HIV reverberated in my head.

The doctor spouted off some words in garbled Russian.

"Teeem, hee geeev anteee-heeestameeen," translated Jonathan's counterpart. "Heee neeed put you booottocks. Pleeez..."

She pointed to my pants, gesturing me to expose my butt. I cautiously obliged.

My hands were sweaty, and my heart raced. I watched the nurse closely to make sure the needles weren't the re-used infected kind. I saw plastic wrappings torn open. Syringes were pulled from them. I smelled rubbing alcohol.

The nurse swathed my right butt cheek clean.

I clenched my butt. I couldn't relax.

Gasp!

With one sharp prick, the needle went in.

"Oookay, now arm," commanded Jonathan's counterpart.

"*Davay*, Teem," started the doctor. "*Vash adres?*"

He had a clipboard and pen in hand.

The nurse fiddled with another syringe.

"My address?" I blurted.

Why ask me this now? I couldn't stop thinking how stupid of a question it was. My thoughts were getting cloudy. *They know I'm in the Peace Corps. Just write down the Peace Corps...*

"*Davay! Vash adres?*"

I glanced at the nurse, needle in handle.

"Uhh..." My mouth moved but no words came out.

Survival

The nurse took a rubber band. She tied it around my bicep.

The vein that pulsed through the inside of my elbow became plump and ripe, perfect target for the next injection.

"Heee ask you *adres*," exclaimed Jonathan's counterpart.

"Uhh... Nevada... Carson City... No... Uhh... Renooo..."

I caught one final glance as the needle slid into my arm. Things began to get fuzzy. My world became darker. My head felt nauseous.

Whaaat thaaa...

The Wilderness

A week before things started to unravel in Balkhash, I had taken the train with Sam from Petropavlovsk to Kokshetau. In Kokshetau, we boarded a *marshrutka* heading southwest out of town.

We told the driver our stop. He looked at us perplexed but nodded as if understanding the destination in our garbled and unintelligible Russian.

The van's destination was a small town called Atbasar, a remote outpost in the middle of the steppe. Our stop was long before Atbasar.

Leaving the outskirts of the city, we passed derelict buildings and dump yards scattered among the rubble of the post-industrial chaos of Kokshetau. These hollow shells of concrete abandoned buildings, apartments mostly, were common sights in much of Kazakhstan. They usually inhabited the spaces between man and nature—the places that ebb and flow between the flux of civilization and the eroding forces of wind, water and time. The locals often called these sights "Chechnya," a reference to the ill-fated and destructive wars that Yeltsin and Putin unleashed on the Caucasus region of Russia in the 1990s.

An hour and a half outside of Kokshetau and the bombed out remains of "Chechnya," our marshrutka slowed. It came to a stop at a dirt road that led off into nowhere. Grassy fields, small lakes and forests dotted the area.

"Hey a-yooo!" yelled the driver. "*Dikaya mestnost*! Here na-tooora!" *Welcome to the wilderness.*

We opened the door and stepped down from the vehicle. The van sped off down the asphalt road.

"I hope this is the spot," started Sam. "If not, we're screwed."

The summer's daylight was finally coming to an end. The sun was getting lower in the sky, and here we were on the edge of the wilderness, far from civilization. The last village we passed was at least ten miles behind.

We began walking down a dirt road that bisected the main highway. It felt like it was almost a mile down the way as we walked. A group of trees stood far off in the distance next to a small lake.

As we approached the lake, we saw tarps and tents set up. A fire was blazing, and people were sitting around it. A tall blonde man stood up from the group and began running towards us.

"Welcome, bros!" exclaimed a joyous Simon. "Welcome to my 'Into the Wild English Camp,' sponsored by Shell!"

"Shell?" I laughed. "Like the gas company?"

"Yeah, dude, Shell! They gave me a ton of money to put on this camp. They paid for all of the camping equipment and food. All the gas companies give out money to the locals, and I found a grant to pay for this."

It was true. Petroleum companies, like Shell, gave out money to Kazakhstani education and development programs such as the "Into the Wild Camp." Aside from what kickbacks the Kazakhstani politicians received, these grants were a way for the oil industry to "repay" the people of what they reaped from their lands. Kazakhstan was wealthy in natural resources, and the consumer world pined for many of the treasures that could be ripped out of its ground, especially oil.

"Dudes, we've got some sick equipment," continued Simon.

"Come check this out! Everything you need to be comfortable in nature. This is glamping!"

"Glamping?" laughed Sam.

"Dudes! Glamor meets camping!" proclaimed Simon. "It's the only way camping should be done."

He led us into camp. A large group of teenagers sat around a fire-pit. They all stared at us newcomers and smiled.

"Oh, yeah," interjected Simon, "meet the kids!"

We were here at this camp in the wilderness, after all, to speak English with these Kazakhstani youths and to facilitate camp activities. Here in the natural setting, away from the distractions of the modern world, theoretically, these kids would learn English. That was according to Simon. They were required to speak English, and only English, and the volunteers were not allowed to speak Russian to them.

"Check this out," demanded Simon. "Command central."

Two large canopy tents had been erected side by side. Tables and chairs were set up underneath the shelter. A couple of gas stoves and coolers were placed around the tables. Board games had also been left out for kids to play. An electric generator stood nearby.

"What's the generator for?" I asked.

"Dude, that's glamping at its finest," said Simon. "Anyways, all this was paid for by Shell, plus my counterpart's son insisted we buy it. He brought our office's laptop to watch movies and play video games out here—also paid for by Shell."

It turned out that Simon's counterpart and her son accompanied us to the camp. She was a Russian woman in her fifties. He was a greasy long-haired twenty-something. The son played video games most of the time. Neither of them spoke English.

I quickly picked up that they had also reserved the best tent and sleeping equipment for themselves: a plush, mega tent with a comfortable, two-foot-high air mattress inside. The rest of the camp equipment was standard: canopy two- and three-person tents; thin foam sleeping pads; cheaply made sleeping bags. Each camper had been paired up with one or two others, and the volunteers shared a couple tents with each other.

On that first night, it felt good to be out in nature. It felt good for the spirit and the soul. We sat around the fire and cooked hotdogs and made s'mores with imported Hershey's chocolate, marshmallows and graham crackers. American delicacies. We sang camp songs and told scary stories. It was like being in America, but thousands of miles away in the middle of the vast Kazakh Steppe.

The second night things started to turn sour, though. The food situation became most apparent. It was lacking. Simon's counterpart had paid a good penny for their tent, air mattress and other equipment, but it appeared that they had scrimped on food. The volunteers and campers began to starve.

While we starved, the mosquitoes came out in swarms. The beautiful lake that stood at our doorstep was apparently a cesspool for mosquito breeding. While we starved, the mosquitos feasted. I got thoroughly bit up.

By the third day, the rains came. At first, we were thankful for the rain for washing away the mosquitoes, but the rain wouldn't relent. We all crowded in our tents and played card games for hours. We told stories and talked with the campers for hours. There wasn't any place for us to go, so we huddled down in our tents.

For three more days it rained, and we went hungry. Simon's counterpart and her son remained mostly confined to their tent playing video games and watching movies.

This was nature. This was the grand adventure into the wilderness, sponsored by Shell.

It wasn't all misery, though. In the brief moments when the rain let up, we were able to run around outside, playing games and tossing the football. We even attempted to swim in the freezing lake one of the afternoons when the sun broke through the clouds.

After six days on the steppe, over half of which we spent huddled in our tents wet and starved, we were slated to spend four more nights in this wilderness.

On the evening of the sixth day things took a turn from bad to worse for the camp, sponsored by Shell.

Woosh! The winds came suddenly and violently from the north. *Boom!* Thunder echoed. *Zap!* Lightning pierced the sky, electrifying and illuminating the dark clouds. It was as if a hurricane appeared out of nowhere.

Most of our group was sitting underneath the canopy tents at the command central. We were playing cards and waiting for the remaining food to be cooked up for dinner when the storm rolled through. Our cards blew away. Trash bags blew around in cyclonic motions. Tent stakes were pulled from the ground and tarps began flying away. We all took hold onto the canopy tent we sat underneath, holding on so it wouldn't fly off. The second tent was picked up by the wind and blew five feet into the air. The metal frame twisted and bent with ease when it smashed back down into the ground and rolled away. A torrent of hail came next. Chunks of ice fell in a veil of white pellets. Hail pelted the already windswept tents, collapsing and flooding whatever structure remained. There were few places to escape the fury the sky had unleashed.

What seemed like hours, was mere minutes, but the forces of nature were enough to destroy our small encampment. Tents and sleeping bags were strewn across the area, soaking wet. Tables and kitchen supplies had blown away. One of the canopy tents was destroyed and had been smashed into a twisting pile of metal. The one tent that remained undamaged was Simon's counterpart's. However, they had left the door of the tent unzipped and the hailstorm had soaked everything inside, includeing the office laptop the son had brought for movie watching and video games.

At first, when we surveyed the damage, we were dismayed and distraught. Then one of the campers, a boy named Chingeskhan, grabbed one of the smashed up metal canopy tent legs that once made up the command central. He pulled a plastic grocery bag from his back pocket. The Shell logo was firmly printed on the bag. He latched the bag to the pole like a make-shift flag, and he began to hoist the new flagpole upright into the air. The rest of the volunteers ran to help him raise the makeshift pole high and mighty. Like the marines who raised the American flag on Mount Suribachi during the Battle of Iwo Jima, we courageously raised our own camp colors. We were heroes for the moment. We felt invulnerable.

We told Mother Nature: "We will triumph and survive! We are the Peace Corps, sponsored by Shell!"

The next morning Simon's counterpart informed us that she had contacted the campers' parents. Vans were heading our way to pick us up. Our time in the wilderness was coming to an end.

We cleaned up the campsite, and we loaded up the vans when they arrived. In Kazakhstani fashion, we burned the trash. Burning trash has a distinct smell to it.

Smell

"Teem! Teem! Teem!"

I woke to the nurse and the doctor yelling my name. I came back from a cloud of darkness.

A foul smell permeated the air. The nurse used smelling salts to revive me.

I lied on the hard exam table. My pants and shirt had been stripped off.

"Wow! You were out cold," laughed Liam. "I've never seen someone faint before."

"I fainted?" I asked in confusion. "I guess I've never fainted before. What did they put in those shots?"

"I don't think anything that would've knocked you out like that," replied Liam.

"I must really hate needles."

"The doctor said you should wait here for a few minutes," continued Liam, "just to make sure you're not going to pass out again. Looks like your eye isn't swollen anymore. Whatever they gave you is working."

At that moment Dr. Bluma called my cell phone. I answered.

"Doktooor Bluma here." She tersely stated. "I hope you are alvriiight now."

"Uhh... I guess I fainted, but the hives are disappearing."

I looked at my exposed torso. The rash subsided like magic before my eyes.

"This is veeery good!" shouted Dr. Bluma. "I vaaant you to leave Balkhash tonight. Say fareveeell to your friends and board a bus south to Almaty. I veeell see you in the morning at the Peace Corps office, medical unit."

I left the hospital, and I did as I was told. I said goodbye to my friends.

Rebecca was still celebrating her birthday when I left. The other volunteers played along to placate her.

Jose walked me to the bus station.

"So Rebecca is already complaining that you and Liam ruined her birthday," sighed Jose.

"What? Are you serious?" I laughed. "She's mad because we went to the hospital?"

"Yep, you took the attention from her 'special' day," replied Jose. "It's just Rebecca. It's the way she is. You have to forgive her for it."

"Liam and I were on our deathbeds, and she's mad about her birthday." I continued to laugh. "There's no winning with her!"

"Her intentions are good, but..." paused Jose for a moment, trying to find the right words. "You know? Kazakhstan? It's just hard on everyone. It's just tough."

"I understand." I replied.

"Well, we are almost to the end of our service here in Kazakhstan," lamented Jose.

"Although it's been tough at times, it was worth it." I told him.

"It was worth it," agreed Jose. "To think, the life we built in Kazakhstan will end shortly. The friends that we've made, the experiences—it'll all end soon. If any of us ever come back after Peace Corps, it'll never be the same as it is right now."

"Change happens, I guess." I replied. "Change is inevitable."

"Change is inevitable," repeated Jose.

"Well, here we are, the station!" I was surprised that the bus station was closer to Jonathan's apartment than I remembered.

"Take care of yourself, and I hope the allergic thing is all done for," wished Jose.

"I hope so too. I'll see you soon at COS."

With a farewell handshake to Jose, I turned and entered the bus station office.

By the time I headed out of town on the bus to Almaty, the hives and rash had disappeared. It was a miracle of modern medicine. After days of suffering, my skin was back to normal!

I will arrive in Almaty, and Dr. Bluma will think I made up the whole ordeal. I thought to myself. *First, though, a ten-hour drive ahead—a long and boring one too.*

I fell asleep as the bus drove out of Balkhash onto the steppe.

Dr. Bluma

Even at seven in the morning, the distinct smell of Sairan, the long-distance bus station in Almaty, was that of barbecued *shashlyk*. The station served domestic and international destinations all over the former Soviet Union and even into China.

My overnight bus from Balkhash pulled up to the terminal.

Survival

I scratched my chest as I exited the bus. My skin had become irritated and itchy again. The hives and rash had returned with a vengeance.

Despite the terrifying, yet effective treatment I received in the Balkhash hospital, the effects were short lived. The infestation had returned in the early morning hours while the bus was still driving to Almaty. I awoke to the feeling of hives crawling over my skin. They itched and burned underneath my clothing. I felt them creep up my body and up my neck.

As I exited the bus, I grabbed my luggage from the storage compartment. I was hounded by taxi drivers. I had less than five dollars' worth of *tenge* (T) in my wallet, far too little for a taxi ride to the Peace Corps office. I made my way for a city bus.

The Peace Corps office was located on the far southern edge of the city. It was in an area of town that was largely under con-

struction with glass high rises and nice luxury apartments for the *nouveau riche*—far, far removed from the city's earthquake-prone Soviet-era center built of prefab concrete slabs and bricks. The closest monument to gauge where to get off the bus in this largely unpopulated part of Almaty was an enormously large department store called Ramstore. Though resembling an American-style, warehouse store for the middle-class, Ramstore and its prices were anything but.

At Ramstore, I exited the bus. The office was located past Ramstore and across a busy street called Al-Farabi. The street, named after a philosopher from the Middle Ages with an obscure connection to Kazakhstan, was always congested with cars. I played Frogger across Al-Farabi and headed down a sketchy-looking alley.

Behind a dingy slum of falling-apart houses and new high-rise construction sites, situated next to a dried-up riverbed that descended from the Tien Shan, there sat the Peace Corps office. The office was in a random location, but the budget-conscious Peace Corps couldn't afford many other options in Almaty, a city with a sky-rocketing cost of living. The office was a two-building compound surrounded by walls and barbed wire. The operations office was housed in one building while the program office and volunteer lounge were located in the other. A guard checked IDs at the gate.

When I arrived, I reported to the medical office. I found Dr. Bluma. She was a Russian woman in her middle age. She spoke English well, but with a high-pitched voice and odd intonation.

"Teeem," started Dr. Bluma, "veeelcom to Almaty. Let us look at the situation."

She motioned me to the examination bed. I took off my shirt.

"Oh, my," gasped the doctor.

She began touching the rash on my chest and arms. The reddish hives turned white with the pressure of her finger, but quickly turned back to red when she pulled back.

"Yes, you have vaaary, vaaary bad hives. Vhaaat could you be allergic to? Vhaaat did you eat before this happened?"

"Uhh, I had some candy from a café on my bus ride to Balkhash." I replied. "They had nuts in them and also dried fruits. I also had an eggplant salad the afternoon I left Karaganda."

"Yes, you veeell not eat those things again! Veee veeell put you on a strict diet! Nothing but *kasha* and water for you. Have you had hives before this time?"

"When I was a kid."

"I see. And did you have any bug bites? Maybe you veeere

bitten by mosquitos?"

"At an outdoor camp I worked at a week before. We were next to a lake, and I got bit up bad one night."

"Interesting…"

"What about the water in Balkhash? I was in the shower there when the hives popped up. Could there be something in the water?"

"No! I don't think it is vaaater."

"Well, there is a large factory in Balkhash. I think it spews wastewater into the lake. I can show you pictures of the weird bluish-green tinge to the lake water."

"No, that isn't necessary," dismissed Dr. Bluma, strangely. "*Ladno*, I know vhaaat veee veeell do," she continued. "Veee veeell get started. The nurse veeell give you some anti-histamines and she veeell also give you an IV with steroid treatment, prednisone."

"IV, steroids?" I gasped.

"Yes, veee veeell flush out the allergen from your blood…"

Al-Farabi

"**V**ooctoor Blllooma." I mumbled into the phone—words impeded by a turgid lisp.

"Vhaaat is vrooong?" replied Dr. Bluma, sounding as if I had unexpectedly interrupted her evening at home.

"My vipsss vare svooven and numv."

My tongue had swollen, and my throat was scratchy and inflamed. It was becoming more difficult to talk past the wall of inflammation growing in my head.

"Stay vheeere you are, Teem! I come to you now."

With that Dr. Bluma hung up the phone.

The Peace Corps had put me up in the Sanatorium Kok Tobe for my stay in Almaty.

I decided to head down to the lobby of the hotel while I waited for Dr. Bluma. I sat patiently on a stiff couch in the dimly lit lobby.

With my hands, I touched my numb lips and surveyed my inflamed throat. On one end of my nerve endings, my fingers could feel the subtle touch of skin on skin. My fingers felt a slight tickle and tender touch with the curve and the cracks of my lips. My lips, however, felt nothing past the numbing wall of inflamed flesh as I pressed my fingers down around my mouth. It was a mind trick. At this point, I felt more intrigued than worried by the numbing sensations.

After waiting for almost an hour, Dr. Bluma arrived with Pasha, the Peace Corps office's driver. I was rushed into their car, and away we went.

"Veee are going to the hospital," explained Dr. Bluma when she turned towards me from the front passenger seat. "Unfortunately, it is far from here. Hospital № 1, it is veeery popular and big hospital. It has allergic reaction specialty center."

Instantly upon leaving the hotel parking lot we encountered the ubiquitous and pervasive traffic of Almaty. Pasha inched along Al-Farabi Avenue.

"*Blya suka!*" spouted off Pasha. Pasha, frustrated with the mass of cars and rush hour traffic, mumbled Russian obscenities under his breath.

As I waited in the back of the car, I continued to touch and rub my inflamed lips. I quietly pondered my fate, trying to silence out the grumbles of the driver and congestive noise of traffic. I experienced a strange calmness in my mediation.

Like Al-Farabi, the medieval philosopher himself, I contemplated the events that were taking place around my being. Worry seemed to fade in that moment. After all what would worrying have done for me? I was stuck in traffic. I could only go as fast as fate, time and the flow of cars allowed. Patience became my virtue, as well as ignorance.

I would learn later from Dr. Bluma that my body was inching

towards anaphylactic shock. My body had been in a state of a hyper-allergenic stasis for so long that it had finally hit the tipping point.

But at that time, as we sat in traffic on Al-Farabi, I didn't realize the seriousness of my ordeal.

"Vooctoor Blllooma!" I broke the silence. "Whav did yoov do bevoor yoov woorked foov Peave Corpv?"

My swollen lips and tongue continued to grow. It made it difficult to speak.

"I vooorked in the oil fields," responded Dr. Bluma. "Vheeenever a foreign vooorker sickened, like American or Japanese, the company flew me out veeest to the Caspian.[49] I lived in Astana."

"Anyone viff my provlemv?"

"No," answered Dr. Bluma. "But," she continued, "veee had some veeery interesting cases."

My calmness dissipated. I started to worry.

---

[49] The Caspian Sea is the largest landlocked body of water in the world. It is on the western boundary of Kazakhstan.

"Don't vooory, Tim," she said when she saw the look on my ballooned face. "It is veeery *foolish* to vooory. Veee veeell get you all better! Veee are almost at the hospital. Don't be a *durak*!"

Durak

"*D*urak!" cried my host brother, Ağasi, with glee as he shoved all his playing cards into my deck.

We had been playing the game of *Durak* (Fool) for an hour on the living room couch. I just lost a round of this card game.

Durak was one of our brotherly rituals while I lived with the Zheltoqsans in my first year of service. We would play *Durak* on the living room couch while we watched Russian TV.

"Timati," started Ağasi, "let's *igra*... I mean, play mooor!"

I shuffled and dealt out the cards onto the sofa's surface.

"You know my faahterrr he in ghospital?" asked Ağasi.

"What? Hospital?" I shook my head in disbelief.

Ağasi's statement was news to me. I just realized I hadn't seen my host father, Äke, in a day or two, but no one had told me that he was in the hospital. It often felt like I was given information from my host parents on a need-to-know basis—and, usually, it seemed like they didn't think I needed to know much.

"*Da*! He over der," pointed Ağasi to the window in the direction of the hospital a few blocks away.

"Why is he in the hospital?" I was confused about the situation. "Is he okay?"

"He hafff bad blood." Ağasi explained more. "Much head hooort. Maybe you call it, in English, sterrresss? We go to him today in ghospital!"

When we finished up our round of *Durak*, we decided to leave. We put on our winter coats and boots at the door as we ventured outside into the March chill. The winter of my first year in Kazakhstan may have been coming to an end, but it was still below freezing outside. Dirty snow still covered everything.

The village hospital in Yavlenka was not far from the house, just a few minutes' walk from the homestead at Four Soviet-skaya Street. It was one of the largest buildings in town—two floors, spanning a large block of the village center. There was a derelict-looking park and smaller hospital buildings surrounding it, including a clinic specializing in tuberculosis treatment.

Tuberculosis plagued the former Soviet Union, and the Peace Corps warned its volunteers that this was a real threat to the locals and to our own health. The bacterial infection was becoming more resistant and difficult to treat around the world, especially in places like Kazakhstan.

We walked into the main building from what appeared to be a side entrance. There was no lobby at the hospital, and there definitely wasn't security to watch the door. In fact, the hallway we entered was devoid of any worker or patient. The fluorescent lights of the hall flickered. Ağasi seemed to know where he was supposed to go. We went up a cold stairwell with cracked and crumbling concrete steps. The second floor of the hospital seemed a bit livelier. Doctors and nurses went about their business, checking on patients. Ağasi ignored them, just as much as they ignored us. We came to an open door.

"Here his room," said Ağasi.

We entered.

There he was, lying on the bed looking weak and weary. Äke was a small man in stature. Lying in the large lumpy hospital bed made him look even smaller.

Where was the man I knew, the one who used military strength with that Siberian spirit? I asked myself. *Where had he gone?*

"Ahh... *Moi syn,*" started Äke in a quiet voice. "Ahh... *Moi amerikanskiy syn.*"

His real son and his American son had arrived to pay homage. Ağasi and I stood at his bedside. Äke smiled.

"My faahterrr hafff bad blood," repeated Ağasi.

"*Da,*" started Äke, talking in his unique high-pitched rasp of a voice. "Bloood! *Blut gutte, nein!*"

Äke often tried speaking to me in German. He spouted off some Kazakh to Ağasi.

"My faahterrr say he in ghospital only one... uhhh... *raz*..." Ağasi struggled to remember the English word.

"Time?"

"Yesss! He in ghospital one time befooor, when in *voina*... uhhh... war Afghan. Dat only *raz*... uhhh... time befooor."

Äke was from the last generation of Soviet men, the men who rushed into the fires of Chernobyl and the boys who were sent to Afghanistan to fight the Mujahideen. They were men who gave their country everything; they were the brave men who sacrificed themselves for the good of the Soviet nation. However, the nation they thought they were protecting would dissolve and crumble. Many would pass away from the cancers that emerged from the wreckage of Reactor Four. The veterans of the Soviet's incursion into Afghanistan would return home to a nation falling apart. Many who returned were broken. Many would never return. They were *durak*, fools left in the dust of the Hindu Kush.[50]

Äke rattled off some more Kazakh to Ağasi.

"He say no, he no hooort in *voina*... uhhh... war," translated Ağasi. "No hooort by Afghan. No blood. No trooo hooort. He hafff much sterrresss... uhhh... over der. Afghan hafff mind trick."

"I'm confused."

Ağasi wasn't making much sense in his broken English.

"It okay. My faahterrr happy we here. We his *syn*... uhhh... we his sons! Me his blood son and you his American son!"

Ağasi gave a smile as he looked at his dad lying in bed. Äke smiled back. He seemed happy to have the support of family.

I didn't realize it then, but now, years after leaving Kazakh-

---

[50] The Hindu Kush is a mountain range in Afghanistan.

stan, I figured it out. Äke had a mental break of some sort. His "bad blood" was stress. His stay in the hospital in Yavlenka was a repeat of what had happened to him during the war in Afghanistan in the 1980s. Stress had caught up with him in his tiny corner of Kazakhstan, his little Yavlenka. The best cure was a visit from his two sons.

Our American Son

"Sam came by to visit on my second night here." I explained to John Sasser while he sat on the opposite hospital bed from mine. "He was heading out of country for a trip to Turkey. I think to meet his brother there."

"That's great that you've had visitors," exclaimed the country director in a deep drawl. "It sounds like Dr. Bluma has also kept you good company."

The grey-haired director glanced over to Dr. Bluma. They had arrived together. This was John's first, and only, visit to me in the hospital.

"Rebecca," I continued, "came by too. Rebecca's visit was a surprise, I guess."

Rebecca's visit was a surprise for me. She had been in Almaty for an unexpected and sudden exit or Close of Service (COS). Apparently, she had been accepted into graduate school, which was starting in September. She was leaving two months earlier than the planned COS that the remaining Kaz 19 group was scheduled for in November.

The time for the Peace Corps was coming to an end for the fifty or so volunteers remaining from Kaz 19. Two years of service and life in Kazakhstan was ending. We would leave our communities and schools, our colleagues and host families. For better or worse, we were all going to be leaving the people we had come to live with and grow with over the course of two years. We would leave those we had come to love. The Americans would depart, hopefully leaving some mark on the hearts and minds of those we had met here.

Over the two years of service, we had lost twenty-five volunteers from our original group of seventy-five. Most who left early had left on their own accord—perhaps, a family obligation at home, or a girlfriend or a boyfriend left behind. A few left early because the Peace Corps had graciously given them the option to leave the country with some dignity left intact. For these few it was either leave by their own "choice" or have their stay be terminated by the Peace Corps—essentially, a dishonorable discharge from service.

"Sounds like Rebecca veeell enjoy school," interrupted Dr. Bluma. "She vaaas veeery excited to leave."

"I've heard a few other volunteers have left for grad school already." I explained.

I learned that, while not officially sanctioned by the Peace Corps, the organization wouldn't necessarily penalize volunteers from leaving a few months earlier than their official COS in November. Many volunteers after all were becoming anxious to start the next chapter in their lives, post Peace Corps. The fall terms for most graduate schools started a month or two before COS—an inconvenience for some.

"Yes," replied the country director, uncomfortably. "A few have left already. Let's cut to the chase," continued John. "You may suspect why I'm here today, and I don't mean to be the bearer of bad news, especially on my first visit to the hospital."

My stomach sank, and my eyes began to tear up. In the back of my mind, I knew this would be the likely outcome of his visit, but I refused to accept it until I heard it. I held out hope that I would be sent back to Yavlenka to finish up my final two months of service once I was out of the hospital.

"The Medical office in DC just informed me and Dr. Bluma of their decision. They gave us a few options, but they all involve sending you home early."

Survival

Although I could tell that John had tough conversations before mine—after all, he had owned a company before he retired to the Peace Corps—he still didn't like this part of the job.

"But," my voice quivering, "I'm all better. The hives are all gone! I am all better!"

I had been in the hospital for over a week. Twice a day involved IV treatments of prednisone to fight the rash of hives on my skin. My diet had been restricted to oatmeal and *kasha*. I lost over ten pounds.

"Well, Tim, Medical is afraid that your condition may return while in Yavlenka," said John while he gave me a look of concern. "They don't want to risk it. There just aren't the facilities and doctors in Yavlenka to treat an emergency."

"I get it." I replied, understanding that I had become a liability—and after two weeks of dealing with my situation, I was exhausted. "What are my options? Can I go back to Yavlenka to get my things? All my stuff is at my site. I need to say goodbye to my counterpart and *babushka*!"

"That," John's tone was one of sincerity and sympathy, "won't be possible. Medical will not authorize that. Washington is calling the shots on this case, and frankly I must agree with their call. Safety is our primary concern."

"What about my things?" It was a shallow question to ask, especially with the severity of everything else happening to me. "People expect me to return to teach in a couple weeks."

"We just can't risk sending you back after this latest episode. Your life versus your things—we have to go with the obvious on that one. We understand that your work will have to be flexible—roll with the punches—and your regional manager will convey the message to your school."

I could tell this wasn't an easy conversation for him, and he had a genuine concern for me. This was something I admired about John Sasser. He truly cared for the volunteers who served under him.

"For your things," continued John, "we will have your site mates pack up your stuff and Peace Corps will ship it home."

"It's going to be hard to explain this to my counterpart, and even harder for my *babushka*."

"Sounds like you're their American son," smiled John. "I remember visiting you and your host family last summer. We had that *dastarkhan* lunch. Great food. The whole family came out for lunch. I saw you were their American son. I could tell back then, and I can barely speak a lick of the language here."

Sasser gave off a deep chuckle. It was reassuring.

"The people here were good to me. They were family."

"There are a lot of good people in Kazakhstan. It's a country that can use some work, but with a lot of good people."

"I think I took more from them than I could've given back."

I felt guilty and remorseful for this fact.

"You're only one person," replied Sasser. "It's a big world and just you. Sometimes we must accept the path that we face, and we often must do it alone. Other times we have help, and let's pray in times of need, we get good people on our side."

I had prayed during this whole ordeal—something I didn't do often, but I felt my health needed all the extra help. At the hospital, I wished and hoped and thought so hard for anything but this outcome. In the end, this was my end in Kazakhstan.

"I guess I need to accept what has happened and what needs to be done next." I told John Sasser.

"Tim"—responded Sasser as he looked at me intently—"you're a good volunteer. Accept it. You did a good job here in Kazakhstan. It's time to go home."

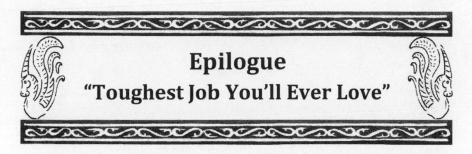

Epilogue
"Toughest Job You'll Ever Love"

"One always begins to forgive a place as soon as it's left behind."

From Little Dorrit
by Charles Dickens

Two Years Passed

The sun had yet to break over the Tien Shan. Outside was dark, quiet and cold.

Like musical notes drifting weightlessly in the early morning air, the faint melodious call of an *imam* woke the faithful to prayer. Prayer is better than sleep...

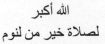

"Allahu Akbar... Al-salatu khayru min an-nawm..."
The harmonious call resonated from a distant minaret, rous-

ing me from sleep. I was vaguely intrigued, slightly confused. I lifted myself from my makeshift bed, a couch in the Peace Corps office, and I turned on the lights.

In less than an hour I would leave for the airport. I prepared my bags, and I waited for Pasha, the Peace Corps' driver. I sat, waiting, feeling pangs of tired sadness, yet happiness.

Pasha arrived at the office at 4:30 a.m. He was a stout and slightly chubby man, round and jolly. While most would be miserable waking so early, when Pasha greeted me, he had a big smile, untypical for a Russian.

I loaded my bags into the vehicle. Its red license plate indicated it was an official caravan used by the US government. We exited through the gates of the compound, and we hit the road to the airport.

Cognitive Development

Before I left for Kazakhstan, I was excited for an adventure. I was twenty-two and fresh from college. I was naïve. The Peace Corps offered an opportunity to broaden my horizons. I knew next to nothing about this strange and distant country. It was a nebulous blank spot on the map of my mind. The only face I could put to its people was that of a British comedian whose character spoofed the nation of sixteen million.

Although excited for this journey into the unknown, I came to Kazakhstan nervous as hell. I was anxious. I had no "real" work experience to offer Kazakhstan. I generally lacked in most life experiences.

Many years after leaving Kazakhstan in 2009, I often think back on my two years in that country, two years of some of the most important experiences of my life. And it almost didn't happen. It took encouragement by my dad to not be swayed by my own self-doubts.

His words still reverberate in my memory: "If you don't go, you may regret it for the rest of your life. At least, give it a try."

I am glad I went—even after the roller coaster ride ended, with its ups and downs, trials and tribulations.

I think back on the memories as if they were yesterday. They are vivid memories. Sometimes they are fond memories, and other times they are anything but. Yet, they are ingrained into my brain. I suppose travel to foreign lands does this to memory. It heightens and etches itself into the brain.

While I was often confused by the cultural and linguistic nuances of Kazakhstan, on that last morning's drive to the Almaty airport, I understood Kazakhstan better than I ever would at any point in my life. On that morning's car ride, I understood the world much better than I had two years prior.

With two years of Peace Corps service, the blank spot on the map of my mind quickly filled with the names of real places: Almaty, *KIZ*, Petropavlovsk, Yavlenka... The blank spot filled with experiences, most mundane and too numerous to list off, but so many cherished. The face of Borat quickly changed into the faces of those who helped me along the journey: Ağasi (brother), Äke (father), Ülkenapa (older sister). The faces of Kazakhstan became very human ones to me with friendly smiles and kind eyes, with hospitality and love. For two years, these people helped guide me. They helped me grow into the person I have become today.

Throughout my two years of Peace Corps service, Kazakhstan tested my own wits and my endurance. The Peace Corps was a wild ride of emotions and physical endurance. It tested who I was and what I believed. A shot of vodka with pepper keeps away the flu. Never refuse food by your hospitable elders. The list of peculiar beliefs and idiosyncrasies, and sometimes annoyances, goes on and on. There were moments of great joy, followed by countless hours of boredom. Sometimes it was lonely. Sometimes it was cold. Sometimes the food tasted like the finest caviar, but it was mostly soup and potatoes. Nevertheless, I came to love and appreciate the uniqueness and many intricacies of Kazakhstan and its people.

Like many volunteers in the Peace Corps, the work was tough and the goals of that "work" were nebulous at best. For the most part, I was lucky to have a job that had a set work schedule and job title as an English teacher. It made my task in the Peace Corps easier to understand. For two years, I was Meester Sachland. I had so many great students and a wonderful counterpart. My former students really give me hope for the future. I am still in touch with some of them today, even as they have left Yavlenka for the broader world.

As part of my job, I had the opportunity to work with my counterpart. As a new teacher, with no teaching experience, she was vital for my crash-course education in teaching. Though it wasn't always easy having a volunteer under her wing, she helped me with everything I needed. We were a great team. I learned from her, and she learned from me. This was sustainable development at its best. "Sustainable development" was one of those phrases the Peace Corps beat into every volunteer's brain during training. Our partnership worked. She was not only a coworker and a mentor, but she became my friend and family. My counterpart and her husband brought me into their family. We still talk all these many years later.

I learned what hospitality really was in Kazakhstan, especially from the three host families I lived with during training and service. I learned the most from my host *babushka*. She was a strong Siberian woman. It didn't matter that I was an American and spoke rudimentary Russian, she took me in when I needed a home. Every day she fed me the best homemade food. She kept the house's wood stove lit on the coldest nights. We kept each other company as we watched Russian soap operas together. She loved to talk my ear off about everything from the days of the Soviet Union to the specifics of planting tomatoes in her garden.

When I left Kazakhstan, the Peace Corps didn't even allow me to return to Yavlenka to collect my things and say goodbye in person to my counterpart and *babushka*. This was one of the saddest moments of my life

Пока, Корпус Мира

During my last few weeks in Kazakhstan, I learned that life is full of changes. Sometimes things change quicker than we can react. Sometimes things change faster than we can understand. With this change, we don't always get our resolve.

In November 2011, only two short years after I had departed Kazakhstan, the Peace Corps decided to "indefinitely suspend" its program in Kazakhstan. The speedy closure of the Peace Corps' program and the exit of its hundred-plus volunteers made international news. Officially, the government in Astana and the Peace Corps cited the high levels of development that Kazakhstan had attained in the eighteen years of Peace Corps' time in the country.

Beyond the official reasons, I learned much more through my network of returned Peace Corps volunteers. In 2011, there had been unprecedented attacks in Kazakhstan by Islamic terrorists. There were many stories of volunteers being harassed by police and the KNB. The Kaz 18 I referenced in this story, who had been arrested and put under house arrest, was just one of many examples of the police meddling with the Peace Corps. He was eventually released six months after his arrest—and, from what I heard later, pardoned by Nursultan A. Nazarbaev himself. Other stories circulated where the job security of volunteers in schools became jeopardized, with some asked by their organizations to resign over baseless accusations. They were accused of teaching "controversial topics" and subverting the youth with "devious" ideas. Stories of violence towards volunteers also surfaced. A few volunteers were jumped in a discotheque during my final months in the country. Volunteers being assaulted by local drunks and hooligans while walking down the street was another common theme. There had been several reports of female volunteers being raped. The Peace Corps' reasons for ending the program in Kazakhstan were much more complicated than the official one given.

Hearing the news of the Peace Corps' departure gave me mixed feelings. On the one hand, Peace Corps had worked in the country for nearly twenty years. It had been a force for good. Kazakhstan had made great strides in its development since the fall of the Soviet Union. The country did have its flaws, and volunteers, unfortunately, got mixed into the intrigue and madness. It was sad to see it go, because I knew there was still more good work to be done there.

"We few, we happy few, we band of brothers..."

From 1993 to 2011, 1,176 Peace Corps volunteers and trainees served in Kazakhstan. They came from everywhere in America. They came from all walks of life in America, but they had a common mission to serve the Peace Corps in Kazakhstan. They had a mission to help, offer whatever means they had, whether this was by their own ingenuity, their education or by their own brute strength. They had a mission to educate themselves about Kazakhstan and to bring back what they learned to other Americans. They had a mission to make Kazakhstan and America better places, better friends.

While the material work and output of volunteers was limited and ephemeral at best, a legacy of the human factor remains. It will hopefully remain beyond the years ahead. We made true friends and family with the people of Kazakhstan. Indeed, some really did make families there with many international marriages happening.

As volunteers, we created deep friendships with each other. Some of my best friends today are the ones I served alongside in Kazakhstan. We shared a common experience that only returned Peace Corps volunteers, and maybe even those who just served in Kazakhstan, can truly appreciate and understand. In the Peace Corps, many of us were new graduates straight out of college. While highly educated, most of us lacked life experience. The experiences we created together in Kazakhstan bonded us. We laughed together and we suffered together.

We came to Kazakhstan together on that bus from the mountains at Tabagan, but two years later we left Kazakhstan in our own different ways. Some left early to tend to family matters at home in the States or to return to a boyfriend or girlfriend or a fiancé that they left behind. Others couldn't handle it, the Peace Corps that is—too much pressure from the locals or maybe too much pressure from within. Boredom, fatigue, depression, exhaustion, etc., etc., etc., these were facts of life in Kazakhstan. Some were forced to leave by the Peace Corps staff for not following the rules. Others were made to leave because of medical necessity. The seventy-five of Kaz 19 who left that American bubble up in the mountains high above Almaty in the summer of 2007 dwindled down to less than fifty by the end of two years of service in 2009. No matter how long we were there, Kazakhstan impacted us all in our own unique ways.

Конец (The End)

Pasha rushed down Al-Farabi. The street was lined with the glow of streetlamps. The light of dawn had barely begun to brighten the morning darkness. The awful traffic of Almaty had yet to emerge from the morning slumber as we passed under the gleam of the city's new business district. Down Almaty's sloping streets to the airport we went.

As we drove along, the Russian pop music playing from the radio helped rouse me from my sleepy state. I attempted to make small talk with Pasha.

"How do you like driving for Peace Corps?" I asked.

"It okay. I like. It pay good money." He replied. A few awkward seconds passed when he asked, "Vat vill… ah… you do now in Ameeerika?"

"I don't know." I replied curtly.

"*Udachi*!" replied Pasha with a simple good luck.

Just before we entered the airport gates, I glimpsed back one last time at Almaty, a city under the shadow of the Tien Shan. I gave one last glance at Wonderland, and out the rabbit hole I began to emerge.

Our IDs were checked at the airport gates by guards with large-brimmed hats. We were waved on through.

Pasha drove up the ramp toward the glimmering neon glow of the airport's lights. He pulled up to the drop-off zone.

There was no party, no last toast or fireworks for my departure from Kazakhstan. I simply stepped out of the vehicle, thanked Pasha for the ride and began towards the airport doors.

Конец (The End)

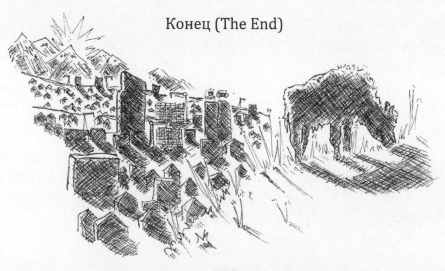

Acknowledgments

I want to acknowledge those I served in the Peace Corps, the people of Yavlenka. I say "served" in the lightest sense of the word. In reality, it was those same people who helped me more than I could've ever done for them. I owe no greater debt than to the people of Yavlenka and Kazakhstan. My three host families took care of me and kept me safe. My counterpart taught me how to survive in Kazakhstan. Thank you to the Peace Corps staff there and the work they did for me and the other 1,175 Peace Corps volunteers and trainees who passed through their program. I thank my friends and fellow volunteers of Kaz 18, Kaz 19 and Kaz 20. Without them, I would've never been able to make it through the two years of service. To my friends at home, the care packages and the support meant the world to me, especially on the darkest and coldest of winter days. Lastly, to my parents, for being there for me... always.

Regarding the production of this book, which took me a decade to write from start to finish, I start by thanking a family friend, Judy. During my Peace Corps service, she wrote to me, encouraging me to use the many emails I sent home as fodder for a future book. This was the spark that lit the fire. To my friend Casey, we both served in Kaz 19, though only as acquaintances. When I moved to Seattle several years after we both left Kazakhstan, we reconnected. Our many good times of reminiscing about our service, *Semper Fi*, helped provide many insights as I wrote this book. I want to thank my friends James and Shelby, whose critical, yet thoughtful review of my stories, ideas and writings helped me question and rethink parts of this book. To my wife Monica, she gave me constant support through the process of publishing *A Five Finger Feast*. Lastly, and most importantly, I need to thank Cody Salinas, one of my oldest friends and the editor of this book. His critical eye and review of my book was most essential in getting *A Five Finger Feast* edited. It was his help and hard work that pushed me to finally get this book finished and published.

A Brief Chronology

4th Century BCE: The Golden Warrior is buried near Almaty.

334-327 BCE: Alexander the Great conquers the Achaemenid (Persian) Empire.

482 CE: The city of Kiev is founded

632: Muhammad dies.

1220s: Genghis Khan's armies invade Central Asia.

1274 CE: Marco Polo visits Kublai Khan's court at Xanadu.

1336: Timur (Tamerlane) is born.

1480: Moscow overthrows the "Tatar Yoke."

Circa 1500s: Kazakhs emerge as a distinct ethnic group.

1703: St. Petersburg is founded by Tsar Peter the Great.

1718-1895: Turkestan is conquered by the Russian Empire.

1752: Petropavlovsk is established as a Russian fort.

1917: October Revolution is launched by the Bolsheviks.

December 1922: The Soviet Union is founded.

June 1941: Operation Barbarossa is launched by Nazi Germany.

May 8, 1945: The Great Patriotic War (WWII) ends in Europe.

1949: The Soviet Union sets off its first nuclear bomb near Semey, KZ.

October 14, 1960: John F. Kennedy gives his University of Michigan Peace Corps speech.

March 1, 1961: Kennedy signs Executive Order 10924, authorizing the creation of the Peace Corps.

April 12, 1961: Yuri Gagarin is the first person in space.

September 22, 1961: The Peace Corps Act is signed into law by the US Congress.

1979: The Soviet Union launches its war in Afghanistan.

1985: Author Tim Suchsland is born.

April 1986: The Chernobyl nuclear disaster begins.

December 1991: Kazakhstan declares independence, and the Soviet Union dissolves.

1993: The Peace Corps is invited to Kazakhstan.

1999: Vladimir Putin becomes president of Russia.

Sept. 11, 2001: Terrorist attack the World Trade Center in New York City.

August 2007: Kaz 19 arrives in Kazakhstan.

November 2011: The Peace Corps ends its program in Kazakhstan after eighteen years of service.

Maps

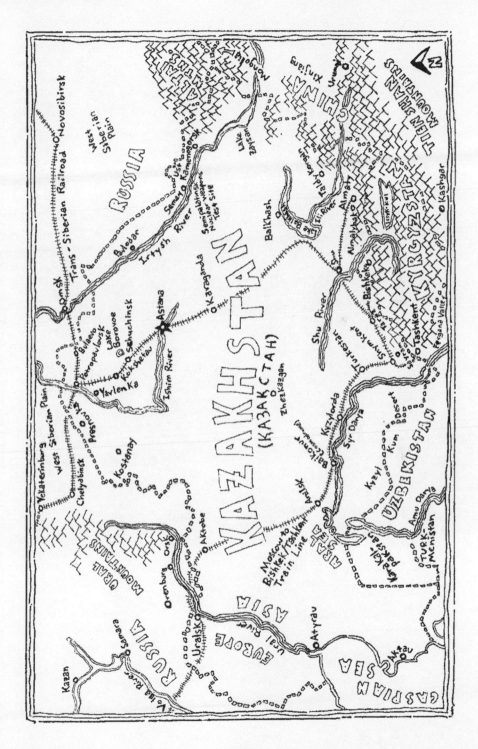

A Five Finger Feast

The Almaty Region

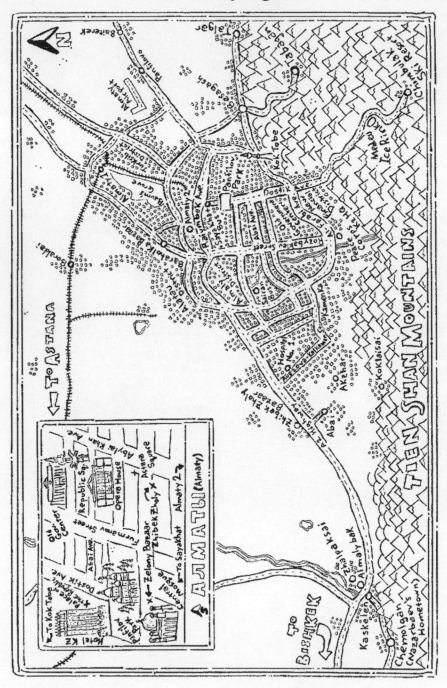

Maps

The Aral Sea (1960 and 2009)

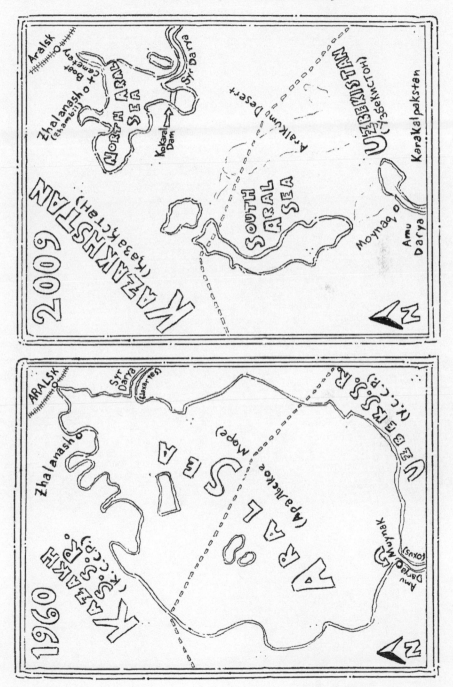

A Five Finger Feast

Northeast Kyrgyzstan
(Bishkek, Lake Issyk-Kul and Karakol)

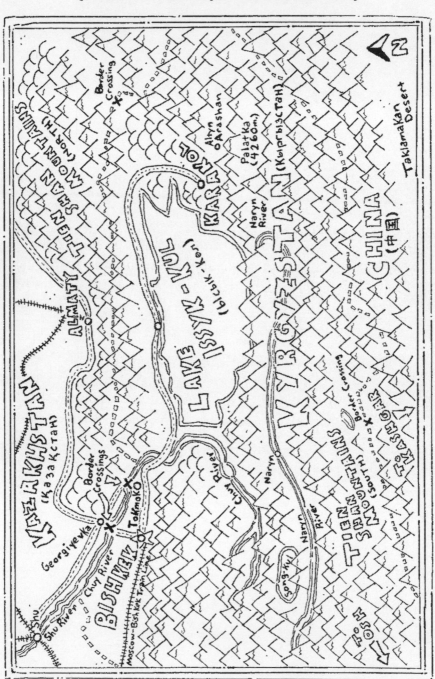

Glossary

Akim (Kazakh - әкім): mayor, city director

Akimat (Kaz. - әкімат): townhall, municipal center

Al humdu lil allahil lazi at'amanaa wasaqaana waja'alana minal muslimeen (Arabic): a traditional Muslim prayer said after dinner; "thank you, oh *Allah* (الله - God) for feeding us and making us amongst the believers"

Allahu akbar al-salatu khayru min an-nawm (Arb.): part of the *salah*, the prayer Muslims say five times a day; "*Allah* is the greatest, prayer is better than sleep"

Alles gut (German): all is good

Alles klar (Ger.): all is clear

Amerika (Russian - Америка): America

Amerikanets (Rus. - американец, pl. *amerikanskiy*): American

Amerykański (Polish): American

Armyanin (Rus. - армянин): Armenians

As-salam aleykum (Kaz. - ассалам алейкум): formal greeting, "peace be upon you;" reply, ***wuleykum as-salam*** ("also with you")

Avtobusa nyet (Rus. - автобуса нет): no bus is coming

A vy? (Rus. - а вы?): and you?

351

Äwejayi (Kaz. - әуежайы): airport

Babushka (Rus. - бабушка): grandmother

Babye leto (Rus. - бабье лето): "grandmother's summer," a period of warm dry weather in the fall

Bagazh (Rus. - багаж): luggage

Banya (Rus. - баня): a wet sauna, bath

Baran (Rus. - баран): sheep, ram, mutton

Bauyrsakh (Kaz. - бауырсақ): a type of fried doughy bread

Bes (Kaz. - бес): five

Beshbarmak (Kaz. - бешбармак): "five fingers," the national dish of Kazakhstan made from boiled mutton and noodles

Bez shapki (Rus. - без шапки): without a hat

Bir (Kaz. - бір): one

Blitzkrieg (Ger.): lighting war

Blut gutte (Ger.): good blood

Blyat (Rus. - блять, also spelled *blya* or *blyah*): fuck

Bogatye (Rus. - богатые): rich

Borscht (Rus. - борщ): a type of beet soup

Brat (Rus. - брат): brother

Brüder (Ger.): brothers

Brüderschaft (Ger./Rus. - брудершафт): brotherhood; a type of drinking ritual, where two people link arms while toasting

Buran (Rus. - буран): blizzard

Buterbrod (Rus. - бутерброд): a type of open-face sandwich

Chai (Rus. - чай): tea

Chashki (Rus. - чашки): mug, teacup

Chetyre (Rus. - четыре): four

Chto? (Rus. - что; colloquial *cho*): what?

Chto hotite? (Rus. - что хотите): what do you want?

Chto vash znak? (Rus. - что ваш знак): what's your astrological sign?

Chut-chut (Rus. - чуть-чуть): a little bit/amount

Ciao (Italian): hello, goodbye

Coupe (Rus. - купе): the second-class ticketed area of a train

Da (Rus. - да): yes, yeah

Dacha (Rus. - дача): a small country house used by many urbanites for spending holidays and growing vegetables

Dastarkhan (Kaz. - дастарқан): a low table often used for parties and dining

Davay (Rus. - давай): come on

Dengi (Rus. - деньги): money

Desyat (Rus. - десять): ten

Deti (Rus. - дети): children

Devochka (Rus. - девочка): young girl

Dikaya mestnost (Rus. - дикая местность): wilderness

Diplom (Rus. - диплом): diploma, degree

Dom (Rus. - дом): house, home

Dombra (Kaz. - домбыра): a two-string banjo-like instrument

Dom kultury (Rus. - дом культуры): "house of culture," community center

Dorogie druzya (Rus. - дорогие друзья): dear friends

Druzya (Rus. - друзья): friends

Druzya pyut vmeste (Rus. - друзья пьют вместе): friends drink together

Dublenka (Rus. - дубленка; pl. *dublenki*): a winter coat

Durak (Rus. - дурак): fool; also a Russian card game

Dva (Rus. - два): two

Dvadtsat (Rus. - двадцать): twenty

Dvesti pyatdesyat (Rus. - двести пятьдесят): two hundred fifty

Dyed Moroz (Rus. - дед мороз): Grandfather Frost (Santa Claus)

Dyen Kosmonavtiki (Rus. - День Космонавтики): Day of the Cosmonauts (April 12)

Dyen Pobedy (Rus. - День Победы): Victory Day (May 9), a holiday celebrating the defeat of Nazi Germany

Dyesert (Rus. - десерт): dessert

Eta liniya (Rus. - эта линия): this line

Eto zhizn (Rus. - это жизнь): such is life, *c'est la vie*

Fotografiya (Rus. - фотография; also, *foto*): photograph

Für (Ger.): for

Geroy (Rus. - герой): hero

Glück (Ger.): luck

Govorite po-kazakhski? (Rus. - говорите по-казахски): do you speak Kazakh?

Gulag (Rus. - ГУЛаг; гла́вное управле́ние лагере́й): a Soviet prison camp

Gusi (Rus. - гуси): geese; in Russian geese say "*ga-ga-ga*"
Gut (Ger.): good, well
Gute gesundheit (Ger.): good health
Guten abend (Ger.): good evening
Guten tag (Ger.): good day
Hozyayka (Rus. - хозяйка): hostess
Idi syuda (Rus. - иди сюда): come here
Idti (Rus. - идти): go (command)
Idti na khui (Rus. - идти на хуи): suck my dick
Igra (Rus. - игра): play, game
Imam (Arb.): the spiritual leader of a mosque
Insha'Allah (Arb.): God willing
Izviniti, slova zabila (Rus. - извините, слова забыла): excuse me, I forgot some words
Ja (Ger.): yes, yeah
Kak dila? (Rus. - как дела): how are you?
Kak familiya? (Rus. - как фамилия): what's your surname?
Kak voda (Rus. - как вода): like water
Kasha (Rus. - каша): buckwheat (cereal)
K chortu (Rus. - к чорту): go to hell
Khleb (Rus. - хлеб): bread
Khorosho (Rus. - хорошо): good
Khorosho nyet (Rus. - хорошо нет): not good
Khui (Rus. - хуй; also spelled *khuy*): penis, dick
Kirieshki (Rus. - кириешки): flavored crouton snacks
Klasno (Rus. - класно): cool, classy
Kommen (Ger.): to come
Komm zu mir (Ger.): join me
Korpusa Mira (Rus. - Корпуса Мира): corps of the world/peace (US Peace Corps)
Krasivy volocy (Rus. - красивые волосы): beautiful hair
Krishenia (Rus. - Кришеня): the Christening, the Epiphany holiday (January 19)
Kto on? (Rus. - кто он): who is he?
Kupey (Rus. - купей): second-class ticketed area on a train
Kushay (Rus. - кушай): eat (command)
Ladno (Rus. - ладно): okay, alright
Lagman (Rus. - лагман): a Uyugr noodle dish

Glossary

Lepeshka (Rus. - лепешка): a round flatbread from Central Asia

Luchshaya tekhnologiya (Rus. - лучшая технология): better technology

Magazin (Rus. - магазин, pl. *magaziny*): shop, store

Makhabbat ishu (Kaz. - махаббат ішу): drink/toast to love

Manti (Kaz. - мәнті): a steamed meat dumpling

Marshrutka (Rus. - маршрутка): minibus

Mashina (Rus. - машина): car

Maslo (Rus. - масло): butter, grease, oil

Men kazakhsha suylemeymen (Kaz. - мен қазақша сөйлемей-мін): I do not speak Kazakh

Mentalität (Ger.): mentality, personality

Mezhdu pervoy i vtroy pererivchek ne bolshoi (Rus. - между первой и второй перерывчик небольшой): between the first and the second toast, there is no break

Mnogo (Rus. - много): many

Mobilnik (Rus. - мобильник): cell phone, mobile phone

Moi nomer (Rus. - мой номер): my (telephone) number

Moi pervi amerikanets (Rus. - мой первый американец): my first American

Molodyets (Rus. - молодец): good job

Moroz (Rus. - мороз): frost

Moya devochka, lublu tebya (Rus. - моя девочка, люблю тебя): my girl, I love you

Musey (Rus. - музей): museum

My (Rus. - мы): we

Nakazanie (Rus. - наказание): punishment

Naprimer (Rus. - например): for example

Nash volontur iz Korpusa Mira (Rus. - наш волонтер из Корпуса Мира): our volunteer from the Peace Corps

Na stadion (Rus. - на стадион): to the stadium

Nastoyaschoye lekarstvo (Rus. - настоящее лекарство): real medicine

Nastoyashiy (Rus. - настоящий): real, authentic

Nauryz (Kaz. – Наурыз): Kazakh New Year (March 21-23)

Nein (Ger.): no

Nelzya (Rus. - нельзя): it's forbidden

Ne ponimau (Rus. - не понимаю): I don't understand

Nu (Rus. - ну): well (participle)

Nul (Rus. - нуль): zero

Nyemtsy (Rus. - немцы): Germans

Nyet (Rus. - нет): no

Nyet korovy (Rus. - нет коровы): no cow

Oblast (Rus. - область): region

O bozhe moy (Rus. - о боже мой): oh, my god

Odin (Rus. - один): one, alone

Ogurtsy (Rus. - огурцы): cucumbers

Pakistanets (Rus. - пакистанец): Pakistani

Paritsya (Rus. - парится): "steamed up," *paritsya* is the act of whipping the body with a *venik* in the *banya*

Pelmeni (Rus. - пельмени): a type of boiled dumpling

Perchatki (Rus. - перчатки): gloves

Pivo (Rus. - пиво): beer

Platzkart (Rus. - платзкарт): "reserved seat," third-class ticketed area of a train

Plov (Rus. - плов): "pilaf," an Uzbek rice dish

Pochemu? (Rus. - почему): why?

Pochti zabyla (Rus. - почти забыла): I almost forgot

Pogrom (Rus./Yiddish - погром/פּאָגראָם): a violent attack on a Jewish community

Poka (Rus. - пока): bye

Politburo (Rus. - Политбюро): the Soviet Union's executive leadership of the government and the Communist Party

Pomidory (Rus. - помидоры): tomatoes

Poshli na khui (Rus. - пошли на хуй): fuck you

Posle banyi budem vodku i pivo pyet (Rus. - после бани будем водку и пиво пьет): after the *banya* we drink vodka and beer

Potseluy (Rus. - поцелуй): kiss

Privet (Rus. - привет): hi

Priyatnogo appetita (Rus. - приятного аппетита): *bon appetit*

Prodyetsya dom (Rus. - продётся дом): house for sale

Pyat (Rus. - пять): five

Pyechka (Rus. - печка): wood-fire stove

Rabotaet (Rus. - работает): he/she works

Rakhmet (*Kaz.* - рахмет): thank you

Rauchen kann tödlich sein (Ger.): smoking will kill you

Riba (Rus. - рыба): fish

Ruski (Rus. - русский): Russian.

Ryzhiy (Rus. - рыжий): redhead

Ryzhiy, ryzhiy konopatyy, ubil dedushku lopatoy (Rus. – рыжий, рыжий, конопатый, убил дедушку лопатой): children's saying translated as "redhead, redhead with freckles, you killed your grandfather with a shovel"

Salam/salem (Kaz. - сәлем): hello

Samsa (Rus. - самса): a fried pastry with meat

Segodnya my poydem na rynok (Rus. - сегодня мы пойдем на рынок): today we will go to the market

Segodnya vash dyen (Rus. - сегодня ваш день): today is your day

Serdtse (Rus. - сердце): heart

Shapka (Rus. - шапка; pl. *shapki*): hat

Shashlyk (Rus. - шашлык): shish kebab of Armenian origin

Shchelchok po sheye (Rus. - щелчок по шее): "neck flick," a finger motion to indicate if someone is drunk or drinking alcohol

Shche ne vemerly Ukraina ni slava ni volya (Ukrainian - ще не вмерли Україна ні слава ні воля): the glory and freedom of Ukraine has not perished

Shproti (Rus. - шпроты): canned sardines

Shubat (Kaz. - шұбат): fermented camel's milk

Siber (Rus. - Сибирь): Siberia

Skolko? (Rus. - сколько): how much?

Skolko stoit (Rus. - сколько стоит): how much does this cost?

S legkim parom (Rus. - с легким паром): "enjoy the bath," a traditional greeting

Soldat (Rus. - солдат): soldier

Spasibo (Rus. - спасибо): thank you

SPID (Rus. - СПИД): AIDS

Spokoi (Rus. - спокой): shush, calm down, be quiet

SSHA (Rus. - США): acronym for the USA

Sto gramm (Rus. - сто грамм): one hundred grams, a large serving of vodka

Subbotnik (Rus. - субботник): Saturday cleanup

Suka (Rus. - сука): bitch

Sve budet khorosho (Rus. - все будет хорошо): all will be good

Sve normalno (Rus. - все нормально): all is ok

Syn (Rus. - сын): son

Tak (Pol.): yes

Tarelka (Rus. - тарелка): plate

Tenge (Kaz. - теңге): Kazakhstan's money (Ṯ)

Tört (Kaz. - төрт): four

Tost (Rus. - тост): toast, honor

Tovarishch (Rus. - товарищ): comrade

Tozhe (Rus. - тоже): also

Tri (Rus. - три): three

Trinken (Ger.): to drink

Trista (Rus. - триста): three hundred

Tsygane (Rus. - цыгане): gypsies

Ty (Rus. - ты): you (informal)

Ubili (Rus. - убили): we killed

Udachi (Rus. - удачи): good luck

Udachnyy (Rus. - удачный): lucky

U menya (Rus. - у меня): I have

U menya yest zhelanie kupit dom, no ne sredstvom (у меня есть желание купить дом, но не средством): I have a desire to buy a house, but not the means

Umnyy (Rus. - умный): clever

U nas nyet (Rus. - у нас нет): we don't have

Ush (Kaz. - үш): three

Vash adres (Rus. - ваш адрес): your address

Venik (Rus. - веник): a bundle of branches for the *banya*

Vilka (Rus.- вилка): fork

Vnimanie (Rus. - внимание): attention

Voina (Rus. - война): war

Vory (Rus. - воры): thieves

Vse (Rus. - все): all

Vy (вы): you (formal)

Vy zhenati? (Rus. - вы женаты): are you married (for men)?

Ya chempion (Rus. - Я чемпион): I'm a champion

Yavlyatsya (Rus. - являться): to appear

Yaytsa (Rus. - яйцо): eggs

Ya zamuzhem (Rus. - я замужем): I'm married (for women)

Glossary

Ya znayu, chto eto pravda (Rus. - я знаю, что это правда): I know that this is true

Yeda (Rus. - еда): food

Yeki (Kaz. - екі): two

Za druzhbu (Rus. - за дружбу): a toast to friendship

Za druzhbu mezhdu narodami (Rus. - за дружбу между народами): drink/toast to friendship between nations

Za lubovyu (Rus. - за любовью): drink/toast to love

Za more (Rus. - за море): drink/toast to the sea

Zavuch (Rus. - завуч): dean, assistant school administrator

Za zdravie (Rus. - за здравие): drink/toast to good health

Zdorove (Rus. - здоровье): health; also an informal greeting

Zdravstvuyte (Rus. - здравствуйте): hello (formal greeting)

Zharko (Rus. - жарко): hot

Zhena (Rus. - жена): wife

Zhyuri (Rus. - жюри): jury

Zloy (Rus. - злой): evil

Yaytsa (Russian. - яйцо): eggs

A (host) father with his most-prized possessions

Bibliography

Bissell, Tom. *Chasing the Sea: Lost Among the Ghosts of Empire in Central Asia*. New York: Random House, 2003.

Carrol, Lewis. *Alice's Adventures in Wonderland*. 1865. New York: Dover, 1993.

Chekhov, Anton. "The Bet." 1889. *Best Russian Short Stories*, edited by Thomas Seltzer, Boni and Liveright, 1917, pp. 147-154.

Dickens, Charles. *Little Dorrit*. 1857. New York: The Modern Library, 2002.

Frankl, Viktor. *Man's Search for Meaning: An Introduction to Logotherapy*. 1959. New York: Simon and Schuster, 1984.

Frost, Robert. "Nothing Gold Can Stay." 1923. Wikipedia, en.wikipedia.org/wiki/Nothing_Gold_Can_Stay_(poem). Accessed 27 Feb. 2022.

Hopkirk, Peter. *Setting the East Ablaze: Lenin's Dream of an Empire in Asia*. 1984. New York: Kodansha, 1995.

—. *The Great Game: The Struggle for Empire in Central Asia*. 1990. New York: Kodansha, 1994.

Olcott, Martha Brill. *Kazakhstan: Unfulfilled Promises*. Washington, DC: Carnegie Endowment for International Peace, 2002.

—. *The Kazakhs*. Stanford, CA: Hoover Institution Press, 1987.

Remnick, David. *Lenin's Tomb: The Last Days of the Soviet Empire*. New York: Vintage, 1994.

—. *Resurrection: The Struggle for a New Russia*. New York: Random House, 1997.

Shakespeare, William. *Hamlet*. New York: Simon and Schuster, 1992.

—. *Henry V.* New York: Simon and Schuster, 1995.

Solzhenitsyn, Aleksandr. *One Day in the Life of Ivan Denisovich*. 1962. Translated by Ralph Parker. New York: New American Library, 2009.

—. *The Gulag Archipelago: 1918-1956: An Experiment in Literary Investigation*. 1973. Translated by Thomas P. Whitney. New York: Harper Perennial, 2007.

Stevenson, Robert Louis. *Treasure Island*. 1883. Orinda, CA: SeaWolf Press, 2018.

Swift, Jonathan. *Gulliver's Travels*. 1726. New York: Signet Classics, 1960.

Twain, Mark. *Roughing It*. 1872. New York: Signet Classics, 1962.

Yeats, William Butler. "The Second Coming." 1919. Wikipedia, en.wikipedia.org/wiki/The_Second_Coming_(poem). Accessed 27 Feb. 2022.

Index

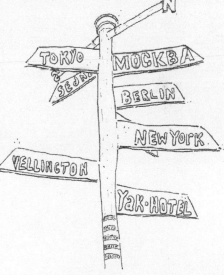

Index

Index

Index

Index

About the Author

Tim Suchsland was raised in California and Nevada. He attended the University of Nevada, Reno, where he studied history and art. He spent two years (2007-09) in Kazakhstan teaching English with the US Peace Corps. In 2012, he began writing about his time and experiences in Kazakhstan. From this reflection, came *A Five Finger Feast*. Today, he lives in Seattle, Washington with his family, where he works as a counselor and an artist. To learn more, visit TimSuchslandArt.com.

From Yavlenka's *Ishim* newspaper: "Volunteer from the Peace Corps" (December 7, 2007)

373